PENGUIN BOOKS

I DON'T NEED YOU ANY MORE

Arthur Miller was born in New York City in 1915 and studied at the University of Michigan. His plays include *All my Sons* (1947), *Death of a Salesman* (1949), *The Crucible* (1953), *A Memory of Two Mondays* (1955), *A View from the Bridge* (1955), *Collected Plays* (1958), *After the Fall* (1963) and *Incident at Vichy* (1964); his most recent play, *The Price*, was performed in New York in 1968 and in London in 1969. He has also written two novels, *Focus* (1945) and *The Misfits*, which was filmed in 1960. He has twice won the New York Drama Critics' Award, and in 1949 he was awarded the Pulitzer Prize.

Arthur Miller, who was married to Marilyn Monroe, has been married three times.

I DON'T
NEED YOU ANY MORE

Stories by Arthur Miller

PENGUIN BOOKS
in association with Secker & Warburg

Penguin Books Ltd, Harmondsworth, Middlesex, England
Penguin Books Australia Ltd, Ringwood, Victoria, Australia

—

First published in the U.S.A. 1966
Published in Great Britain by Secker & Warburg 1967
Published in Penguin Books 1969

—

Copyright © Arthur Miller, 1951, 1957, 1958, 1959,
1960, 1961, 1962, 1966, 1967

—

Made and printed in Great Britain by
Cox and Wyman Ltd, London
Reading and Fakenham
Set in Intertype Plantin

Four of these stories first appeared in *Esquire*,
two in *The Noble Savage*, and one each in
Atlantic Monthly and *The Saturday Evening Post*

To the memory of Pascal Covici

Contents

Foreword: About Distances

THESE stories were written over the past fifteen years; all but one, which is published in this book for the first time, appeared in magazines. They were not, of course, conceived as a series (although reading them together now I am surprised at a certain continuity). They were done for my own pleasure, if indeed that can be possible when one intends writing to be published at all. In comparison to playwriting, however, writing stories is undoubtedly more pleasurable if one connects that word to something done primarily for its own sake. After all, we in this country pay small attention to stories, which are squeezed in between the magazine ads, and are ranked more or less as casual things at the lower end of the scale of magnitude, like bungalows in the architectural world.

But I would just as soon see that attitude remain unchanged. The premium on grandiosity leaves us this form of art in which a writer can still be as concise as his subject really requires him to be. Here he need not say more than he knows for form's sake. There is a short-story tone of voice which, amid the immodest heroics of the day, still invites whoever wishes to speak or blurt out his truth in a single breath. For a playwright it has certain affinities; its economy and formal decorum – at least it *can* have those qualities – offer a vessel for those feelings and tales which, unelaborated, are truer, and yet for one reason or another do not belong on a stage.

Of course, a playwright is expected to say that he enjoys writing stories because he is rid of actors, directors, and the nuisance of the theatrical machinery, but in all truth I rather like actors and directors. What I have found, though, is that from time to time there is an urge not to speed up and condense events and character development, which is what one does in a play, but to hold them frozen and to see things isolated in stillness, which I

9

think is the great strength of a good short story. The object, the place, weather, the look of a person's shift of posture – these things can have but secondary importance on the stage, where action makes truth evident; in life, however, and in the story, place itself and things seen, the mood of a moment, the errant flight of apprehension which leads nowhere, can all register and weigh.

Some of these stories could never be plays, but some perhaps could have been. The latter were not written as plays partly because they seemed to me to reject the theatrical tone of voice, which is always immodest, at bottom. The playwright, after all, is performer *manqué*; thoroughly shy and self-effacing philosophers do not write plays – at least not playable ones. That is probably why playwrights at middle age so often turn to fiction and away from the unseemly masquerade. All the world's a stage, but the point comes when one would rather be real and at home. In my case, over the years I have found myself arriving at that point once or twice a week (although not always lucky enough to seize a subject at these ripe moments), and it is then that I have found short-story writing particularly fitting. The mask, in short, is of another kind when one sits down to write a tale. The adversary – audience and critic – will be taken off guard in the dentist's waiting room, on a train or plane, or in the bathroom. They have less to resent. It is paradoxical but true, for me at least, that even as the short story falls, so to speak, into a well of silence once published, while a play is always accompanied by every kind of human noise, it is in the story that I find myself feeling some connexion with the reader, with strangers. There is an aggressiveness in playwriting; if there is a friendly and familiar form of art it is the story. I feel I know Chekhov better from his stories than from his plays, and Shakespeare through his sonnets, which analogously at least are his stories. Certainly Hemingway is more palpable in his stories than in his novels, less covered up and professional in the icy sense. There is less to sweep one away in 'The Cossacks' or 'The Death of Ivan Ilyitch' than in *War and Peace*, to be sure, but there is also less that one cannot possibly believe. Maybe that is the attraction – one stretches truth a little less in a story if only because the connective arcs of interpretation are shorter, less remote from the concrete; one can more quickly catch wonder by surprise, which is after all why one writes – or reads, for that matter.

None of which is to denigrate drama or the theatre, but merely to point to some of the differences. It has always been a curious thing to me, for example, that I should find dialogue so much harder to write in a story than in a play, and from time to time I have imagined various explanations for this strangeness. Perhaps, I thought, I know that no actor is going to speak these lines, so there is an absurdity in writing them. Then, it seemed that there might be some half-conscious objection to putting dialogue into a form where it was not absolutely necessary, and thus a feeling of arbitrariness had intervened. But I think now that there is a conflict of masks, a clash of tonalities. The spoken line is 'speech', it is something said to a crowd and must therefore be peculiarly emphatic and definite, and implicitly must call for reply; every line of stage dialogue is one half of a dialectical conflict. But this kind of pressure laid upon dialogue in a story distorts everything around it. It is as though one were being told an incident by a friend who suddenly stands up, and casting his gaze beyond the room, continues his tale by imitating the voices of the participants in it. The sudden injection of formality, of this kind of formality, is the threatening imminence of the actor. This, perhaps, is why it is impossible to lift scenes of dialogue from novels and put them on the stage. They may seem perfectly stageworthy on paper, and on occasion they really are, but for the most part the novelist's dialogue is pitched toward the eye rather than the ear and falls flat when heard. Conversely, the dialogue in a story needs to sacrifice its sound in order to be convincing to the eye. And this is another enticement stories have for a playwright – as one writes dialogue for the eye, the stage becomes a wonderful thing all over again and the thirst returns for playwriting, and the 'right' to tell a story through sounds once more. That is odd and ironical to me because as a schoolboy I was first taken with books in proportion to the amount of dialogue a quick flip of the pages revealed. It was for the sake of the dialogue, I supposed, that the rest of the book was written; certainly it was for the dialogue that the book was read. This was when the author, I thought, stopped chattering and got out of the way; his own comment was like opinion as opposed to fact.

A primitive notion, but it reflects a truth nevertheless. All these forms we have inherited – story, novel, play – are degrees of distance writers need to take between themselves and the dangerous audience which they must cajole, threaten, and, in one way or another, tame. The playwright is all but physically on stage, face to face with the monster; the writer of fiction, however meagre his covering, is most safe in this sense, but out of hearing of the applause, out of sight of the mass of strangers sitting spellbound in a theatre, sucked out of themselves by his imaginings. Thus, when a novelist takes to writing a play, or a playwright a story, he is shifting his distance toward or away from the terrible heat at the centre of the stage. Sometimes a Dickens, a Mark Twain, striving to rip clear all masks, will come forward in person on the lecture platform, and a Sinclair Lewis as a member of Actors Equity, a Hemingway as a personality in his own right, his work to one side. But there is no end to masks; the one we put down only leaves the one we have on. The problem is, therefore, not one of sincerity – who can know that of himself? It is rather the rendering of a particular vision at its proper distance, the discovery of the tone appropriate to one's feeling for a thing, a person, an event. No single form can do everything well; these stories are simply what I have seen, at another distance.

November 1966   A.M.

I Don't Need You Any More

SEVERAL times in the previous days he had been not exactly warned but instructed, in a certain thickly absolute way, that God forbade swimming on Friday this week. And this was Friday now. He had been watching the ocean many times a day, and sure enough it had been getting rougher and rougher all the time and the colour of the water was getting funny. Not green or blue but kind of grey and even black in certain places, until now, when the water was running with sins, the waves were actually banging down on the sand so hard that the curb on which he was sitting shuddered up faintly through his spine. Some connexion ran under the beach and came up here where the street ended.

The waves were skidding in like big buildings that swayed drunkenly and then toppled over on their faces and splattered all over the hard sand. He kept his watch along the curved faces of the breakers for a sign of the bearded sins he knew were floating around in there like seaweed, and for a second now and then he got a glimpse of them. They were like beards, except that they were yards long and you couldn't see the man's face from which they grew. Somehow there were several beards, but they all belonged to the same face. It was like a man in there floating just a foot or so underneath the water or sometimes moving as fast as a fish and then floating again in another spot. It was because today and tomorrow were Tishebuf or Rosh Hashonoh or Yom Kippur or one of those holidays which Grandpa and the other old men somehow knew had arrived – days when everybody got dressed up, and he had to wear this tweed suit and tie and new shoes, and nobody was allowed to eat all day except him, because he was still only five and had not had Hebrew lessons yet. He would also have piano or violin lessons when he would be six, and once he started playing the piano or the violin he would not be allowed to eat on this holiday either, like his brother couldn't. Meantime, though,

13

he could go to the synagogue and sit with his brother and father, but he didn't have to. It was better to, but if he got impatient and wanted to go outside in the fresh air he could and not be blamed or even noticed. He could do practically anything because he was still only five.

This morning after he had finished breakfast, eating all alone on the oilcloth-covered kitchen table after his father and his brother had gone off to pray, he had decided not to eat a single thing again the rest of the day. At eleven o'clock, though, his mother, as always, had come out of the bungalow looking for him with a piece of jam-spread rye bread, and at first he had refused to eat it. But then she had said, 'Next year . . .' and he had compromised for her sake and eaten it. It tasted good but not delicious, and he got angry a moment later remembering how she had forced it on him. Then at lunchtime she had come out again looking for him, and he had eaten lunch in the same frame of discontent. But now he openly wished, as he sat staring at the ocean and listening to its booming roar, that his father or his brother had forbidden him outright to eat at all. He could have stood it. Side by side with his great father and his good brother he would have been able to go without even water all day. Just as he wouldn't dream of going into the ocean now, for instance, even though his tweed suit was scratching his neck and thighs, even though he could not stop himself from imagining how fine the water would feel on his skin. His mother had said it was all right if he got into a pair of cotton shorts, but he would not think of taking off his itchy suit. A holiday was a holiday. He tried now to wipe out of his mind that he had eaten lunch. He tried to make himself feel very hungry, but he could not remember the feeling exactly. At least he had not gone back into the bungalow since lunch for a glass of milk. He counted and, half believing, assured himself that he had fasted three times today, and then brushed some sand off the top of his shoes to make himself perfect. But after a moment a vague restlessness returned; he could not believe in anything alone, and he wished his brother or his father were here to see his perfection. Suddenly he realized that without even trying to stop himself he had not picked his nose all day, and felt silvery at the knowledge. But there was not a soul around to see.

The ocean went on booming. The beach, white as salt, was deserted. There was no tinkle of the ice-cream-man's bell, hardly any cars were parked on the bungalow-lined street now that September was here, and the little front porches, each one exactly like the next, were almost all empty. Practically no garbage cans stood out on the curbs any more. He felt, pressing against his thigh inside his pocket, the rusted penknife he had found in the Levines' vacated bungalow last week. It was the best treasure he had ever found at the end of the season when he had followed the other boys to ransack. He wondered idly why the mothers always left so many bobby pins and hairy pieces of soap. Fathers left razor blades, but these were not hidden in the crevices of drawers and under the mattresses. He wondered why mothers stopped talking or changed the subject whenever he came into a room. Under their skirts it was dark. Fathers kept right on talking, hardly noticing a little boy coming in, and there was always more light around.

A new strangeness on the ocean scattered his memories. He saw its surface tilting up. Far, far out a crest was rising as wide as the sea itself, and a new rumbling, deeper than any he had heard before, was beginning to sound. He got to his feet, ecstatically frightened, ready to run. Higher and higher the crest rose up until it was a straight wall of blackish water. No one else was seeing it, he knew, only he and the sand and the empty porches. Now it leaned forward, hard as stone and compact, and he could hear it kind of screaming to itself as it pounded over on its head, the spray shooting upward like fifty garden hoses going at once. He turned, happy to have escaped death, and started for his house to tell it. Already the joyful words were forming in his mouth. 'The water got like hard, like the street, and then it stood up in the air and I couldn't even see the sky, and then you know what? I saw the beard!' He halted.

He was not sure, suddenly, whether he had seen the beard. He remembered seeing it, but he was not sure he had really seen it. He visualized his mother; she would believe it if he told her, as she always believed everything he reported that happened to him. But a sadness crept into him now, an indecision, as he remembered that lately she was not as excited about the things he told her. Of course she didn't say he was lying, like his brother did, or question him the way Ben did so that contradictory details turned up to ruin everything. But there was something about her now that was not exactly listening, the way she always used to. So that even with her now he was finding himself having to add things he knew were not true in order to make her really pay attention. Like about the milkman's horse stepping on the fly. It really had stepped on that fly, but when she had merely nodded at the news he had gone on and told how it had raised its hoof again, looked down at the ground, waited, and then clomped down on another fly, and then a third. His sallow face frowned. If he went to her now with the news of the ocean he would probably have to say he had seen not only the beard but even the face under the water, and maybe even tell how the eyes looked. In his mind he could clearly see the eyes – they were blue with fat white lids, and they could stare up through the salt water without blinking; but that was not the same as knowing he had actually seen the eyes. If she believed it, then probably he had seen it, but if she merely nodded as she was doing lately, and without gasping and being full of astonishment, then he would end up feeling vagrant and bad that he had said a lie. It was getting to be almost the same as telling things to his brother. Anger against her grew in him as he paused there, aching to tell her at least about the wave. For him, nothing happened if he could not tell it, and lately it was so complicated to tell anything.

He went to his front door and entered the small living room, his uncertainty filling him now with bitterness. He saw her through the kitchen doorway working over the pots. She glanced out at him and said, 'Have a glass of milk.'

Milk! When his father and his brother were standing right now praying to God in the synagogue with parched lips, yellow with hunger. He did not answer. He could not even bring himself to go into the kitchen, that blessed place where he always loved to sit with his chin on the cool oilcloth tablecloth, watching her while she cooked, telling her all the amazing things he had seen

16

in the world outside. He hoisted himself on to a chair at the living-room table where he had never sat alone before.

After a few moments of silence she turned and saw him there. Her eyebrows rose as though she had discovered him suspended from the ceiling. 'What are you doing there?' she asked.

As if she didn't know! He bitterly lowered his eyes to the table top. Now she came out of the kitchen and stood a few feet from him, mystified. He was not looking at her but he could see her, and once more, as though for the first time, he recalled that she had a strange look lately, her face was somehow puffy. Yes, and she walked differently, as if she were always in a slowly moving line of people.

She kept looking down at him without speaking, her eyebrows creasing together, and he was suddenly aware that he was the only one in the whole family, including his cousins, whose ears stuck out. 'Pull in your ears, Martin, we're going through a tunnel!' And his uncles looking down at him, grinning – 'Where did *he* come from? Who does he take after?' He did not look like any-body, he recalled as he sat there with his mother before him. The sensation grew in him now that there was a space through which he and his mother were looking at each other all the time, and he did not remember it before. 'Are you sick?' she said at last, laying a hand on his forehead.

He brushed her hand away, lightly striking her belly with the side of his finger. Instantly his finger felt hot, and fright stabbed his stomach like a sliver of glass. She covered her belly with a silent gasp, a deep contraction within her body that he could al-most hear, and she turned to go back into the kitchen. He took the chance and looked up at her turning face. It was shut away in silence, and in silence she went back to the stove. She never even screamed at him lately, he realized, and she never dressed any more if he was in the bedroom but went into her closet and talked to him through the nearly closed door. He knew he was not sup-posed to notice that, just as Ben and Papa didn't. And now he knew that he was not supposed to notice that she was not scream-ing at him any more, and he slid down off the chair, not knowing where to go next, his secret knowledge frosting his skin.

'Why don't you get into your shorts?' she said from the kitchen.

A sob started to convulse his stomach. Shorts now! When Ben and Papa had to be standing up and sitting down in the synagogue a million times a day in their wool suits! If it was up to her people would be allowed to do anything they wanted – and the long beard floating in the water and the ocean so rough! He would like to dare her to go and tell Papa or Ben to put on their shorts!

'Go ahead, dear,' she said, 'they're in your top drawer.'

The chair he had been sitting on skidded away, squealing along the floor. He realized he had kicked it and glanced across to the kitchen doorway; she had turned, a frightened amusement in her eyes.

'What's the matter?' she asked. Her falseness buzzed like insects around his face.

He sluffed out the front door, flinging it wide so that the spring meowed.

'Martin?' She was coming through the living room faster than he had expected, and he moved across the porch, wanting to run but keeping to a prideful stroll. He felt a certain amount of rightness for somehow he had enforced the law on her. Behind him the door spring meowed, and he was starting adamantly down the stoop when she reached out and grasped his shoulder. 'Martin!' Her voice was a complaint, but it was also accusing now, reaching and spreading into his most silent thoughts, blasting his rectitude. He tried to wriggle out of her grasp, but she held on to his jacket, pulling so that his jacket button was up to his chin. 'Martin!' she screamed now into his face.

The indignity flamed up in him that she should be so disrespectful of his suit, which he wore so carefully, and he struck at her arm with all his might. 'Let me go!' he screamed.

His blow unleashed her. She cracked his offending hand, holding it by the wrist, again and again, until it stung, and trying to get away he stumbled and landed on the porch, sitting up. 'Papa'll take his strap to you!' she yelled down at him, tears in her eyes.

Papa! She was going to tell Papa! His contempt pushed her

distorted, yelling face a mile away, and he felt a calm road of light opening before him. His jaw trembling, his black eyes edged with hatred, he screamed, 'I don't need you any more!'

Her eyes seemed to spread open wider and wider, like scandal. He was astonished; even now it did not seem a bad thing to say, only the truth; she didn't need him so he didn't need her. But there she was, her mouth open, her hand to her cheek, looking down at him with a horror he had never dreamed a person could show. He did not understand; only lies were horrible. She stepped away from him, looking down at him like a strange thing, opened the door, and quietly went into the house.

He heard the sea crashing behind him, the sound hitting him in the back familiarly. He got up, strangely spent. He listened, but she was not making any noise or crying that he could hear. He walked down the stoop and along the few yards of sidewalk to the sand, hesitated about ruining his shine, and continued on to the beach. He knew he was bad, but he did not know why. He approached the forbidden water. It seemed to see him.

There was a privacy here. The brisk breeze would cut off her voice if she called to him, and, he remembered, she could not run after him any more. Just as she did not dance around the table with him or let him jump on to their bed in the mornings, and if he came up behind her any more to clasp her around she would slip quickly out of his embrace. And nobody but he had noticed these new ways, and the knowledge was somehow dangerous. Papa didn't know, or Ben, and as he walked along the edge of the wet sand, his body wrapped in the roar of the falling waves, he pressed one ear against his head, silently speaking his wish. If only he *looked* like his father and his brother! Then he wouldn't know what he was not supposed to know. It was his ears' fault. Because he looked so different he saw different things than they saw, and he had knowledge of things a fine boy could never know. Like the dentist.

His breath turned to pebbles in his throat as he tried to fend off the memory of that terrible day. A sudden wash flowed up and lapped at his shoe, and he leaped away. He bent over, trying to concentrate on drying his shoe with his hand. Suddenly he realized that he had actually touched the evil water. He smelled his hand. It did not smell rotten. Or maybe it was God who was in the water today, and you must not get in with Him, so that the water was not stinking rotten even though it was forbidden. He moved back several yards and sat on the sand, the image of the dentist mingling with his thrill of fear at having touched the water, and he gave way to a certain frightening pleasure.

He clearly saw the sidewalk before their apartment house in the city – his mother walking home, he at her hip, hearing the creaking of the brown-paper grocery bag she was carrying. And he remembered the feeling of walking with her and not having to think where to turn next, when to stop, when to hurry, when to go slow. They were as though connected, and he was simply there. And then, suddenly, they had stopped. Looking up, he saw the strange man's face close to hers. And a tear fell from the man's cheek past Martin's nose. She was talking with such a strange laughter, a dense excitement, posing very straight. And he called her by her first name, the stranger. And afterward, in the lobby as they waited for the elevator, she laughed and said, still with that same high-breathing laughter, 'Oh, he was so in love with me! I was ready to marry him, can you imagine? But Grandpa made him go away. He was only a student then. Oh, the books he brought me all the time!'

Through the waves' roar he could still hear her excited voice over his head exactly as it had sounded in the lobby. And he reddened again with embarrassment, a humiliation which did not come from any thought or even from the incident itself. He could not imagine her really being married to the dentist since she was Papa's wife, she was Mama. In fact, he barely remembered anything she had said that day, but simply her laughter and the excitement in her breath when she had left the dentist and entered the apartment house. He had never heard her voice that way and it had made him resolve instantly never to let on that he had noticed the new tone and the rather strange woman who had made it. And the horror which lay behind his embarrassment was that she had thoughts which Papa did not have. He had felt since that day like a small shepherd guarding big animals that must be kept from understanding their own strength, and if he played out of their sight for a moment or even joked or fought with them, he never forgot that his flute would really be no match for their unrealized violence if they once became aware that they were not the same person but separate, not joined in their minds as they thought they were but capable of talking and breathing differently when out of each other's sight. Only he knew this and only he was in charge of guarding them from this knowledge and keeping them unaware that they were not as they had been before the dentist had come up to Mama on the street.

As it always happened when he recalled the stranger, he thought now of the day following, a Sunday, when the whole family had gone for a walk, and as they approached that particular square of pavement he had held his breath, certain that when Papa's shoe came down on it a roaring and a crashing would break the air. But Papa had walked right over the concrete, noticing nothing, and Mama had noticed nothing either, so that Martin at that moment saw his duty clearly; it was that he alone had the vigil to keep. For even though Mama had actually acted that way with the stranger, she was somehow not aware of its real meaning, as he was aware of it. He must never let her know, in any conceivable way, the true meaning of what she had done; that instead of laughing excitedly when she said, 'He was so in love with me, I almost married him,' she should have howled and screamed and been horrified. He would never tell her this, though.

Now his mind trembled and flickered out as it always did when he came to the last part, when he imagined what would happen if Papa should ever find out not only what had happened, but that he knew this secret. Papa would look down at him from his height and roar with terrible hurt and horror, 'Mama almost married the dentist? What kind of a boy are you to make up such a thing! Waaaaaahhh!' And he would be swallowed up in the roaring and the agony raised him to his feet.

He walked beside the ocean, picking up tiny snail shells and crushing them to powder; he threw stones, broke sticks, but a threat would not leave him alone. Slowly it returned to him that he had never seen his mother as horrified as he had just left her.

He had driven her crazy many times, but not like this, not with that look in her eyes. And her teeth had showed when she hit him. That had never happened – not with the teeth showing.

Her teeth showing and her widened eyes. . . . He looked at the sea. Maybe it had to do with today being a holy day? He already believed that his badness sent out a sort of invisible ray, a communication that passed beyond his family and entered a darkness somewhere far away; it was not something he ever thought of, it was something he had always known. And the retribution would come out of that darkness as from an unalterable judgement, which could not be stopped or entertained or deflected. Her scandalized eyes seemed now to be frightened for him, for what he had drawn down upon himself from the darkness. She hadn't been merely mad at him on the porch, she had been afraid with him. He must have said something to her that was not only an insult to her but a sin. And he could not remember what it was that he had said. His failure to remember frightened him in itself; it opened up some awful possibilities.

The dentist! His heart contracted; by mistake had he told her that he knew she had acted that way with the strange man? Or maybe she believed he had already told Papa? He wanted to run home and tell her, 'Mama, I never told Papa about the dentist!' But as soon as he envisioned it he was stopped, realizing he could not tell her either that he knew. And if he told Ben, Ben would be horrified that he could even say such a thing. He sluffed along the empty beach as lonely as his duty, unknowingly sharing his secret with the bearded sea in whose forbidden depths there were eyes that saw, and saw him, and saw through his skull. And, walking, he remembered how it would be to lose his visibility; if Papa should ever discover what he knew, and roared, he would gradually disappear. But that was not the end. He would actually be there, hearing everything and seeing them all the time, except that they would not see him. He suddenly felt he would burst out weeping for them at having lost him, and he quickly corrected his vision. The fact is, he would be visible when they looked at him, but as soon as they turned their backs he would disappear. It was very fine. At night, for instance, he might get up out of bed and invisibly go into their bedroom and just sit there comfortably, and they would never know he was there. And if he got tired when it got very late, he could just lie down in bed between them and everybody would have a good sleep. Except – he carefully amended – he must remember not to wet the bed, or they would wake in the morning and see it and accuse each other and fight.

He found himself standing still, facing the ocean. As if it were a very old thought that never went away, he saw that he could walk into the water and drown. For the moment there was no fear in it, and no hope, but only the pleasure of not longing. And now he recalled the time earlier in the summer when he and his brother had gone in before breakfast when no one was on the beach. And they had played around in the water for a while, and then it came time to go back, and he could not. The undertow pushed him out as hard as he tried to swim against it. And then he had turned himself around in the water, already vomiting, and started to swim with the current. How easy it was, how fast! And soon he would have got to Europe. Then he was lying in his bed all bundled up, with the doctor there, and everybody saying he would have drowned except that the milkman happened to notice him.

He had never openly denied it to them. But, standing there now, he knew he had not nearly drowned at all. He would have made it to Europe, because he had a secret strength nobody knew he had. And suddenly he remembered: 'I don't need you any more!' His own words came back, shrill and red with fury. Why was that so terrible? He didn't need her. He could tie his laces now, he could walk forever without getting tired. . . . She didn't want him, why did he have to pretend he wanted her? The horror in it escaped him. Still, it probably was horrible anyway, only he didn't understand why. If only he could know what was horrible and what was only terrible! How fine it would be to sink into the ocean now, he thought. How she would plead with his dead, shut-eyed face to say something. Ben would be frantic too, and Papa. . . . Papa would probably be waiting in the background not wanting to interfere with the doctor, waiting to be told what had happened. And then his lips would move a little, and they would all gasp. 'He's going to speak!' she would cry. And he would open up his eyes and say, 'I was by the ocean, walking. I saw a wave, and in the wave I saw the beard. It was a whole block long. All grey. And then I saw the face. It had blue eyes, like Grandpa, only much bigger. And it has a very, very deep voice, like whales hooting in the bottom of the ocean. It's God.'

'It's God,' his mother gasps, clapping her hands together the way she used to.

'How can it be God?' Ben asks, disgusted with his lies.

'Because He kissed me.'

'Prove it!' Ben says, laughing warmly.

And he opens his mouth, and they look in, the way they all did when he had a toothache New Year's Eve and had to call up so many dentists. And in his mouth they see the whole ocean, and just beneath the surface they see the blue eyes and the floating beard, and then from his mouth comes a deep, gigantic roar, just like the ocean. In the corners of his eyes he saw a movement. A man was there, dressed in black.

He did not dare to turn fully, but even in that first instant he saw that the man had on black shined shoes, a white satin prayer shawl over his shoulders, and a black skullcap on top of his head.

Now he forced himself to face the man; a terror sucked his tongue an inch back into his throat, but quickly he was relieved – the man was really there, because there were other men standing behind him in a little crowd. They were as far away as he could throw a ball. The wind was whipping the white fringes of their prayer shawls. They were facing the sea, praying aloud from the black prayer books they held, and they were swaying backward and forward a little more urgently, he thought, than he had ever seen them do in the synagogue, and he saw his father and brother among them. Did they know he was standing here? Nobody even glanced at him; they kept addressing the air over the sea.

He had never seen so many men with shined black shoes on the beach. He had never seen prayer shawls in open sunlight. It was out of order to him, pulsing in a vague alarm. He feared for them, doing this, as though the roof had been lifted off the synagogue and God might really appear and not just the Scrolls of the Ark. They were facing Him, and He must be very near, and it was terrible. Seeing their inward stares, he wondered if they maybe did not realize they were out on the beach only a yard from the rough ocean. Maybe he should sneak quietly over to Papa and tell him, and then Papa would look up from his book, see where he was, and yell, 'What did we do! How did we get out of shul!' And they would all turn around and run back, with prayer shawls flying, to the synagogue and then thank him for saving them from having looked into God's naked face.

Or maybe he wasn't even supposed to watch this, like the time last year in the synagogue when his grandfather had said, 'You mustn't look now,' and had made him cover his eyes. But for one second he had peeked through his fingers, and there up front on the raised platform he had seen a terrible sight. The cantor, or the rabbi, or somebody with a long beard, with three or four other old men, was covering his face with his silk prayer shawl. He had no shoes on, only white socks. All of them had white socks, and they started singing crazily and then they were *dancing*! And not a beautiful dance but an old man's dance, mainly up and down and rocking stiffly from foot to foot like a group of moving tents, and from under the shawls came squawking and crying and sudden shouts. Then they all faced the closet where the Scrolls of the Ark were kept and got down on one knee, then on the other knee, and, like buildings bending over, they lay down right on their faces, all stretched out. Right up there on the altar, where usually the rabbi or the cantor or whoever he was always stood so stiff and didn't even look directly down at anybody. He was embarrassed at the thought of grave old men dancing.

Nobody in the little crowd was looking at him, not even Ben for a second, and not Papa either. 'They know that I peeked that time at the cantor dancing,' Martin thought, and they knew that he could not be saved any more; it did not matter whether he watched this now because he was not good. In fact, they might all have come here to mourn him, that he was such a bandit. If a good boy like one of his cousins with regular ears were here now, they would probably rush over and make him close his eyes and not watch. He turned his face from the men to concentrate on the roar of the sea, trying not even to hear them praying. But there was no reward, and still no reward, and suddenly the voice of the cantor, the man he had seen first, rose high and then higher in the wind, until it was like a girl's voice, and Martin had to look.

They all were praying louder now and crying out frighteningly toward the waves, the cantor and then the other men with him hitting themselves on the chest with their fists. The blows sounded like separate drums in the ground, making them grunt or cry out across the water again and again, and Martin saw some sparkling thing fly out of the cantor's hand and arch into a wave. A dead sardine? Or was it a speck of spray glistening? Now there was silence. No one moved. All their lips opened and closed, but there was only a deep humming that merged into the roaring of the waves.

Martin waited, and suddenly he felt fright at the thought that the cantor, as he had done in the synagogue last week, would draw out the curved ram's horn and blow on it. 'Ahoooo-yah!' Martin's flesh moved at the memory of the raw, animal cry, which he prayed would not happen now, not now when God was so close that the noise would go right into His ear and drive Him up out of the ocean to burn them all in His blue-eyed gaze. Oh, what a clashing pillar of foam would break the surface of the sea, rivers of green water pouring down the great fall of beard!

Without warning, everybody started shaking hands. Now they were talking, so relieved and familiarly, and laughing, nodding, folding up their satin prayer shawls, closing their books, sounding like neighbours. Martin felt a singing in him that God had stayed where He belonged. Thank God He hadn't come out! He hurried over and squeezed through the crowd toward his father, forgetting all about whether he was supposed to have watched. He saw Ben first and called him excitedly as he tried to get through to him. Ben, seeing him, pulled his father's sleeve, and Papa turned and saw him, and both of them smiled down at him proudly, he felt. And before he could think he cried out, 'Ben! I saw it! I saw him throw it in the water!' How fine it was to have seen a wonder, and not alone! 'I saw it fly into the waves!' He felt as clear and fine as Ben, with nothing at all hidden inside him.

'What, in the water?' Ben asked, puzzled.

Terror snapped its nail lightly on Martin's eye. He blushed at the rebuff, but his desire would not be stopped. 'The cantor – what he threw just before.' He looked up quickly for corroboration at his father, who laughed down at him warmly and surprised, not understanding, but only loving him.

Ben shook his head to their father. 'Boy,' he said, 'what he can make up!'

Papa laughed, but kind of crediting him, Martin thought, and he lived on the credit for a few moments as he walked with them across the beach toward the bungalow. At least he had made Papa laugh. But he *had* seen something arching into the sea – why wouldn't they admit it? A sallowness was creeping into him. He could feel his ears sticking out farther and farther, and he could not bear his loneliness, being thrown back into the arms of his secrets. 'I saw it, Ben,' he insisted, trying to stop Ben with his hand. 'Pa? I saw him throw, I swear!' he yelled suddenly.

His father, alarmed, it seemed, looked down at him with his kind incomprehension and his wish for happy behaviour. 'He just throws out his hand, Marty. When he hits himself.'

That was something anyway. 'But what's in his hand, though? He threw, I saw him.'

'He throws his sins, dopey,' Ben said.

'Sure,' Papa said, 'the sins get thrown in the ocean.'

Martin sensed a shy humour in his father's tone. He wondered if it was because this was not supposed to be talked about. And then he wondered if it was that Papa did not absolutely believe they were sins in the cantor's hand.

'And they shine, don't they, Pa?' he asked avidly. More than anything, he wanted Papa to say yes, so that they could have seen something together, and he would no longer be alone with what he knew.

'Well – ' Papa broke off. He sighed. He did not laugh but he wasn't serious enough.

'Don't they shine?' Martin repeated anxiously.

Papa seemed about to answer but he didn't, and Martin could not bear for it to end in silence. 'I saw like' – his inner warnings rattled but he could not stop – 'like a sardine fly out and go in.'

'A sardine!' His father burst out laughing.

'Oh, God!' Ben groaned, knocking himself on the head with his fist.

'Well, it wasn't live! I mean dead!' Martin amended desperately.

'Dead yet!' Ben laughed. 'You know what he said last week, Pa?'

'Shut up!' Martin yelled, knowing well what was coming.

'The milkman's horse – '

Martin grabbed his brother's sleeve and started to pull him down to the sand, but Ben went on.

' – kills flies with his foot!'

With all his strength Martin beat his brother's back, pummelling him with his fists.

'Hey, hey!' Papa called in his reedy voice that was just like Ben's.

'I saw him!' Martin tore at his brother's arms, kicked at his legs, while their father tried to separate them.

'All right, you saw him, you saw him!' Ben yelled.

Papa pulled Martin gently clear of his brother. 'All right, cut it out now. Be a man,' he said and let him go. And Martin struck his father's arm as he was released, but his father said nothing.

They walked on across the beach. Martin tried to quell his throat, which kept squeezing upward to cry out. Before he knew he would speak he said with a sob, There's a lot of flies on a horse.'

'Okay,' Ben said, disgusted with him but saying no more.

Martin walked on beside him, and his anger pumped in him. A woman in an apron was at the end of their street, looking off toward the dispersing crowd of men, probably for her husband. Seeing her there, Martin moved closer to his father so that maybe she would think he too had been fasting all day in the synagogue and praying on the beach with the others. She glanced at them as they approached the macadam and respectfully said, '*Gut Yontef.*'

'*Gut Yontef,*' Papa and Ben said together, weightily. Then Martin started to say it, but it was too late; it would sound naked, his voice all by itself, and maybe laughable since he had eaten so many times all day. They mounted the steps of their bungalow, and suddenly he was weak with uneasiness at not being one of them.

The door spring meowed, and his innocent father held the door open for Ben to go in and then pressed his great hand on Martin's back, warming it with pride. It was only when the door banged shut behind him that he remembered his mother's bared teeth and scandalized eyes.

'Ma?' Ben called.

There was no answer.

The stove was steaming, unattended. Martin's father went into the kitchen, calling her name in a questioning voice, and came back into the living room, and Martin saw the perplexity, the beginning of alarm in his face. Martin blushed, afraid of being aware of what his father did not know. And he envisioned that she had gone away forever, disappeared, so that they, the three men, could sit down quietly and eat in peace. And then Ben would go away and only he and Papa would be left, and how he would obey! How perfectly grave he could always be with his father, who would discuss with him seriously the way he did with Ben, making him get a shine the way Ben had to every Saturday, and conversing with him about holidays so he would always know way in advance, and not just suddenly the day before, that it was Rosh Hashonoh or Tishebuf or whatever it was, and sharing together the knowledge of what was or was not against the Law at all times.

The bathroom door opened and Mama came out. He saw at once that she had not forgotten. Her eyes were red, like after Uncle Karl had died from bending over to pick up a telephone book. Martin's neck prickled at the relentlessness of her present grief. It was no joke, he saw – Papa was really frightened and Ben's eyes were big.

'What happened?' they asked her, already astounded.

She looked from them down to Martin, powerless incomprehension, dried grief, glazing her eyes. 'I shouldn't have lived to hear it,' she said and turned back to Martin's father.

Even now Martin could not believe she was going to tell on him to Papa. Again he could not remember exactly what there was to tell, but for her to reveal anything that passed between them was obscurely horrifying and would leave him all alone to face his father's and Ben's awakening eyes and a crashing and screaming that would crush him out of sight.

'You know what he said to me?'

'What?'

' "I don't need you any more." That's what he says to me!'

It seemed that no one could breathe. Ben's face looked so hurt and astonished he seemed about to faint. And Martin waited for her to go on, to set forth some final fact about him that would fall like a stone or a small animal from her mouth; and, looking at it, they would all know, and he would know, what he was.

But she was not going on. That was all! Martin had no clear idea what more she might say, but the final, sea-roaring evil was not brought into the room, and his heart lifted. She was talking again, but only about how he had hit her. And although Papa was standing there shaking his head, Martin saw that he was abstracted already.

'You shouldn't say a thing like that, Marty,' he said and went into the bedroom, taking off his jacket. 'Let's eat,' he said from in there.

He wanted to run and kiss his father, but something kept him: a certain disappointment, a yearning for and a fear of a final showdown.

And suddenly his mother yelled, 'Didn't you hear what I told you? He's driving me crazy every day!'

Papa's footsteps approached from the bedroom. Now, now maybe it would come, his thunderstruck roar of down-looking disgust. He appeared in the doorway in his shirt sleeves, enormous, immovable. 'I'll take my strap to you, young fella,' he said and touched his belt buckle.

Martin thrilled and got set to run around the table. Papa sometimes took his belt off – and Martin would have to dodge out of his way, keeping the dining-room table between them for a minute or two. But Papa never actually hit him, and one time his pants had started to fall down and everybody had laughed, including Mama and Papa himself.

But now he was unbuckling his belt, and a surge of pity for his father brought tears to Martin's eyes. He pitied his father for having so unworthy a son, and he knew why he was going to be beaten and felt it was right, for it was disgusting that a boy should know what he knew. He backed away from his father, not because he feared being hurt but to save him the pain of having to be cruel.

'I didn't mean it, Mama!' he pleaded. Maybe she would let Papa go, he hoped.

'You'll kill me!' she cried.

But instantly Martin knew it was his release. Papa's having unbuckled his belt was enough for her, and she went into the kitchen with her hand on her belly to stop a pot cover from rattling.

'Be a man,' Papa said, buckling his belt again, and he went to the sideboard and filled a tiny glass with whisky and carried it over to the rocker by the window and, with a sigh, sat down.

The tablecloth and silverware sparkled. Martin noticed suddenly that Ben had gone out of the room, and he wondered if he had gone outside to cry. This wasn't finished yet, he knew.

Papa raised his glass toward the kitchen and said, 'Well? A New Year!'

Mama called out from the stove, *'Mit glick!'* And she closed her eyes for an instant. Martin never made any noise at these times because they were addressing some unseen ear.

Papa swallowed the glassful in one gulp and exhaled. 'I tell you,' he said toward the kitchen doorway, 'that cantor is a horse.' Martin saw the cantor with his long beard harnessed to the milkman's wagon. 'Never sat down all day. The man didn't stop for five minutes.'

'Because he's not one of those fakers. He's a religious man.'

'Well, say,' Papa grudgingly agreed, 'he's got all year to rest up.'

'Oh, stop that.'

'If I had two days' work a year I'd stand up too.' Martin saw the warm humour in his father's eyes, his peaceful blinking.

'What are you talking about?' Mama said. 'They could drop

dead that way, singing all day with nothing in their bodies, not even a glass of water.'

'He won't drop dead,' Papa said. He always knew the evenness of things, Martin felt, the real way it always was going to turn out, and he prayed to be good. 'His boss takes good care of him.'

'Don't be so smart,' Mama said, and she raised her eyebrows and closed her eyes for a second to ask God to pay no attention to what He had just heard.

'I wouldn't mind that either – a two-day year.'

'That's enough already,' Mama said with a little unwilling smile. She brought in Papa's big, gold-bordered soup plate filled with yellow chicken soup in which matzoh balls floated. 'Eat,' she said and returned to the kitchen.

Papa got up and hoisted up his pants, letting out his long brown belt two holes. Quickly Martin went to his place, climbed on to his chair, and put his skullcap on. Papa sat down at the head of the table and put his cap on. Mama brought Ben's soup and went back into the kitchen.

'Who's his boss?' Martin asked.

'Who?'

'The cantor's.'

Papa shrugged. 'God. Who knows?' Then, dipping his spoon into his soup, he stirred it and mumbled a prayer.

'Does he see God?' Martin asked. The hope was flying through his heart that the cantor and possibly Papa too had seen the beard in the ocean, and then he would be able to tell how he also had seen it floating there, and with this secret wiped out it would somehow take all secrets with it.

'Where's Ben?' Papa asked. The spoon was not quite to his lips.

Mama instantly came out of the kitchen. 'Why? Where's Ben?' She looked at Martin with alarm, and his mouth hung open and he blushed.

'I don't know. I didn't do anything to him,' he said.

'Ben?' Mama called, hurrying to the bedroom and looking in. 'Ben?'

Papa watched her, his spoon still raised and dripping. 'Take it easy, for God's sake,' he said, irritated. But he was awakening to trouble too, and Martin felt alarmed that he maybe had done something to Ben which he had forgotten.

'What do you mean?' she said indignantly. 'He's not in here!' And she hurried to the bathroom and found the door locked. 'Ben? Ben!' she commanded an answer in fright, and with a shock Martin saw what a loss Ben would be.

The turning of the lock was heard, and the door opened. Ben came out, his hair wet and freshly combed, his blue tie still in place even though Papa had taken his off. Martin saw the hurt in his brother's face and that he was still not looking at him and that he had been crying for Mama's sake as a good son should.

'There!' Papa said. '*Now* what've you got to cry about?' And he gulped his soup, spoonful after spoonful.

'I thought something happened,' she queried Ben.

'I was just in the bathroom,' Ben said, his voice husky.

'Why didn't you report to her that you were going to the bathroom?' Papa said.

'All right, all right,' Mama warned.

Ben tried to smile and sat down in his place.

'If you don't report,' Papa went on, 'you might've got killed – '

'Stop it,' Mama said, grinning and angry.

'You could've got run over. After all, there's a lot of traffic in this house.'

'Will you stop it?' she asked him, losing her grin.

'Place is full of trucks,' Papa continued, as he ate his soup. 'Person should ask her permission before they go to the bathroom.' Then he looked up at her and shook his head, ready to laugh. 'I'm telling you, young lady – ' He broke off with a weary laugh and went back to his soup.

Ben adjusted his satin cap on his head and stared meaningfully at the silver centrepiece, which was full of fruit, and Papa stopped eating. Now there was quiet. '*Boruch ahto adonai . . .*' Ben monotoned, and without faltering or moving at all he went into the blessing. Mama stood there listening in the doorway, caught by his gravity, her hands clasped together, her face raised toward the air overhead, where Martin knew her secret wishes floated, aroused to life by Ben's power of prayer and his immaculate memory, which never left out a single holy word. Martin pressed one ear against his head, pretending he had a slight itch, while Ben continued unswervingly to the prayer's end. Only then did Papa resume eating and Ben, without rushing to break his terrible fast, selected his spoon, stirred his soup so long that it seemed he was even reluctant to eat at all, and finally he ate in grief. Mama took his grave permission to move and went silently into the kitchen and in a moment came out with her plate and sat down opposite Papa.

Martin's hand was still sticky from the salt water with which he had cleaned off his shoe, but he knew it was invisible, and he drank his soup, his chin just clearing the rim of his bowl. It was quiet in the room. He drew the soup through his lips with the same soft sound his father made, sniffing the way Papa did after each swallow. Now he calculated his matzoh ball. The edge of the spoon had to cut it exactly down the middle or it would slip out from under, spring out of the bowl, and his hand would come down sharply and spill the soup. He set the edge of his spoon on top of the matzoh ball, knowing his mother was watching him from the end of the table. With his left hand gripping the bowl he started to press down. The matzoh ball began to slide under the pressure.

'Martin,' his mother began, 'let me – '

Surprised at his own sharpness, he shot back, 'I can do it!' Ben seemed stabbed but said nothing. Papa glanced up but went on eating.

He lifted his spoon and set its edge on the hard-packed ball again, slightly to one side of the previous mark. He knew that now Papa and Ben were also watching, even though they were not looking up. His face was getting rigid and red, his raised elbow trembling with his effort as he started to press down to cut the ball. Again it began to slide, but he knew that sometimes a sudden, swift, downward push could slice through before it flew out of the bowl, although sometimes this only sent it spinning out on to the table or into his lap. He hesitated, struggling with his dignity, which might collapse if he should start still a third cut, and he was about to raise the spoon to try again when he saw his mother's hand reaching toward his own to take the spoon away.

With all his might and anger he pushed the spoon down, drawing together his powers of mystic command to make the matzoh ball stand still and obey as it did for Papa and Ben, and at the same instant Mama's hand grabbed his. The ball shot out of the bowl and his hand banged down on the bowl's edge. The soup first warmed, then suddenly burned into his thighs through his good tweed pants, the smoky smell of wet wool alarming his nostrils. Out of the screaming he heard Ben's yell – the ball had toppled one of the candles into Ben's wine and he had knocked over the glass trying to save it. The tablecloth was bleeding through a red wound spreading down its middle. Martin was jumping up and down, hitting his hands against his burning thighs and trying at the same time to keep his mother's hands away from him, for she was trying to loosen his belt in order to get his pants off.

'You made me do it!' he screamed at her.

'He's burning! Get your pants off!' she yelled.

Ben was now in front of him, pulling at his pants to lower them. This further indignity infuriated him. 'Don't do that!' he screamed, but he could feel his pants being drawn down past his hips and he kicked out. Mama gasped, and Ben fell back to a sitting position on the floor. It was quiet. From somewhere up high he could hear Papa's reedy, questioning voice.

Mama was straightening up, her hand cupping one of her breasts, her alarmed eyes looking into the future over Martin's head. He heard the ocean booming as if it were underneath the floor and felt the house trembling as the waves struck. Papa, murmuring questions, followed Mama into their bedroom. Her breath was coming in short gasps. The door closed.

Ben stood facing the closed bedroom door. Fright and concern were rigid in his eyes.

'Why is she that way?' Martin asked softly.

'You kicked her!' Ben shouted in a whisper, glancing at Martin with contempt, then turned back to the door to listen.

Martin had no memory of kicking her. He knew he had kicked, but he had not hit anything, he thought. But it was impossible to explain, and shame gathered in him, and he saw a blackened sky.

'Pa?' Ben called softly through the door. There was no answer, and Ben's breathing quickened, close to sobbing, as he listened. Now Ben turned down to his brother, disbelief and disgust in his face. 'How could you ever *say* that to her?'

'What?'

'What you said. You don't need her any more. To your own mother!'

Martin sobbed aloud but softly, standing there.

'You have to go to her and apologize. You have to beg her pardon,' Ben said, as though Martin did not know anything at all about behaving. 'Did you even apologize?'

Martin shook his head, sobbing.

'You didn't even apologize?'

Martin wept, covering his face with his hands. He wept because he had hurt his mother and did not understand anything and was alone outside the circle of a fine family. His pants were getting cold now.

'Pa?' Ben called again, more insistently now. Then he carefully turned the knob and peeked inside. 'Pa?' he asked. Papa's deeper voice spoke from within, and Ben entered the room, closing the door behind him. Martin listened for any sound of the window being opened and all of them climbing out to leave him forever. But they were still talking in there.

He waited. His soup bowl lay overturned on the floor; the wreckage of the table seemed to make a screeching, disorderly noise at him; one candle still burned its holy light while the wick of the other lay in Ben's overturned glass, and all the chairs stood facing in odd directions. He took a step toward his bowl to pick it up, but his thigh touching his cold wet pants stopped him, and he busied himself trying to re-form the vanished crease. Again he tried to walk, but the coldness of the tweed clinging to his skin disgusted him and brought tears to his eyes. It was like waking up between wet sheets, and it brought the same resentment and mystification into his heart. Vaguely he felt it was his mother's fault, and he felt stronger, having blamed her, and walked stiff-legged into his and Ben's room.

Using his fingertips, he unbuttoned his pants and let them down, then sat on the floor to slip them over his shoes. They smelled like a wet dog. He stood up, trying to decide what to do with them, and he started to cry. He went about the room crying softly, the pants hanging heavily from his fingertips. He draped them over the back of the only chair in the room and stepped away, but their weight pulled them down to the floor. Then he started to lay them on his bed but feared they would wet the blanket; he had not wet his bed in a long time, maybe two weeks ago or a month or three months, and he did not want to give them any new ideas now. He crossed the room to the closet, but the hangers were impossibly high; and, besides, he vaguely recalled a time when he had been scolded for having put his wet bathing suit in the closet. Standing there sobbing softly, he looked around the room for a place to leave his pants, and a hand seemed to reach in and squeeze his stomach. 'Ma!' he called softly, careful not to let his call penetrate the wall to her room. But he was really crying now, and in raising his hands to wipe his eyes he dropped the pants on the floor; he looked at them there and, giving himself up to his fate, walked out into the living room.

The bedroom door was still shut. He walked over to it, still sobbing, and said, 'Ma?' and tried to stifle his sobs in order to hear. But it was silent in there now. They had left him! 'Mama!' he called louder and stamped his foot. Maybe they had wet his pants so he would go into his bedroom, giving them time to get away. For the first time in his life he did not dare turn the door-knob without first hearing permission; he dared not open it and find an empty room. He banged on the door, calling his mother, his shouts blinding him. A sudden rage flung itself up into his head, the way the ocean sometimes spews a wave deep on to the beach. 'I didn't kick that baby!' he yelled, the skin on his temples crawling, 'I didn't see it!'

As though in reply a chair scraped angrily inside the room and the door opened, and Martin was already half across the living room in flight. Papa appeared in the doorway. His fair face was darker than Martin had ever seen it. He was frowning, with no trace of a smile even in his eyes. It was no joke. He looked down at Martin. He was going to say, 'Nobody's ears stick out in this family but yours! Nobody in this family stands around trying to see the beard in the ocean! Nobody peeks through his fingers at the cantor dancing in his white socks! Nobody goes around with his shoelaces opening all the time and throwing matzoh balls all over the clean tablecloth and wetting his pants from McCreery's and making up about dentists! And nobody knows anything about babies! *Nothing is happening at any time in this house, Martin!*'

And then Martin would disappear. He saw, with great relief, how he would vanish, like that time when he had accidentally turned the electric fan on the egg-white his mother had whipped, and it flew off the dish into the air and was not there any more. He would always be around watching, but they would not see him, and he could sit with his mother or Papa or lie down between them in bed on Sunday mornings the way he used to, and they wouldn't know.

'Sit down,' his father said, partly to him and partly to Ben, who was coming out of the bedroom, red-eyed.

Martin went and picked his bowl off the floor, carefully avoiding the puddle, and set it neatly at his place and climbed up on to his chair. Everything was far away. Ben sat at his place, righted his wineglass, and put back the fallen candle in its silver holder, handling it as though it stood for his mourning. But Papa, instead of sitting, went into the kitchen. Martin could hear dishes being moved in there. Ben stared down at the red gash in the tablecloth. Mama's empty chair twisted Martin's heart, and he began to sob softly again, trying not to attract either sympathy or blame or any notice at all. Papa came out of the kitchen and gave them each a plate of chicken piled on top of the peas and carrots. Martin never ate white meat but he did not complain. In a moment Papa came out again with his own plate and sat down.

Martin ate through his sobs, but the chicken was being wetted by his tears, the water from his cold nose, and the saliva flowing loosely inside his mouth. Papa reached into his back pocket, drew out his great handkerchief, and reached over and held it under Martin's nose. It was warm. He blew. 'Again,' Papa said. Martin's pleasure started his sobs pulsating again, but he adamantly controlled himself and blew for Papa's sake.

'Should I cut your chicken?' Papa asked.

Martin hesitated; Papa's newly respectful tone freshened his memory of the pain he had caused him, his treason, and he did not want to go even further now and turn down his kindness. But he could not bear the injustice of having his chicken cut when Ben was cutting his so easily. 'I can do it, Papa,' he whispered apologetically.

'Okay. Be a man.'

Papa ate rapidly for a few minutes, thinking. Ben kept his eyes on his plate. Now the table looked even worse than before, like a desecration of a holiday. There was no sound from the bedroom. At last Papa put down his knife and fork, drank some wine, and tilted his body to one side with his hand gripping his chair arm. He was going to talk. He looked at Martin with a clear look, a shyness and an unspoken pride in him. 'So you're going to go to school soon, eh?'

'I think next week,' Martin said, glancing toward Ben for correction. But Ben was not looking up and would not give way to Papa's lightness.

'You going to go with the gentleman together?' he asked Ben.

'I'll take him in the beginning,' Ben said after a moment.

Papa nodded. Martin had not known Ben was to take him to school in the mornings. Again he realized that Ben and Mama must be having secret talks when he was not around – when he slept, maybe. In that thought he felt the warmth of being cared for, but uneasy again at finding things out only after they had happened.

'So now you'll have to wash your face in the morning and get your shoes shined. You going to have to tend to your business now.'

'Yes, Pa,' Martin said, elated, hoping Papa would continue on with further commands. But there were none. 'I think I have to have my own fountain pen,' he suggested, knowing how carefully a fountain pen had to be taken care of. Oh, how he would care for his pen!

'You don't need a fountain pen in the first grade,' Ben said.

'Well, I mean in the second grade.' Martin blushed.

'As long as you don't need a secretary,' Papa said. Then he added, 'Third grade you can have a secretary.' He laughed, but Ben would not be fooled, and Martin laughed with his father, feeling how fine it would be to keep him just like this. But Ben was immovable, and his mind searched rapidly for a marvel to distract his brother's judgement. 'You know what?' he said, avidly now, his brown eyes darting back and forth between them. He had no idea what he was going to say yet, but he was adamant – he was going to keep Papa amused even if Ben refused to forget his sins.

'What?' Papa asked.

'They're going to have Indian's summer!'

'You don't say! Who?'

He saw that Ben was starting to turn pink trying not to laugh, and he felt a strange power over his brother that he could force him out of his condemning sulk, a power that was evil because it could bedazzle Ben's righteous condemnation. He kept his eyes on his father, feeling close to him now because Papa was listening, yet somehow traitorous as he sensed he was about to astound him. 'I think in the hotel,' he said.

'Oh,' Papa said, throwing his head up overmuch, 'in the hotel they going to have Indian summer?'

Martin nodded eagerly. Now there was nothing but the pleasure of his vision. 'The milkman told me.'

Ben went 'Ts' and turned his head away.

'He did!' Martin shouted angrily, yet happy that Ben was coming out to oppose him openly and not mourning remotely any more.

'Every time he can't think what to say he blames it on the milkman,' Ben said scoffingly, but his eyes were amused and interested to hear more.

Martin reddened. 'He told me! They didn't have it last year, but they're going to have it this year. So they have to have more milk.'

'To feed the Indians,' Papa said.

'He told me,' Martin said.

'Well, sure.' Papa turned to Ben. 'They're probably expecting a lot of Indians.'

'From the country,' Martin added, clearly seeing a file of feathered Indians emerging from the woods near the railroad station.

'In other words,' Papa said, 'country Indians.'

With a spray of spittle flying from his burst-open mouth, Ben laughed helplessly.

'Well, they are!' Martin yelled indignantly, but strangely happy that he was making them laugh at his lies and not at something worse.

'Hey, hey!' Papa frowned at Ben, but with laughter in his eyes. 'Cut it out, don't laugh.'

'Country Ind – ' Ben choked hysterically.

Martin giggled, infected. 'It's when everybody goes back to the city,' he explained, desperately meticulous. 'That's how come nobody sees them.'

Ben's arms suddenly flew up as he slipped off his chair on to the floor, and his fall made Martin burst out in clear, victorious laughter. He jumped down, thrilling with love for his brother's laughter, and he ran around the table and flung himself on Ben, tickling him under the arms with all the strength in his fingers. Ben fell back on the floor helplessly, pleading for Martin to stop, but his suffocating gasps were like soft wet sand to dig into, and Martin kneaded his brother's flesh, straddling him now, darting from his ribs to his belly to his neck until Ben was not laughing any more. But Martin kept on, feeling a delightful fury and a victorious power. Ben's neck was stretched and his face contorted, tears on his cheeks, unable to take a breath. Martin struggled against being lifted into the air and heard his father calling, 'Ben? Ben?' And then, 'Ben!' And Ben at last drew a breath and lay there gasping, laughing with tears in his eyes, and he wasn't dead.

Papa put Martin down. 'Okay, Indian, that's enough. Go and say good night to your mother and go to sleep. We've got to start the packing tomorrow early. Ben, you too.'

Ben, still breathing heavily, got to his feet, his expression sobering as he brushed off the seat of his pants and inspected his shoes. Martin happily began to brush his pants too, his brother's equal, but discovered he was in his underwear, and his mind darkened with the memory of his wet pants still lying in the middle of his and Ben's bedroom. Papa had already gone into the other bedroom where Mama lay.

'You have to apologize to her,' Ben whispered.

'Why?' Martin asked in all innocence. Anger stirred in him again as he felt himself slipping back.

'For what you did, you nut,' Ben whispered. 'Before.' Then he went into their parents' bedroom. He always knew exactly what had to be apologized for.

Martin followed, moving toward his parents' bedroom as slowly as he could without actually coming to a halt. First he moved one foot an inch or two and then the other. He searched in his mind for a clue to sadness; he was inwardly still happy. He thought of his Uncle Karl dying and it sobered his face, but he could not precisely recall what he was to apologize about, and his forgetting left voids that frightened him. He knew it was not about his pants lying in the middle of his room, because nobody had seen them yet, and the memory of his mother standing up holding her breast had splintered in his mind; he could see her doing that and gasping, but he could not quite recall what had caused her pain. The fear he felt as he approached the open doorway of her bedroom was that he had done something he did not even know about. Things were always being remembered that he had forgotten. Only Ben never forgot; Ben remembered everything.

He entered the bedroom, feeling his ears growing foolishly bigger and heavier; his mother was looking at him from her

42

pillow, and Papa and Ben, standing on either side of the bed, turned to look at him as though they had all been discussing him for an hour and knew what he was supposed to do.

At the foot of the bed he stopped, trying not to let his eyes be caught by the hill over her stomach. In the silence the ocean's hiss and boom came into the room, surprising him with its sudden presence. He could smell the water in here and see the bearded thing floating just beneath the heaving water like seaweed.

She smiled at him now, tiredly; his lips parted tentatively in reply. His father, he saw, was crooking his arms to stand with his hands bracing his back, elbows out. Martin's hands slipped down off his hips when he tried it, so he lowered his hands and rested one on the soft yellow blanket.

'So?' she asked, without turning from him, but smiling. 'He ate – my bandit?'

'Sure he ate,' Papa said, 'he's a big man. Leave him alone, he eats.'

Hearing her call him her bandit – which she never called Ben – he lowered his eyes with pleasure, distinguished by his crimes. He knew exactly where he was now, and he loved all of them.

'You ate your peas too?'

'Uh-huh.'

'And the carrots?'

'Yeah.' In this expectancy he saw his recognition, his uniqueness expanding before his mother, and Papa too, and even Ben seemed magnanimously vanquished and kind of showing him to her. But he kept his eyes on the blanket, not knowing why he was beginning to feel embarrassed.

'So now you're going to be good, heh?' she said.

'Uh-huh.' He glanced at her face; she was serious and still hurt. Then he looked down at the blanket and plucked at it, growing wary about the next five minutes, for he knew once again that something was still unfinished.

'You bother him too much,' Papa said. 'He's practically a professor and you still – '

'He's going to cut his own matzoh balls? You crazy?'

'A man is got a right to cut his own matzoh balls.'

'Oh, shut up.'

'Specially a professor with his own fountain pen.'

'What do you know about it?' she said. Martin glanced at her and saw that she was angry but smiling. Fear moved into him. 'I slave like a dog all day and you come home and he should do whatever he wants!' Papa looked up high to make little of it, but she was going toward an underlying darkness, and dread flew into Martin's chest, so he grinned. 'I don't bother him,' she denied. 'I'm just trying to help him. A boy five years old can't – '

'A boy five years old! I was six I was out selling newspapers.'

'Sure,' she said, 'that's why you got such a good education!' She turned to Ben, as she always did at this point in the story. 'Not even to let a boy go to school so he could maybe read a book in his life.'

Papa sat there slightly blushing for his upbringing, his family, and Martin kept grinning and plucking in agony at the blanket. Through the corners of his eyes he saw the three books on her bed table, and his heart got cold; were these the books the weeping dentist had given her? 'Oh, the books he used to bring me!' Her voice in the lobby sang over his head with all its longing, and the memory reddened his face. Oh, Papa must never know! 'When I grow up – ' he said.

They turned to him, smiling at his sudden statement. 'What, when you grow up?' his mother asked, still flushed with her feelings.

He lowered his eyes to the blanket; he had not meant to say anything aloud, and his face burned with shame. 'What, darling?' his mother persisted. He did not know if he wanted to say that he would teach Papa so he could read books in a chair the way she did, or whether he would grow up and bring her books himself, so she would not remember the dentist, and then they wouldn't argue any more, she and Papa. He only knew for certain that he wanted her never to make Papa ashamed.

She kept asking what would happen when he grew up, and he knew he had to say something quick. 'Papa gave us chicken,' he said. They all laughed in surprise, and he felt relieved, and he laughed although he did not know what was funny about it. 'Right on top of the peas and carrots!' he added.

'Some waiter!' Mama laughed. They all laughed louder, but Papa was blushing, and Martin wanted to run to him and apologize.

She was proud of Martin now, and he knew she ought not to be. 'Come here, give me a kiss,' she said, holding out her arms. He lingered in place, crunching his toes inside his shoes. 'Come!' she smiled.

Fearing to affront her again, he moved an inch toward her outstretched arms and writhed to a halt, pulling at the blanket with his fingertips. 'Ben's taking me to school,' he said, keeping out of her reach.

'He can't wait to go to school, you see?' she boasted directly to Papa, and in the instant Martin glowed under her pride in his taking after her. But when he saw how pleased and innocently Papa nodded, his mind quickly darkened; he only knew she must not so blatantly make him her own in front of Papa, and in the air between his mother and himself he felt an evil compact growing, a collusive understanding, which he lusted for and could not bear.

'I can spell "beach"!' he said suddenly and immediately felt afraid.

'Oh, you! You'll spell everything!' She waved the words at him with her hand. 'Go – spell, "beach".'

' "Beach," he said, in the approved way of saying the word before starting to spell it. He saw Ben grinning; was it because he was proud of him or doubtful he could really spell the word? Martin's memory sharpened around each letter. ' "B" . . .'

'Right!' she said, nodding with satisfaction.

' "e" . . .'

'Very good!' she said, glancing with pride at Papa.

' "a" . . .' he said less strongly.

She seemed to sense a wavering in him and kept silent. He was looking at his father now, his warm, magnanimous smile, his wholly selfless gaze – and he knew in that instant that Papa did not know how to spell 'beach'. He and Ben and Mama knew how, but Papa was sitting out there all alone with his patient ignorance.

' "B-e-a" what?' his mother prompted. He could feel the embracing power of her demand like a wind on his back, and he dug in his heels against it. But Papa saw nothing, only the wonder that was about to come out of his son's mouth, and the sense of his own treason burned in him.

'What, darling? "B-e-a" . . .'

' "B-e-a" . . .' Martin began again, slowly, to make more time. He lowered his eyes as though searching for the final letters, but the realization stuck to him that he was teaching his father. How dare he teach Papa! She must shut up or something terrible would come down upon them. Because . . . he did not know why, but he did not want to be standing there in front of Papa, teaching him what he had learned from her or. . . . His mind drowned in the consequences as in the trough of an incoming wave. 'I can spell "telephone",' he said. They all laughed. Somehow 'beach' was forbidden now. He remembered suddenly that he had once spelled 'telephone' off the cover of the phone book to Papa. He wanted deeply to spell 'telephone' for him again and to wipe out the memory of 'beach'.

'First spell "beach",' she lightly complained. 'You can spell it.'

Ben spoke. 'It's the same as "teach".'

'I know!' Martin shot out at his brother. His heart quickened at the fear that Ben was about to spell 'beach' himself.

'Or "reach",' Ben said.

'Shut up!' Martin yelled, and both his father and mother were starting to laugh.

'I can spell it!' he shouted at his father and mother.

'Well, go, spell it,' his mother said.

He got himself set, but now it was he who was alone, pleading with them, all three of them, to be allowed to show what he could spell. And he could not bear the indignity, the danger, that lay in having to produce something in exchange for their giving him a place among them. The golden aura was gone from his head; he was merely standing there stripped of his position, and he started to sob, and he did not know why, except that he hated them all, as though he had been somehow betrayed and mocked.

'What's the matter, darling?' she asked and reached toward him. He struck at her falseness, and she withdrew her hand.

'Come on, let's go to sleep,' his father said, coming over to him.

He pushed his father's belly away but not with his full force. 'I don't want to go to sleep!' Something, some battle, remained unfought, and he lusted for it now as for peace.

The feel of his father's belt buckle remained impressed on his hand. He looked up at Papa's perplexed, fading grin. Now, now he would take his belt off and whip him! Through the red webbing of his anger Martin saw the promise of an end, of peace. Swiftly he saw that now he would be really whipped, and then the thoughts of the dentist would be driven out of his mind and he would never again hear the sound of his mother's high and excited laughter that day. Oh, yes – it would all be cracked away by the snap of that leather and Papa in fury roaring out, 'I ... I ... I ... I!'

Now, now he would do it! And then Papa would turn and knock Mama against the wall, and she would never dare to make him teach Papa anything again.

But Papa was bending over him, patting his back, saying, 'It's late, professor, come on,' and Martin felt his father's great hand folding around the back of his neck and allowed himself to be walked to the doorway of the room. And as he was going out into the living room he heard his brother's voice, weighted down by the responsibility for teaching him. 'It's "b-e-a-c-h", Marty.'

The injustice fell on his head like a shower of nails. He heard the crash first, then saw the tablecloth cascading down over his feet, the dishes rushing toward him and smashing on the floor, fruit rolling across the room, the falling arc of the lighted candle, a smack of a palm across his forehead, another on his behind, and he was running, running into Ben first and dodging out of his grasp, then into Mama's thigh, and then he was high in the air, his legs kicking beneath him, his face toward the ceiling where the marks of three flies his father had once squashed still showed. Everything was red, as though he were looking through his own blood, and he could feel the thuds of his toes inside his shoes as he kicked against his father's body. 'Hey!' He was let down, dropped to his feet, and he glimpsed his father's hand going to his belly as though it hurt, and the pain he had caused his father caught at his throat but he was strangely free, full of himself – bad, agile, swiftly glancing at them at bay, knowing he could never be caught and held if he did not want himself to be. For an instant no one moved, and he could only hear himself gasping.

He ran into his room, picked up his crumpled pants, rushed back into the living room and flung them down on the floor before his family. The next thing, he knew, would be that he would run out the door and down the street and never come back. No – he corrected – he would run across the beach and go swimming! Into the bearded ocean where he belonged – he was not afraid like they were! His mother moved one foot to approach him and he stiffened, gasping for his breath. The words pitched upward from his stomach – *I don't need you any more!* His mouth was open and he was yelling, but nothing came out because his tongue was crouching flat in the back of his throat.

'Martin!'

He yelled again. 'Aaahhg!' came out. The root of his tongue felt cold now. He felt frightened. They were all coming closer to him, carefully. He swallowed, but his tongue would not come up to where it belonged. He felt himself being carried, and his pillow came up under his head.

His bedroom was dark, and their faces were cut in half by the moonlight coming through the window. For a long time he did not see them, but he could hear their talking and worried murmurings. He could not move his mind out of his mouth, where it groped and felt for his tongue. He felt a hand on his arm and turned to his bedside, expecting his mother to be there, but it was his father who was seated in the chair. He looked toward where Mama's voice was coming from, and she was down at the foot of his bed with Ben. It was strange; Papa always stood at the foot of the bed when he was sick, and Mama sat at his side. Turning back to his father, he felt helpless and grateful, striving to understand their novel positions.

'Say something, Martin,' his mother said fearfully from her distance.

He kept his eyes on the half-dark face of his father, waiting. But his father, alarmed as he looked, did not speak; he was there merely holding on to Martin's arm, communicating some new, unfathomable thought. And Martin in his silence pleaded with his father to speak, but his father did not.

'What's the matter, darling? It's all right. Nothing happened. Say something. Say "boy". Can you say "boy"?'

The root of his tongue was turning icy. With his mind groping inside his mouth he could hear her voice only distantly, and her faraway quality made it easier for him not to answer her. Unable to answer back, he felt strangely relieved of all thought and strategy. A remoteness from all of them, and from his own feelings, set him afloat, and unawares he grasped the powers of invisibility – he had no doubt he was on his bed, but nobody could get mad at him when he could not reply to their demands, and his enforced silence gave him a new, smoothed-out view that was cleared of the necessity to be thinking at every instant what he should or should not say next. All of a sudden in his life nothing seemed to be happening, and everything was about to happen. Beauty seemed to be forming around him, all of them gently rising and falling together in an imminence, an about-to-be that was like an unsung but audible singing. The distance his mother fearfully kept struck him as vaguely respectful, and his father's hand on his arm held some kind of new promise he could not understand. His mother continued asking him to speak, and he heard Ben's voice too, and under their words a pleasantly steady astonishment at him that carried no blame. Had he broken his tongue? he wondered. Oddly it did not terrify him but only held him in suspense, and there was no pain.

He felt time passing and passing, and there was still no anger in them, only a worried curiosity, which he felt was gradually bringing him a little closer to them – until there was something quite new for him in this half darkness, a new sense forming in him of his own truthfulness. The fact was spreading through his mind that this was a wonder they had all discovered at the same moment as he had. It was not something he had half made up and half believed, it was a real happening that had overcome him and yet was astounding to them too. They were all sharing the single belief together, and this sudden unity, fusing them without warning, burned away his sense of having secrets. He felt supported in space, with them suspended around him, and in this moment there was no Mama or Papa or Ben but three congealments of warmth embracing him with no thoughts of their own. And it seemed to him now that this was all he had been trying to find, this was actual and perfect, while everything else, the whole past of arguments and fights and smiles and shouts, was a dream.

She was telling him to try to close his lips now and say 'b'. But a secret winter seemed to have frozen his upper lip, and he could not bring it down. Something strange moved in the moonlight, and he peered to see his father biting on his lower lip. He had never seen him distort his face like that. He watched. Papa, half green in the moonlight, was looking down at him, biting hard on his lip, and his one illuminated eye was oddly widened with fury. The rising and falling steadied and then stopped. Warmth began to flow into Martin's tongue, and his own lip was getting less stiff. He felt fear flowing into his chest. Papa's hand was now gripping his arm, through which he could sense a living power in his father's great body. A thunder seemed to be gathering, expanding his father, infuriating him, like a whole sky suddenly drawing a storm into itself. A popping sound burst from Martin's lips, and his neck prickled with a sudden sweat. He saw himself swept away now, flung outward into the night like a lump of cloth. 'Papa!' he cried, backing into his pillow.

'He's all right!' his mother's voice screamed, startling him. He could hear her hurrying toward him alongside the bed, saw her arms reaching toward him, and fright broke his silence. 'Mama!' he sobbed, and she fell on him, kissing him frantically, calling into his face, 'Yes, yes, speak, my baby, speak! He's all right!' Her thankfulness, so unexpectedly pure, swept him out of the reach of punishment he had expected a moment before; her oneness with him blotted out his last thought, and he seemed to swim with her effortlessly through light. She was weeping now and stood erect, looking down at him, her hands clasped prayerfully together.

And once again now Martin saw his father, and he saw that he was not happy, not thankful, but just as he had been a moment before. And he heard his father's voice before he heard his words, like thunder rumbling before it speaks with a crash. 'Gaaaaooo-dammit!'

Mama swerved to look at him.

'When are you going to stop bothering him!' he bellowed into her face.

'I – ?' she started to defend herself.

'You bother him and bother him till you drive him crazy!' The rumbling was sharpening now, forming the burning white crash, and Martin stiffened against its burst, his brain thrilling to the howl of winds that seemed to be hurling across the darkened air. 'So he spills a little soup! Goddammit, how's he gonna learn if he don't spill something!'

'I only – ' she started weakly.

'You "only"!' Oh, he wouldn't let her even explain! He saw, astonished, that Papa's anger was not at all against him! And how frightened she was, standing there, facing him with her hands still clasped in prayer. His father's thunder hit the earth now, and he could not hear the words, but his mother's fright gave him their message – her fright and Ben's lowered eyes. Both of them were getting it now, both of them being pressed farther and farther from Papa's love.

'You can't treat a boy that way,' he was saying more quietly now, more sternly. 'If he can't eat, don't give him a spoon; if he can eat, stop bothering him.' She did not dare answer now. Papa moved about, towering over her. 'I'm no professor, but that's no way,' he said. 'No way. You're killing yourself and everybody else.'

'I was only trying to – '

'Stop trying so much!' he roared out, with the moon over his ear. 'Now, come. Let him sleep. Come on.' Breathing angrily, he made a commanding gesture with his open hand, and she started for the door. She hesitated, wanting, Martin knew, to kiss him good night, but instead she obediently walked past Papa and went out of the room, and Martin felt her chastised happiness as she silently vanished.

Now Papa turned to him and said sternly as before, 'Less tricks now. Listen to her when she tells you, y'hear?'

'Yes, Papa,' Martin whispered, his love choking off his voice.

Papa reached down. Martin stiffened against a blow, but his father gently straightened his blanket a little and walked out of the room.

For a moment Martin forgot entirely that Ben was still there at the end of his bed. A conviction of valour had come alive in his soul; it felt almost as though he had fasted all day at his father's side, and he was braced by the echoes of that deep voice which had so suddenly smashed the air in his defence. And in a moment he almost believed that he had been the roarer himself; in his mind he imitated the sounds and the expression in his angry father's face and quickly had them exactly for his own. Purified and wanting to act anew, he wished for morning and the chance to walk in daylight beside his father and possibly meet someone and hear his father say, 'This is my son.' His son! For the first time in his life he had the hard, imperishable awareness of descent, and with it the powers of one who knows he is being watched over and so receives a trust he must never lay down. In his mind's eye there rushed past the image of his angry father, and behind Papa was Grandpa and then other men, all grave and bearded, watching over him and somehow expecting and being gratified at the renewal of their righteousness and bravery in him. And in the warmth of their commending nods he began to slide into sleep.

A loud sob woke him. He raised up quickly. Ben! He looked into the darkness for his brother, whom he had forgotten, wanting to tell him – it didn't matter what he would tell him – he merely had nothing to hide any more and he wanted to reach out to his brother.

'Ben?' Unaccountably Ben was not at the end of the bed any more. Martin waited. Again, but softly now, he heard him weeping. How could Ben be sad? he wondered.

'Ben?' he called again. The weeping continued, remote, self-sufficient, and it reached Martin, who felt himself being pushed away. Suddenly he saw that Ben was sitting right next to him, facing him from across the aisle that separated their beds. He was fully dressed.

'What's the matter?' Martin asked.

Moonlight illuminated one cheek and the corner of an eye; the rest of Ben's face was lost in the darkness. Martin could not tell what expression Ben had, and he waited for Ben to speak with only curiosity and no fear. But now he could hear his brother's irregular breathing, and even though he could not remember any sin he had done he felt condemnation gathering in the long silence.

'What happened?' he asked.

In a voice broken by mourning Ben said, 'How could you say a thing like that?'

'Don't cry,' Martin began to plead. But Ben sat there crying into his hands. 'They're *sleeping*!' he cautioned nobly. But Ben wept even more strongly at the mention of their parents, and Martin's fear found him again; and his old sense of his secrets came evilly alive in him once more.

'Don't cry like that!'

He quickly slid off his bed and bent over to see up into his brother's face. Panic was opening a space at his elbows. 'I didn't mean it, Ben. Please!' And yet he still did not know what had been so terrible in what he had said, and his not knowing it itself was a mark of his badness.

Suddenly he reached out to draw Ben's hands down from his face, but Ben pulled himself away and lay over on his bed with his back to Martin. A swirl of clouds, ocean depths, and bearded secrets flowed out of Ben's back and swept around Martin's head. Soundlessly he crept back into his bed. 'I'll never say it again, I promise,' he offered.

But Ben did not reply. Even his sobs were quieting. He waited, but Ben did not accept his promise, and in his brother's silence he saw that he had been cast away. Lying there with his eyes open to the darkness, he saw that even though Papa had yelled out for his sake, it was because Papa did not understand, as Ben did, how bad he was. Papa was innocent so he defended him. But Ben knew.

He could not lie there. He sat up and sniffed loudly to see if Ben would turn to him, but Ben was motionless, quiet. Was he falling asleep in his clothes? This disruption of age-old order spread Martin's vision, and he remembered that the dining room must still be full of his wreckage. How wonderful it would be if he slipped out there and cleaned up without a sound, and in the morning they would all be amazed and love him!

His feet were on the floor. Ben still did not move. He bent low and tiptoed out of the bedroom, his hands stretched out in the empty black air.

In the dining room there was no moonlight, and he moved inch by inch for fear of noise. His hand touched the table, and he stretched his hands out. It was all bare. Only now he remembered it precisely as it had been, and he heard the great crashing for the first time, and the reality of his badness was like a blow on his face. He got down on his knees, fiercely resolved to clean up. His knee descended on a pear and squashed it, repelling him. He sat down to clean off his knee and felt cold meat under him and jumped; it was a chicken leg. Keeping his knees off the floor, he went on all fours away from the table to escape a rising feeling of disgust. At the front window he stood up and looked out and saw a wonder. A silvery greenish glow was hanging over the macadam street.

He had never seen such bright moonlight. It even glistened on windows across the street. In the silence he heard a faint high ringing in his ears, like insects. His eyes swallowed the mysterious glow outside, and in a moment he no longer knew what had brought him out here. A sense of newness was upon him; things to do that he had never done before. It was a secret moment suddenly; with no one watching everything was up to him. No one knew he was standing here, and he had never before been walking around when everyone was asleep. He could even go outside! The illicit freedom exhilarated him – to go outside and be the only one awake in the world! His hand reached up and turned the key in the front door and it opened, surprising him a little. Looking out through the screening, he felt how warm the air was. Now he heard the new gentleness of the falling surf, and he opened the screen door enough to look out to the left, and then he walked on to the porch and faced the ocean. It was flattened out, all the roughness of the preceding days melted away. God was gone?

The magical new calm of the ocean sucked at his mind. When no one was looking God had shot up out of the water with a rush of foam; and when the water had fallen back the waves flattened out and the sea was at rest. God had waited there until they had thrown in their sins, and He had taken them up with Him, leaving the water clean and hairless. How wonderful it was that Papa and the other men knew what to do about God! How to pray to Him and when to throw their sins to Him and when to go home and eat. Papa, and Ben too, with the others, had an understanding with Him and knew what was supposed to happen next and what He wanted them to do.

Facing the glistening beach, the salt-white sand that stretched before him like a sky to walk on and the moon's green river flowing on the ocean toward his eyes, he yearned to know what he should do for God, as the others knew. His body stretched as with a mute vow, a pure wish that quickly changed to fact; as when he had stood up and sat down with the congregation in the synagogue, not knowing why but satisfied to be joined with others in sheer obedience, he now vowed obedience to the sea, the moon, the starry beach and the sky, and the silence that stretched its emptiness all around him. What exactly its command was he did not know, but an order was coming to him from the night, and he was grateful, and it made him better and no longer quite alone. He felt, without any sense of the details, that secretly, unknown to anyone but known to the night, he was the guardian of Ben's and his parents' innocence. Vaguely he felt that with some words which he knew were somewhere in his head he had almost sent them all screaming and roaring at one another and at him, so that – had he said what he could say, they would all be horrified at the mere sight of one another and there would be a terror of crashing. He must keep them from that knowledge, and he knew this and received it like water when he was thirsty, with placid eyes and an inner attention and pleasure, with a yearning that was more than knowledge.

Suddenly he felt exhausted. Sleep was felling him as he stood there holding on to the railing. He held his hand out past the eaves of the porch roof and felt the moonlight. It wasn't warm! Now, washing both his hands in it, he searched for its heat and texture, but it felt no different than darkness. He put his moon-touched hands to his face to feel, but no warmth came out of them. He raised up and tried to lean out over the rail to put his face into the moonlight, but he couldn't reach. With his eyelids heavy he walked unsteadily to the low stoop and went down and walked to the corner of the house, where the beach began, and moved out of the house's shadow into the open moonlight. As he looked up, the light blinded him, and he sat suddenly, falling back on his stiffened arms; then his elbows gave way, and he lay down on the sand.

With the last darkening corner of his mind he sought to feel his face warming, and slowly it was. His eyelids first, then the bridge of his nose, then his mouth, were feeling the spread of the moon's heat. He saw his brother and his father and his mother and how he would tell that the moonlight was so warm! – and he heard their laughter at the impossibility, their laughter that was like a gate keeping him out of their world, and even as he felt angry and ashamed and big-eared he was their protector now. He would let them laugh and not believe him, while secretly, unknown to anyone but the eyes that watched everything from the sea, he would by the power of his silence keep them from badness and harm. In league with rule, in charge of the troubled peace, he slept in the strength of his ministry.

The breeze cooled him, and soon the sand chilled his back, but he summoned more heat from the moonlight and quickly he was warmed. Sinking down, he swam through the deepest sea and held his breath so long that as he came up with the sunlight bursting from his hair he knew he would astonish everybody.

[*1959*]

Monte Sant' Angelo

THE driver, who had been sitting up ahead in perfect silence for nearly an hour as they crossed the monotonous green plain of Foggia, now said something. Appello quickly leaned forward in the back seat and asked him what he had said. 'That is Monte Sant' Angelo before you.' Appello lowered his head to see through the windshield of the rattling little Fiat. Then he nudged Bernstein, who awoke resentfully, as though his friend had intruded. 'That's the town up there,' Appello said. Bernstein's annoyance vanished, and he bent forward. They both sat that way for several minutes, watching the approach of what seemed to them a comically situated town, even more comic than any they had seen in the four weeks they had spent moving from place to place in the country. It was like a tiny old lady living on a high roof for fear of thieves.

The plain remained as flat as a table for a quarter of a mile ahead. Then out of it, like a pillar, rose the butte; squarely and rigidly skyward it towered, only narrowing as it reached its very top. And there, barely visible now, the town crouched, momentarily obscured by white clouds, then appearing again tiny and safe, like a mountain port looming at the end of the sea. From their distance they could make out no road, no approach at all up the side of the pillar.

'Whoever built that was awfully frightened of something,' Bernstein said, pulling his coat closer around him. 'How do they get up there? Or do they?'

Appello, in Italian, asked the driver about the town. The driver, who had been there only once before in his life and knew no other who had made the trip – despite his being a resident of Lucera, which was not far away – told Appello with some amusement that they would soon see how rarely anyone goes up or comes down Monte Sant' Angelo. 'The donkeys will kick and run away as we ascend, and when we come into the town everyone will come out to see. They are very far from everything. They all look like brothers up there. They don't know very much either.' He laughed.

'What does the Princeton chap say?' Bernstein asked.

The driver had a crew haircut, a turned-up nose, and a red round face with blue eyes. He owned the car, and although he spoke like any Italian when his feet were on the ground, behind his wheel with two Americans riding behind him he had only the most amused and superior attitude toward everything outside the windshield. Appello, having translated for Bernstein, asked him how long it would take to ascend. 'Perhaps three quarters of an hour – as long as the mountain is,' he amended.

Bernstein and Appello settled back and watched the butte's approach. Now they could see that its sides were crumbled white stone. At this closer vantage it seemed as though it had been struck a terrible blow by some monstrous hammer that had split its structure into millions of seams. They were beginning to climb now, on a road of sharp broken rocks.

'The road is Roman,' the driver remarked. He knew how much Americans made of anything Roman. Then he added, 'The car, however, is from Milan.' He and Appello laughed.

And now the white chalk began drifting into the car. At their elbows the altitude began to seem threatening. There was no railing on the road, and it turned back on itself every two hundred yards in order to climb again. The Fiat's doors were wavering in their frames; the seat on which they sat kept inching forward on to the floor. A fine film of white talc settled on to their clothing and covered their eyebrows. Both together began to cough. When they were finished Bernstein said, 'Just so I understand it clearly and without prejudice, will you explain again in words of one syllable why the hell we are climbing this lump of dust, old man?'

Appello laughed and mocked a punch at him.

'No kidding,' Bernstein said, trying to smile.

'I want to see this aunt of mine, that's all.' Appello began taking it seriously.

'You're crazy, you know that? You've got some kind of ancestor complex. All we've done in this country is look for your relatives.'

'Well, Jesus, I'm finally in the country, I want to see all the places I came from. You realize that two of my relatives are buried in a crypt in the church up there? In eleven hundred something.'

'Oh, is this where the monks came from?'

'Sure, the two Appello brothers. They helped build that church. It's very famous, that church. Supposed to be Saint Michael appeared in a vision or something.'

'I never thought I'd know anybody with monks in his family. But I still think you're cracked on the whole subject.'

'Well, don't you have any feeling about your ancestors? Wouldn't you like to go back to Austria or wherever you came from and see where the old folks lived? Maybe find a family that belongs to your line, or something like that?'

Bernstein did not answer for a moment. He did not know quite what he felt and wondered dimly whether he kept ragging his friend a little because of envy. When they had been in the country courthouse where Appello's grandfather's portrait and his great-grandfather's hung – both renowned provincial magistrates; when they had spent the night in Lucera where the name Appello meant something distinctly honourable, and where his friend Vinny was taken in hand and greeted in that intimate way because he was an Appello – in all these moments Bernstein had felt left out and somehow deficient. At first he had taken the attitude that all the fuss was childish, and yet as incident after incident, landmark after old landmark, turned up echoing the name Appello, he gradually began to feel his friend combining with this history, and it seemed to him that it made Vinny stronger, somehow less dead when the time would come for him to die.

'I have no relatives that I know of in Europe,' he said to Vinny. 'And if I had they'd have all been wiped out by now.'

'Is that why you don't like my visiting this way?'

'I don't say I don't like it,' Bernstein said and smiled by will.

He wished he could open himself as Vinny could; it would give him ease and strength, he felt. They stared down at the plain below and spoke little.

The chalk dust had lightened Appello's black eyebrows. For a fleeting moment it occurred to Appello that they resembled each other. Both were over six feet tall, both broad-shouldered and dark men. Bernstein was thinner, quite gaunt and long-armed. Appello was stronger in his arms and stooped a little, as though he had not wanted to be tall. But their eyes were not the same. Appello seemed a little Chinese around the eyes, and they glistened black, direct, and, for women, passionately. Bernstein gazed rather than looked; for him the eyes were dangerous when they could be fathomed, and so he turned them away often, or downward, and there seemed to be something defensively cruel and yet gentle there.

They liked each other not for reasons so much as for possibilities; it was as though they both had sensed they were opposites. And they were lured to each other's failings. With Bernstein around him Appello felt diverted from his irresponsible sensuality, and on this trip Bernstein often had the pleasure and pain of resolving to deny himself no more.

The car turned a hairpin curve with a cloud below on the right, when suddenly the main street of the town arched up before them. There was no one about. It had been true, what the driver had predicted – in the few handkerchiefs of grass that they had passed on the way up the donkeys had bolted, and they had seen shepherds with hard moustaches and black shakos and long black cloaks who had regarded them with the silent inspection of those who live far away. But here in the town there was no one. The car climbed on to the main street, which flattened now, and all at once they were being surrounded by people who were coming out of their doors, putting on their jackets and caps. They did look strangely related, and more Irish than Italian.

The two got out of the Fiat and inspected the baggage strapped to the car's roof, while the driver kept edging protectively around and around the car. Appello talked laughingly with the people, who kept asking why he had come so far, what he had to sell, what he wanted to buy, until he at last made it clear that he was looking only for his aunt. When he said the name the men (the women remained at home, watching from the windows) looked blank, until an old man wearing rope sandals and a knitted skating cap came forward and said that he remembered such a woman. He then turned, and Appello and Bernstein followed up the main street with what was now perhaps a hundred men behind them.

'How come nobody knows her?' Bernstein asked.

'She's a widow. I guess she stays home most of the time. The men in the line died out here twenty years ago. Her husband was the last Appello up here. They don't go much by women; I bet this old guy remembered the name because he knew her husband by it, not her.'

The wind, steady and hard, blew through the town, washing it, laving its stones white. The sun was cool as a lemon, the sky purely blue, and the clouds so close their keels seemed to be sailing through the next street. The two Americans began to walk with the joy of it in their long strides. They came to a two-storey stone house and went up a dark corridor and knocked. The guide remained respectfully on the sidewalk.

There was no sound within for a few moments. Then there was – short scrapes, like a mouse that started, stopped, looked about, started again. Appello knocked once more. The door-knob turned, and the door opened a foot. A pale little woman, not very old at all, held the door wide enough for her face to be seen. She seemed very worried.

'Ha?' she asked.

'I am Vincent Georgio.'

'Ha?' she repeated.

'Vincenzo Giorgio Appello.'

Her hand slid off the knob, and she stepped back. Appello, smiling in his friendly way, entered, with Bernstein behind him closing the door. A window let the sun flood the room, which was nevertheless stone cold. The woman's mouth was open, her hands were pressed together as in prayer, and the tips of her

61

fingers were pointing at Vinny. She seemed crouched, as though about to kneel, and she could not speak.

Vinny went over to her and touched her bony shoulder and pressed her into a chair. He and Bernstein sat down too. He told her their relationship, saying names of men and women, some of whom were dead, others whom she had only heard of and never met in this sky place. She spoke at last, and Appello could not understand what she said. She ran out of the room suddenly.

'I think she thinks I'm a ghost or something. My uncle said she hadn't seen any of the family in twenty or twenty-five years. I bet she doesn't think there are any left.'

She returned with a bottle that had an inch of wine at the bottom of it. She ignored Bernstein and gave Appello the bottle. He drank. It was vinegar. Then she started to whimper and kept wiping the tears out of her eyes in order to see Appello. She never finished a sentence, and Appello kept asking her what she meant. She kept running from one corner of the room to another. The rhythm of her departures and returns to the chair was getting so wild that Appello raised his voice and commanded her to sit.

'I'm not a ghost, Aunty. I came here from America – ' He stopped. It was clear from the look in her bewildered, frightened eyes that she had not thought him a ghost at all, but what was just as bad – if nobody had ever come to see her from Lucera, how could anybody have so much as thought of her in America, a place that did exist, she knew, just as heaven existed and in exactly the same way. There was no way to hold a conversation with her.

They finally made their exit, and she had not said a coherent word except a blessing, which was her way of expressing her relief that Appello was leaving, for despite the unutterable joy at having seen with her own eyes another of her husband's blood, the sight was itself too terrible in its associations, and in the responsibility it laid upon her to welcome him and make him comfortable.

They walked toward the church now. Bernstein had not been able to say anything. The woman's emotion, so pure and violent and wild, had scared him. And yet, glancing at Appello, he was amazed to see that his friend had drawn nothing but a calm sort of satisfaction from it, as though his aunt had only behaved correctly. Dimly he remembered himself as a boy visiting an aunt of his in the Bronx, a woman who had not been in touch with the family and had never seen him. He remembered how forcefully she had fed him, pinched his cheeks, and smiled and smiled every time he looked up at her, but he knew that there was nothing of this blood in that encounter; nor could there be for him now if on the next corner he should meet a woman who said she was of his family. If anything, he would want to get away from her, even though he had always gotten along with his people and hadn't even the usual snobbery about them. As they entered the church he said to himself that some part of him was not plugged in, but why he should be disturbed about it mystified him and even made him irritated with Appello, who now was asking the priest where the tombs of the Appellos were.

They descended into the vault of the church, where the stone floor was partly covered with water. Along the walls, and down twisting corridors running out of a central arched hall, were tombs so old no candle could illuminate most of the worn inscriptions. The priest vaguely remembered an Appello vault but had no idea where it was. Vinny moved from one crypt to another with the candle he had bought from the priest. Bernstein waited at the opening of the corridor, his neck bent to avoid touching the roof with his hat. Appello, stooped even more than usual, looked like a monk himself, an antiquary, a gradually disappearing figure squinting down the long darkness of the ages for his name on a stone. He could not find it. Their feet were getting soaked. After half an hour they left the church and outside fought off shivering small boys selling grimy religious postcards, which the wind kept taking from their fists.

'I'm sure it's there,' Appello said with fascinated excitement. 'But you wouldn't want to stick out a search, would you?' he asked hopefully.

'This is no place for me to get pneumonia,' Bernstein said.

They had come to the end of a side street. They had passed

shops in front of which pink lambs hung head down with their legs stiffly jutting out over the sidewalk. Bernstein shook hands with one and imagined for Vinny a scene for Chaplin in which a monsignor would meet him here, reach out to shake his hand, and find the cold lamb's foot in his grip, and Chaplin would be mortified. At the street's end they scanned the endless sky and looked over the precipice upon Italy.

'They might even have ridden horseback down there, in armour – Appellos.' Vinny spoke raptly.

'Yeah, they probably did,' Bernstein said. The vision of Appello in armour wiped away any desire to kid his friend. He felt alone, desolate as the dried-out chalk sides of this broken pillar he stood upon. Certainly there had been no knights in his family.

He remembered his father's telling of his town in Europe, a common barrel of water, a town idiot, a baron nearby. That was all he had of it, and no pride, no pride in it at all. Then I am an American, he said to himself. And yet in that there was not the power of Appello's narrow passion. He looked at Appello's profile and felt the warmth of that gaze upon Italy and wondered if any American had ever really felt like this in the States. He had never in his life sensed so strongly that the past could be so peopled, so vivid with generations, as it had been with Vinny's aunt an hour ago. A common water barrel, a town idiot, a baron who lived nearby. . . . It had nothing to do with *him*. And standing there he sensed a broken part of himself and wondered with a slight amusement if this was what a child felt on discovering that the parents who brought him up were not his own and that he entered his house not from warmth but from the street, from a public and disordered place . . .

They sought and found a restaurant for lunch. It was at the other edge of the town and overhung the precipice. Inside, it was one immense room with fifteen or twenty tables; the front wall was lined with windows overlooking the plain below. They sat at a table and waited for someone to appear. The restaurant was cold. They could hear the wind surging against the windowpanes, and yet the clouds at eye level moved serenely and slow. A young girl, the daughter of the family, came out of the kitchen, and Appello was questioning her about food when the door to the street opened and a man came in.

For Bernstein there was an abrupt impression of familiarity with the man, although he could not fathom the reason for his feeling. The man's face looked Sicilian, round, dark as earth, high cheekbones, broad jaw. He almost laughed aloud as it instantly occurred to him that he could converse with this man in Italian. When the waitress had gone, he told this to Vinny, who now joined in watching the man.

Sensing their stares, the man looked at them with a merry flicker of his cheeks and said, '*Buon giorno.*'

'*Buon giorno,*' Bernstein replied across the four tables between them, and then to Vinny, 'Why do I feel that about him?'

'I'll be damned if I know,' Vinny said, glad now that he could join his friend in a mutually interesting occupation.

They watched the man, who obviously ate here often. He had already set a large package down on another table and now put his hat on a chair, his jacket on another chair, and his vest on a third. It was as though he were making companions of his clothing. He was in the prime of middle age and very rugged. And to the Americans there was something mixed up about his clothing. His jacket might have been worn by a local man; it was tight and black and wrinkled and chalkdust-covered. His trousers were dark brown and very thick, like a peasant's, and his shoes were snubbed up at the end and of heavy leather. But he wore a black hat, which was unusual up here where all had caps, and he had a tie. He wiped his hands before loosening the knot; it was a striped tie, yellow and blue, of silk, and no tie to be bought in this part of the world, or worn by these people. And there was a look in his eyes that was not a peasant's inward stare; nor did it have the innocence of the other men who had looked at them on the streets here.

The waitress came with two dishes of lamb for the Americans. The man was interested and looked across his table at the meat and at the strangers. Bernstein glanced at the barely cooked flesh and said, 'There's hair on it.'

Vinny called the girl back just as she was going to the new-comer and pointed at the hair.

'But it's lamb's hair,' she explained simply.

They said, 'Oh,' and pretended to begin to cut into the faintly pink flesh.

'You ought to know better, signor, than to order meat today.'

The man looked amused, and yet it was unclear whether he might not be a trifle offended.

'Why not?' Vinny asked.

'It's Friday, signor,' and he smiled sympathetically.

'That's right!' Vinny said although he had known all along.

'Give me fish,' the man said to the girl and asked with intimacy about her mother, who was ill these days.

Bernstein had not been able to turn his eyes from the man. He could not eat the meat and sat chewing bread and feeling a rising urge to go over to the man, to speak to him. It struck him as being insane. The whole place – the town, the clouds in the streets, the thin air – was turning into a hallucination. He knew this man. He was sure he knew him. Quite clearly that was impossible. Still, there was a thing beyond the impossibility of which he was drunkenly sure, and it was that if he dared he could start speaking Italian fluently with this man. This was the first moment since leaving America that he had not felt the ill-ease of travelling and of being a traveller. He felt as comfortable as Vinny now, it seemed to him. In his mind's eye he could envisage the inside of the kitchen; he had a startlingly clear image of what the cook's face must look like, and he knew where a certain kind of soiled apron was hung.

'What's the matter with you?' Appello asked.

'Why?'

'The way you're looking at him.'

'I want to talk to him.'

'Well, talk to him.' Vinny smiled.

'I can't speak Italian, you know that.'

'Well, I'll ask him. What do you want to say?'

'Vinny – ' Bernstein started to speak and stopped.

'What?' Appello asked, leaning his head closer and looking down at the tablecloth.

'Get him to talk. Anything. Go ahead.'

Vinny, enjoying his friend's strange emotionalism, looked across at the man, who now was eating with careful but immense satisfaction. '*Scusi*, signor.'

The man looked up.

'I am a son of Italy from America. I would like to talk to you. We're strange here.'

The man, chewing deliciously, nodded with his amiable and amused smile and adjusted the hang of his jacket on the nearby chair.

'Do you come from around here?'

'Not very far.'

'How is everything here?'

'Poor. It is always poor.'

'What do you work at, if I may ask?'

The man had now finished his food. He took a last long drag of his wine and got up and proceeded to dress and pull his tie up tightly. When he walked it was with a slow, wide sway, as though each step had to be conserved.

'I sell cloth here to the people and the stores, such as they are,' he said. And he walked over to the bundle and set it carefully on a table and began untying it.

'He sells cloth,' Vinny said to Bernstein.

Bernstein's cheeks began to redden. From where he sat he could see the man's broad back, ever so slightly bent over the bundle. He could see the man's hands working at the knot and just a corner of the man's left eye. Now the man was laying the paper away from the two bolts of cloth, carefully pressing the wrinkles flat against the table. It was as though the brown paper were valuable leather that must not be cracked or rudely bent. The waitress came out of the kitchen with a tremendous round loaf of bread at least two feet in diameter. She gave it to him, and he placed it flat on top of the cloth, and the faintest feather of a smile curled up on Bernstein's lips. Now the man folded the paper back and brought the string around the bundle and tied the knot, and Bernstein uttered a little laugh, a laugh of relief.

Vinny looked at him, already smiling, ready to join the laughter, but mystified. 'What's the matter?' he asked.

Bernstein took a breath. There was something a little triumphant, a new air of confidence and superiority in his face and voice. 'He's Jewish, Vinny,' he said.

Vinny turned to look at the man. 'Why?'

'The way he works that bundle. It's exactly the way my father used to tie a bundle – and my grandfather. The whole history is packing bundles and getting away. Nobody else can be as tender and delicate with bundles. That's a Jewish man tying a bundle. Ask him his name.'

Vinny was delighted. 'Signor,' he called with that warmth reserved in his nature for members of families, any families.

The man, tucking the end of the string into the edge of the paper, turned to them with his kind smile.

'May I ask your name, signor?'

'My name? Mauro di Benedetto.'

'Mauro di Benedetto. Sure!' Vinny laughed, looking at Bernstein. 'That's Morris of the Blessed. Moses.'

'Tell him I'm Jewish,' Bernstein said, a driving eagerness charging his eyes.

'My friend is Jewish,' Vinny said to the man, who now was hoisting the bundle on to his shoulder.

'Heh?' the man asked, confused by their sudden vivacity. As though wondering if there were some sophisticated American point he should have understood, he stood there smiling blankly, politely, ready to join in this mood.

'*Judeo*, my friend.'

'*Judeo?*' he asked, the willingness to get the joke still holding the smile on his face.

Vinny hesitated before this steady gaze of incomprehension. '*Judeo*. The people of the Bible,' he said.

'Oh, yes, yes!' The man nodded now, relieved that he was not to be caught in ignorance. '*Ebreo*,' he corrected. And he nodded affably to Bernstein and seemed a little at a loss for what they expected him to do next.

'Does he know what you mean?' Bernstein asked.

'Yeah, he said, "Hebrew", but it doesn't seem to connect. Signor,' he addressed the man, 'why don't you have a glass of wine with us? Come, sit down.'

'Thank you, signor,' he replied appreciatively, 'but I must be home by sundown and I'm already a little late.'

Vinny translated, and Bernstein told him to ask why he had to be home by sundown.

The man apparently had never considered the question before. He shrugged and laughed and said, 'I don't know. All my life I get home for dinner on Friday night, and I like to come into the house before sundown. I suppose it's a habit; my father – you see, I have a route I walk, which is this route. I first did it with my father, and he did it with his father. We are known here for many generations past. And my father always got home on Friday night before sundown. It's a manner of the family I guess.'

'*Shabbas* begins at sundown on Friday night,' Bernstein said when Vinny had translated. 'He's even taking home the fresh bread for the Sabbath. The man is a Jew, I tell you. Ask him, will you?'

'*Scusi*, signor.' Vinny smiled. 'My friend is curious to know whether you are Jewish.'

The man raised his thick eyebrows not only in surprise but as though he felt somewhat honoured by being identified with something exotic. 'Me?' he asked.

'I don't mean American,' Vinny said, believing he had caught the meaning of the man's glance at Bernstein. '*Ebreo*,' he repeated.

The man shook his head, seeming a little sorry he could not oblige Vinny. 'No,' he said. He was ready to go but wanted to pursue what obviously was his most interesting conversation in weeks. 'Are they Catholics? The Hebrews?'

'He's asking me if Jews are Catholics,' Vinny said.

Bernstein sat back in his chair, a knotted look of wonder in his eyes. Vinny replied to the man, who looked once again at Bernstein as though wanting to investigate this strangeness further, but his mission drew him up and he wished them good fortune and said good-bye. He walked to the kitchen door and called thanks to the girl inside, saying the loaf would warm his back all the way down the mountain, and he opened the door and went out into the wind of the street and the sunshine, waving to them as he walked away.

They kept repeating their amazement on the way back to the car, and Bernstein told again how his father wrapped bundles. 'Maybe he doesn't know he's a Jew, but how could he not know what Jews are?' he said.

'Well, remember my aunt in Lucera?' Vinny asked. 'She's a schoolteacher, and she asked me if you believed in Christ. She didn't know the first thing about it. I think the ones in these small towns who ever heard of Jews think they're a Christian sect of some kind. I knew an old Italian once who thought all Negroes were Jews and white Jews were only converts.'

'But his name . . .'

' "Benedetto" is an Italian name too. I never heard of "Mauro" though. "Mauro" is strictly from the old sod.'

'But if he had a name like that, wouldn't it lead him to wonder if . . .?'

'I don't think so. In New York the name "Salvatore" is turned into "Sam". Italians are great for nicknames; the first name never means much. "Vicenzo" is "Enzo", or "Vinny" or even "Chico". Nobody would think twice about "Mauro" or damn near any other first name. He's obviously a Jew, but I'm sure he doesn't know it. You could tell, couldn't you? He was baffled.'

'But, my God, bringing home a bread for *Shabbas*!' Bernstein laughed, wide-eyed.

They reached the car, and Bernstein had his hand on the door but stopped before opening it and turned to Vinny. He looked heated; his eyelids seemed puffed. 'It's early – if you still want to I'll go back to the church with you. You can look for the boys.'

Vinny began to smile, and then they both laughed together, and Vinny slapped him on the back and gripped his shoulder as though to hug him. 'Goddam, now you're starting to enjoy this trip!'

As they walked briskly toward the church the conversation returned always to the same point, when Bernstein would say, 'I don't know why, but it gets me. He's not only acting like a Jew, but an Orthodox Jew. And doesn't even know – I mean it's strange as hell to me.'

'You look different, you know that?' Vinny said.

'Why?'

'You do.'

'You know a funny thing?' Bernstein said quietly as they entered the church and descended into the vault beneath it. 'I feel like – at home in this place. I can't describe it.'

Beneath the church, they picked their way through the shallower puddles on the stone floor, looking into vestibules, opening doors, searching for the priest. He appeared at last – they could not imagine from where – and Appello bought another candle from him and was gone in the shadows of the corridors where the vaults were.

Bernstein stood – everything was wet, dripping. Behind him, flat and wide, rose the stairway of stones bent with the tread of millions. Vapour steamed from his nostrils. There was nothing to look at but shadow. It was dank and black and low, an entrance to hell. Now and then in the very far distance he could hear a step echoing, another, then silence. He did not move, seeking the root of an ecstasy he had not dreamed was part of his nature; he saw the amiable man trudging down the mountains, across the plains, on routes marked out for him by generations of men, a nameless traveller carrying home a warm bread on Friday night – and kneeling in church on Sunday. There was an irony in it he could not name. And yet pride was running through him. Of what he should be proud he had no clear idea; perhaps it was only that beneath the brainless crush of history a Jew had secretly survived, shorn of his consciousness but forever caught by that final impudence of a Saturday Sabbath in a Catholic country; so that his very unawareness was proof, a proof as mute as stones, that a past lived. A past for me, Bernstein thought, astounded by its importance for him, when in fact he had never had a religion or even, he realized now, a history.

He could see Vinny's form approaching in the narrow corridor of crypts, the candle flame flattening in the cold draft. He felt he would look differently into Vinny's eyes; his condescension had gone and with it a certain embarrassment. He felt loose, somehow the equal of his friend – and how odd that was when, if anything, he had thought of himself as superior. Suddenly, with Vinny a yard away, he saw that his life had been covered with an unrecognized shame.

'I found it! It's back there!' Vinny was laughing like a young boy, pointing back toward the dark corridor.

'That's great, Vinny,' Bernstein said. 'I'm glad.'

They were both stooping slightly under the low, wet ceiling, their voices fleeing from their mouths in echoed whispers. Vinny held still for an instant, catching Bernstein's respectful happiness, and saw there that his search was not worthless sentiment. He raised the candle to see Bernstein's face better, and then he laughed and gripped Bernstein's wrist and led the way toward the flight of steps that rose to the surface. Bernstein had never liked anyone grasping him, but from this touch of a hand in the darkness, strangely, there was no implication of a hateful weakness.

They walked side by side down the steep street away from the church. The town was empty again. The air smelled of burning charcoal and olive oil. A few pale stars had come out. The shops were all shut. Bernstein thought of Mauro di Benedetto going down the winding, rocky road, hurrying against the setting of the sun.

[*1951*]

Please Don't Kill Anything

THAT beach was golden toward sundown. The bathers had all gone home when the wind got brisk. Gulls were diving just beyond the breakers. On the horizon they could see four stubby fishing boats moving in a line. Then she turned toward the right and saw the two parked trucks and the fishermen hauling on a net. 'Let's see if they caught anything,' she said, with the swift surge of wonder that swept through her at any new sight.

The trucks were battered and rusty, with open backs, and the one they came upon had about twenty-five big, sand-sprinkled bass and small bluefish piled at the tailgate. A man in his sixties was sitting on the truck, holding a rope that was wound around a winch at his side. He nodded to them pleasantly and drew on the rope to keep it wound tightly around the turning winch. At the water's edge another man kept watch over the net, piling it in a heap as it was drawn out of the water.

Sam glanced at the fish as they arrived at the truck and knew she would be startled. She saw them, and her eyes widened, but she even tried to smile in congratulation to the old man who drew on the rope, and she said, 'You catch all these?'

'Yup,' he said, and his eyes warmed at her beauty.

'These are all dead, aren't they,' she said.

'Oh, ya,' the old man said.

She had an excitement in her eyes as she looked, it seemed, at each individual fish to be sure it wasn't moving. Sam started talking to the old man about the probability of a good catch in the net now coming into shore, and she was drawn into the conversation, and he was relieved that her eyes, the colour of the blue sea, were calmed.

But now the old man moved a lever, and the winch speeded up with a rising whine, and he was exerting himself to keep the rope taut. The winch on the other truck also turned faster, and the two net-tenders on the beach moved rapidly from the trucks to the edge of the water, hurriedly piling up the incoming net. Now they could see the curving line of cork floats only a few yards away in the water.

'Why do you pull so fast?' Sam asked the old man. 'Are they fighting the net?'

'Naw,' the old man said, 'just want to keep her taut so they mightn't jump over and git away.'

The waves were breaking into the net now, but they could not yet see any fish. She put her two hands up to her cheeks and said, 'Oh, now they know they're caught!' She laughed. 'Each one is wondering what happened!' He was glad she was making fun of herself even if her eyes were fixed in fear on the submerged net. She glanced up at her husband and said, 'Oh, dear, they're going to be caught now.'

He started to explain, but she quickly went on, 'I know it's all right as long as they're eaten. They're going to eat them, aren't they?'

'They'll sell them to the fish stores,' he said softly, so the old man at the winch wouldn't hear. 'They'll feed people.'

'Yes,' she said, like a child reassured. 'I'll watch it. I'm watching it,' she almost announced to him. But in her something was holding its breath.

A wave receded then, and with one pull the bag of the net was drawn out of the surf. Voices sounded from both trucks; it wasn't much of a catch. She saw the tails of small bluefish writhing up through the net ('They're standing on their heads!'), and a great bass flopping, and sea robins trying to stretch their curved umber wings, and one flounder lying in the midst of this tangled rubble of the sea. She kept pointing here and there at a fish that had suddenly jerked or flopped over, and called out, 'There's one! There's another one!' – meaning they were not dead yet and, he knew, must be rescued.

The men opened the net and pulled out the bass and some bluefish, tossing the sea robins on to the sand and the flounder, and two blowfish, which immediately began to swell. She turned to the old man on the truck and, trying to smile, she called to him with a sharpness in her voice, almost a cry, 'Don't you take those?'

He drew an old man's warmth from the glow of her face and the startling shape of her body under the striped jersey and the beige slacks. 'They're no good, ma'am,' he said.

'Well, don't you put them back?'

The old man seemed to hesitate as though some memory of guilt had crossed his mind. 'Sure. We put them back' – and sat there watching his partner, who was picking good fish out of the net and tossing the winged fish right and left on to the sand.

There were now about fifty sea robins on the beach, some of them gulping, some perfectly still. Sam could feel the tension rising in her, and he walked over to the nearest fish and, feeling a tremor of repugnance, picked it up and threw it into the waves and came back to her. The pulse of its life was still in his fingers. 'If I had something to hold them with,' she began.

'You can't throw all those fish back,' he said.

'But they're alive!' she said, desperately trying to smile and not to separate herself from him.

'No, they're dead. Most of them are dead, sweet.'

'Are they dead?' she turned and asked the old man.

'No, they ain't dead. Most.'

'Would they live again if they had water?'

'Oh, sure, they come to,' he said, trying to assuage her but not moving from his place.

She took off one sandal and went to a fish that was writhing and tried to flip it into the water, but it slipped away. Sam came over and picked it up and flung it into the sea. He was laughing now, and she kept saying, 'I'm sorry. But if they're alive . . .!'

'It's all right,' he said, 'but they're mostly dead by now. Look.' And he picked up one that was motionless; it felt flabby. He threw it into the water, and it arched itself as it struck, and she cried out, 'There! It's swimming!'

Defeated and grinning, now that he saw the fishermen watching him with smiles on their faces, he went about throwing all the sea robins back into the water. He sensed that even with their smiles the men were somehow held by her insistence, and as he threw the slimy fish in one by one he saw each fish separately, each straining for its quart of sea, and he was no longer ashamed. And there were two fish left, both sea robins with white bellies and stiff umber wings and the beginnings of legs sprouting from both sides of their necks. They were motionless on their backs. He did not bend to pick them up because she seemed prepared to sacrifice them, and he went back to her, feeling, somehow, that if he let those two die on the beach she might come to terms with this kind of waste. For he had to open the window at home, once, to let out a moth, which ordinarily he would have swatted, and while part of his heart worshipped her fierce tenderness toward all that lived, another part knew that she must come to understand that she did not die with the moths and the spiders and the fledgling birds and, now, with these fish. But it was also that he wished the fishermen to see that she was not quite so fanatic as to require these two last, obviously dead, sea robins to be given their chance.

He stood beside her again, waiting. He smiled and said, 'You got a job cut out for yourself. There's twenty-five miles of beach we can cruise, throwing back fish.' She laughed and drew his head down and kissed him, and he hugged her, and she said, 'Just those two. Go on, Sam. They might be alive.'

He laughed again and picked up one of the fish, knowing that it was even more unjust for two to die when fifty had been saved, and as he tossed it to the waves a dog appeared. It was a big, brown retriever with sea-matted hair, and it leaped into the waves and dipped its head into the water, raised up with the sea robin gently cradled in its mouth, and came back with great pride to lay it carefully at Sam's feet. 'God, look how gently he brings it back!' Sam said.

'Oh, dear!' She laughed and bent toward the stern face of the buff-eyed dog. The dog returned her a look of athletic determination. 'You mustn't do that!' Helplessly she looked at Sam, who picked up the fish and threw it back. Again the dog leaped in and retrieved it and now with enormous élan and pride nearly danced back to Sam, laid it at his feet, and stood waiting for the next throw, its legs trembling with eagerness.

'Well?' he said to her. 'There you are. There's a whole conspiracy against these two fish. This guy was trained to help man; man has to eat and something's got to die, puss . . .'

As he spoke a silvery minnow slid out of the mouth of the sea robin at his feet. 'Look at that now!' he yelled. 'See? What about *that* little fish?'

'Yes!' she said, like an admission.

'You see? The victims make other victims.'

'Well, hurry, throw it back anyway.'

'But this character keeps bringing it back. This fish is doomed,' he said, and they were both laughing, but she had in her head a clock which was telling her that every second counted, and she started to bend toward the fish at his feet despite her repugnance at touching it. He moved her hand away and picked it up, threw it, and when the dog turned and went into the water for it, he ran a few yards along the beach to the other fish and threw it in.

'Now,' he said a little breathlessly as the dog returned with the first fish, 'now there's one. This is a positively doomed fish on the principle that man has to eat and this dog is part of the scheme to feed him.' But now even he could not take his eyes from the fish, which had taken to breathing rapidly, what with the shocks of being thrown into the water and being picked up by the dog and flying through the brisk wind. 'This fish wishes you'd let it die in peace!' He laughed.

She looked around almost frantically, still smiling and laughing with him, and saw a stick and ran, ran with the dancer's leaping stride, and the dog glanced at her, then watched her as she waved the stick and called to him. She threw it into the sea, and the dog streaked into the water after it; and Sam picked up the last fish quickly and flung it, and it arched with life as it slid into a wave.

The beach was now clean, and the fishermen were busy stowing their nets, and the two walked away toward the road. 'I'm sorry, Sam, but they were alive, and if nobody's going to eat them . . .'

'Well, the tide would have taken them out dead, puss, and

they'd have been eaten by other fish. They wouldn't have been wasted.'

'Yes,' she said.

They walked, holding each other by the hand, and she was silent. He felt a great happiness opening in him that she had laid his hand on the fish which were now swimming in the sea because he had lifted them. Now she looked up at him like a little girl, with that naked wonder in her face, even as she was smiling in the way of a grown woman, and she said, 'But some of them might live now till they're old.'

'And then they'll die,' he said.

'But at least they'll live as long as they can.' And she laughed with the woman part of her that knew of absurdities.

'That's right,' he said, 'they'll live to a ripe old age and grow prosperous and dignified . . .'

She burst out laughing. 'And see their children grown up!'

He kissed her on her lips, blessing her and her wish. 'Oh, how I love you,' she said with tears in her eyes. Then they walked home.

[*1960*]

The Misfits

WIND blew down from the mountains all night. A wild river of air swept and swirled across the dark sky and struck down against the blue desert and hissed back into the hills. The three cowboys slept under their blankets, their backs against the first upward curve of the circling mountains, their faces toward the desert of sage. The wind and its tidal washing seethed through their dreams, and when it stopped there was a lunar silence that caused Gay Langland to open his eyes. For the first time in three nights he could hear his own breathing, and in the new hush he looked up at the stars and saw how clear and bright they were. He felt happy and slid himself out of his blankets and stood up fully dressed.

On the silent plateau between the two mountain ranges Gay Langland was the only moving thing. He turned his head and then his body in a full circle, looking into the deep blue sky for sign of storm. He saw that it would be a good day and a quiet one. He walked a few yards from the two other sleepers and wet the sandy ground. The excitement of the stillness was awakening his body. He returned and lit the bundle of dry sage he had gathered last night, dropped some heavier wood on the quick flames, perched the blackened coffeepot on the stones surrounding the fire bed, and sat on one heel, staring at the fresh orange embers.

Gay Langland was forty-five years old but as limber as he had ever been in his life. The light of his face brightened when there were things to do, a nail to straighten, an animal to size up, and it dimmed when there was nothing in his hands, and his eyes then went sleepy. When there was something to be done in a place he stayed there, and when there was nothing to be done he went from it. He had a wife and two children less than a hundred miles from here whom he had not seen in more than three years. She had betrayed him and did not want him, but the children were naturally better off with their mother. When he felt lonely for them all he thought of them longingly, and when the feeling passed he was left without any question as to what he might do to bring them all back together again. He had been born and raised on rangeland, and he did not know that anything could be undone that was done, any more than falling rain could be stopped in mid-air. And he had a smile and a look on his face that was in accordance. His forehead was evenly tracked with deep ridges, as though his brows were always raised a little expectantly, slightly surprised, a little amused, and his mouth friendly. His ears stuck out, as they often do with little boys or young calves, and he had a boy's turned-up snub nose. But his skin was browned by the wind, and his small eyes looked and saw and, above all, were trained against showing fear.

Gay Langland looked up from the fire at the sky and saw the first delicate stain of pink. He went over to the sleepers and shook Guido Racanelli's arm. A grunt of salutation sounded in Guido's head, but he remained on his side with his eyes shut. 'The sumbitch died off,' Gay said to him. Guido listened, motionless, his eyes shut against the firelight, his bones warm in his fat. Gay wanted to shake him again and wake him, but in the last two days he had come to wonder whether Guido was not secretly considering not flying at all. The plane's engine was rattling its valves and one shock absorber was weak. Gay had known the pilot for years and he knew and respected his moods. Flying up and down these mountain gorges within feet of the rock walls was nothing you could pressure a man to do. But now that the wind had died Gay hoped very much that Guido would take off this morning and let them begin their work.

He got to his feet and again glanced skyward. Then he stood there thinking of Roslyn. And he had a strong desire to have money in his pocket that he had earned himself when he came to her tonight. The feeling had been returning again and again that he had somehow passed the kidding point and that he had to work again and earn his way as he always had before he met her. Not that he didn't work for her, but it wasn't the same. Driving her car, repairing her house, running errands – all that stuff wasn't what you would call work. Still, he thought, it was too. Yet, it wasn't either.

He stepped over to the other sleeper and shook him. Perce Howland opened his eyes.

'The sumbitch died, Perce,' Gay said.

Perce's eyes looked toward the heavens and he nodded. Then he slid out of his blankets and walked past Gay and stood wetting the sand, breathing deeply as in sleep. Gay always found him humorous to watch when he woke up. Perce walked into things and sometimes stood wetting his own boots. He was a little like a child waking up, and his eyes now were still dreamy and soft.

Gay called over to him, 'Better'n wages, huh, Perce?'

'Damn right,' Perce muttered and returned to the fire, rubbing his skin against his clothes.

Gay kneeled by the fire again, scraping hot coals into a pile and setting the frying pan over them on stones. He could pick up hot things without feeling pain. Now he moved an ember with his finger.

'You make me nervous doing that,' Perce said, looking down over his shoulder.

'Nothin' but fire,' Gay said, pleased.

They were in silence for a moment, both of them enjoying the brightening air. 'Guido goin' up?' Perce asked.

'Didn't say. I guess he's thinkin' about it.'

'Be light pretty soon,' Perce warned.

He glanced off to the closest range and saw the purple rocks rising in their mystery toward the faintly glowing stars. Perce Howland was twenty-two, hipless and tall, and he stood there as effortlessly as the mountains he was looking at, as though he had been created there in his dungarees, with the tight plaid shirt and the three-button cuffs, the broad-brimmed beige hat set back on his blond head, and his thumbs tucked into his belt so his fingers could touch the engraved belt buckle with his name spelled out under the raised figure of the bucking horse. It was his first bucking-horse prize, and he loved to touch it when he stood waiting, and he liked to wait.

Perce had known Gay Langland for only five weeks, and Guido

for three days. He had met Gay in a Bowie bar, and Gay had asked him where he was from and what he was doing, and he had told Gay his story, which was the usual for most of the rodeo riders. He had come on down from Nevada, as he had done since he was sixteen, to follow the local rodeos and win some money riding bucking horses, but this trip had been different, because he had lost the desire to go back home again.

They had become good friends that night when Gay took him to Roslyn's house to sleep, and when he woke in the morning he had been surprised that an educated eastern woman should have been so regular and humorous and interested in his opinions. So he had been floating around with Roslyn and Gay Langland, and they were comfortable to be with; Gay mostly, because Gay never thought to say he ought to be making something of his life. Gay made him feel it was all right to go from day to day and week to week. Perce Howland did not trust anybody too far, and it was not necessary to trust Gay because Gay did not want anything of him or try to manipulate him. He just wanted a partner to go mustanging, and Perce had never done anything like that and he wanted to see how it was. And now he was here, sixty miles from the nearest town, seven thousand feet up in the air, and for two days waiting for the wind to die so the pilot could take off into the mountains where the wild horses lived.

Perce looked out toward the desert, which was beginning to show its silent horizon. 'Bet the moon looks like this if anybody could get there.'

Gay Langland did not answer. In his mind he could feel the wild horses grazing and moving about in the nearby mountains and he wanted to get to them. Indicating Guido Racanelli, he said, 'Give him a shake, Perce. The sun's about up.'

Perce started over to Guido, who moved before Perce reached him. 'Gettin' light, Guido,' Perce said.

Guido Racanelli rolled upright on his great behind, his belly slung over his belt, and he inspected the brightening sky in the distance as though some personal message were out there for him. The pink reflected light brightened his face. The flesh around his eyes was white where the goggles protected his face, and the rest

of his skin was burned brown by wind. His silences were more
profound than the silences of others because his cheeks were so
deep, like the melon-half cheeks of a baboon that curve forward
from the mouth. Yet they were hard cheeks, as hard as his great
belly. He looked like a jungle bird now, slowly turning his head
to inspect the faraway sky, a serious bird with a brown face and
white eyes. His head was entirely bald. He took off his khaki army
cap and rubbed his fingers into his scalp.

Gay Langland stood up and walked to him and gave him his
eggs and thick bacon on a tin plate. 'Wind died, Guido,' Gay
said, standing there and looking down at the pilot.

'It doesn't mean much what it did down here.' Guido pointed
skyward with his thumb. 'Up there's where it counts.'

'Ain't no sign of wind up there,' Gay said. Gay's eyes seemed
amused. He did not want to seem committed to a real argument.
'We got no more eggs, Guido,' he warned.

Guido ate.

Now the sky flared with true dawn, like damp paper suddenly
catching fire. Perce and Gay sat down on the ground facing
Guido, and they all ate their eggs.

The shroud of darkness quickly slipped off the red truck which
stood a few yards away. Then, behind it, the little plane showed
itself. Guido Racanelli ate and sipped his coffee, and Gay Langland watched him with a weak smile and without speaking. Perce
blinked contentedly at the brightening sky, slightly detached
from the other two. He finished his coffee and slipped a chew of
tobacco into his mouth and sucked on it.

It was a pink day now all around the sky.

Gay Langland made a line in the sand between his thighs and
said, 'You goin' up, Guido?' He looked at Guido directly and he
was still smiling.

Guido thought for a moment. He was older, about fifty. His
pronunciation was unaccountably eastern, with sharp r's. He
sounded educated sometimes. He stared off toward the squat little
plane. 'Every once in a while I wonder what the hell it's all about,'
he said.

'What is?' Gay asked.

Perce watched Guido's face, thoroughly listening.

Guido felt their attention and spoke with pleasurable ease. He still stared past them at the plane. 'I got a lousy valve. I know it, Gay.'

'Been that way a long time, Guido,' Gay said with sympathy.

'I know,' Guido said. They were not arguing but searching now. 'And we won't hardly get twenty dollars apiece out of it – there's only four or five horses back in there.'

'We knew that, Guido,' Gay said. They were in sympathy with each other.

'I might just get myself killed, for twenty dollars.'

'Hell, you know them mountains,' Gay said.

'You can't see wind, Gay,' the pilot said.

Gay knew now that Guido was going up right away. He saw that Guido had just wanted to get all the dangers straight in his mind so he could see them and count them; then he would go out against them.

'You're flying along in and out of those passes and then you dive for the sons of bitches, and just when you're pulling up, some goddam gust presses you down and there you are.'

'I know,' Gay said.

There was silence. Guido sipped his coffee, staring off at the plane. 'I just wonder about it every once in a while,' the pilot said.

'Well hell,' Perce Howland said, 'it's better than wages.'

'You damn right it is, Perce,' the pilot said thoughtfully.

'I seen guys get killed who never left the ground,' Perce said.

The two older men knew that his father had been killed by a bull long ago and that he had seen his father die. He had had his own arms broken in rodeos and a Brahma bull had stepped on his chest.

'One rodeo near Salinas I see a fella get his head snapped right clear off his chest by a cable busted. They had this cable drawin' horses up on to a truck. I seen his head rollin' away like a bowlin' ball. Must've roll twenty-five yards before it hit a fence post and stopped.' He spat tobacco juice and turned back to look at Guido. 'It had a moustache. Funny thing, I never knowed that guy had a moustache. Never noticed it. Till I see it stop rolling and there it was, dust all over the moustache.'

'That was a dusty moustache,' Gay said, grinning against their deepening morbidity.

They all smiled. Then time hung for a moment as they waited. And at last Guido shifted on to one buttock and said, 'Well, let's get gassed up.'

Guido leaned himself to one side with his palm on the ground, then got to his feet by moving in a circle around this palm, and stood up. Gay and Perce Howland were already moving off toward the truck, Perce heisting up his dungarees over his breakfast-full stomach, and the older Gay more sprightly and intent. Guido stood holding one hand open over the fire, watching them loading the six enormous truck tyres on to the bed of the truck. Each tyre had a twenty-foot length of rope wired to it, and at the end of each rope was a loop. Before they swung the tyres on to the truck Gay inspected the ropes to be sure they were securely knotted to the tyres, and the loops open and ready for throwing.

Guido blinked against the warming sun, watching the other two, then he looked off to his right where the passes were, and the fingers of his mind felt around beyond those passes into the bowls and hollows of the mountains where last week he had spotted the small herd of wild horses grazing. Now he felt the lightness he had been hoping to feel for three days, the bodiless urge to fly. For three days he had kept away from the plane because a certain carelessness had been itching at him, a feeling that he always thought would lead him to his death. About five weeks ago he had come up to this desert with Gay Langland and he had chased seven mustangs out of the mountains. But this time he had dived to within a foot of the mountainside, and afterward, as they sat around the fire eating dinner, Guido had had the feeling that he had made that deep dive so he could die. And the thought of his dead wife had come to him again, and the other thought that always came into his mind with her dead face. It was the wonderment, the quiet pressing-in of the awareness that he had never wanted a woman after she had been buried with the still-born baby beside her in the graveyard outside Bowie. Seven years now he had waited for some real yearning for a woman, and nothing at all had come to him. It pleasured him to know that he was free of that, and it sometimes made him careless in the plane, as though some great bang and a wreckage would make him again what he had been. By now he could go around in Bowie for a week and only in an odd moment recall that he hadn't even looked at a girl walking by, and the feeling of carelessness would come on him, a kind of loose gaiety, as though everything was comical. Until he had made that dive and pulled out with his nose almost scraping the grass, and he had climbed upward with his mouth hanging open and his body in a sweat. So that through these past three days up here he had refused to let himself take off until the wind had utterly died, and he had clung to moroseness. He wanted to take off in the absolute grip of his own wits, leaving nothing to chance. Now there was no wind at all, and he felt he had pressed the sinister gaiety out of his mind. He left the dying fire and walked past Gay and Perce and down the gentle slope to the plane, looking like a stout, serious football coach before the kick-off.

He glanced over the fuselage and at the bald doughnut tyres and he loved the plane. Again, as always, he looked at the weakened starboard shock absorber, which no longer held its spread so that the plane stood tilted a little to one side, and told himself that it was not serious. He heard the truck motor starting and he unfastened the knots of the ropes holding the plane to the spikes driven into the desert floor. Then the truck pulled up, and young Perce Howland dropped off and went over to the tail handle, gripped it, lifted the tail off the ground, and swung the plane around so she faced out across the endless desert and away from the mountains. Then they unwound the rubber hose from the gas drum on the truck and stuck the nozzle into the gas tank behind the engine, and Perce turned the pump crank.

Guido then walked around the wing and over to the cockpit, whose right door was folded down, leaving the inside open to the air. He reached in and took out his ripped leather flight jacket and got into it.

Perce stood leaning against the truck fender now, grinning. 'That sure is a ventilated type jacket, Guido,' he said.

Then Guido said, 'I can't get my size any more.' The jacket had one sleeve off at the elbow, and the dried leather was split open down the back, showing the lamb's-wool lining. He had bombed Germany in this jacket long ago. He reached in behind the seat and took out a goggle case, slipped his goggles out, replaced the case, set his goggles securely on his face, and reached in again and took out a shotgun pistol and four shells from a little wooden box beside his seat. He loaded the pistol and laid it carefully under his seat. Then he got into the cockpit, sat in his seat, drew the strap over his belly and buckled it. Meantime Gay had taken his position before the propeller.

Guido called through the open doorway of the cockpit, 'Turn her over, Gay-boy.'

Gay stepped up to the propeller, glanced down behind his heels to be sure no stone waited to trip him when he stepped back, pulled down on the blade, and hopped back watchfully.

'Give her another!' Guido called in the silence.

Gay stepped up again, again glancing around his heels, and pulled the blade down. The engine inhaled and exhaled, and they could all hear the oily clank of her inner shafts turning loosely.

'Ignition on, Gay-boy!' Guido called and threw the switch.

This time Gay inspected the ground around him even more carefully and pulled his hatbrim down tighter on his head. Perce stood leaning on the truck's front fender, spitting and chewing, his eyes softly squinted against the brazen sun. Gay reached up and pulled the propeller down and jumped back. A puff of smoke floated up from the engine ports.

'Goddam car gas,' Guido said. 'Ignition on. Go again, Gay-boy!' They were buying low octane to save money.

Gay again stepped up to the propeller, swung the blade down, and the engine said its 'Chaaahh!' and the ports breathed white smoke into the morning air. Gay walked over to Perce and stood beside him, watching. The fuselage shuddered and the propeller turned into a wheel, and the dust blew pleasantly from behind the

plane and toward the mountains. Guido gunned her, and she
tumbled toward the open desert, bumping along over the sage
clumps and crunching whitened skeletons of cattle killed by the
winter. The stiff-backed plane grew smaller, shouldering its way
over the broken ground, and then its nose turned upward and
there was space between the doughnut tyres and the desert, and
lazily it climbed, turning back the way it had come. It flew over
the heads of Perce and Gay, and Guido waved down, a stranger
now, fiercely goggled and wrapped in leather, and they could see
him exposed to the waist, turning from them to look through the
windshield at the mountains ahead of him. The plane flew away,
climbing smoothly, losing itself against the orange and purple
walls that vaulted up from the desert to hide from the cowboys'
eyes the wild animals they wanted for themselves.

They would have at least two hours before the plane flew out of
the mountains driving the horses before it, so they washed the
three tin plates and the cups and stored them in the aluminium
grub box. If Guido did find horses they would break camp and
return to Bowie tonight, so they packed up their bedrolls with
sailors' tidiness and laid them neatly side by side on the ground.
The six great truck tyres, each with its looped rope coiled, within,
lay in two piles on the bed of the truck. Gay Langland looked
them over and touched them with his hand and stood for a
moment trying to think if there was anything they were leaving
behind. He jumped up on the truck to see that the cap was
screwed tight on the gas drum, which was lashed to the back of
the cab up front, and it was. Then he hopped down to the ground
and got into the cab and started the engine. Perce was already sitting there with his hat tipped forward against the yellow sunlight
pouring through the windshield. A thin and concerned border
collie came trotting up as Gay started to close his door, and he
invited her into the cab. She leaped up, and he snugged her into
the space between the clutch and the left wall of the cab. 'Damn
near forgot Belle,' he said, and they started off.

Gay owned the truck and he wanted to preserve the front end,
which he knew could be twisted out of line on broken ground. So

he started off slowly. They could hear the gas sloshing in the drum behind them outside. It was getting warm now. They rode in silence, staring ahead at the two-track trail they were following across the bone-cluttered sagebrush. Thirty miles ahead stood the lava mountains that were the northern border of this desert, the bed of a bowl seven thousand feet up, a place no one ever saw except the few cowboys searching for stray cattle every few months. People in Bowie, sixty miles away, did not know of this place. There were the two of them and the truck and the dog, and now that they were on the move they felt between them the comfort of purpose and their isolation, and Perce slumped in his seat, blinking as though he would go to sleep again, and Gay smoked a cigarette and let his body flow from side to side with the pitching of the truck.

There was a moving cloud of dust in the distance toward the left, and Gay said, 'Antelope,' and Perce tipped his hat back and looked. 'Must be doin' sixty,' he said, and Gay said, 'More. I chased one once and I was doin' more than sixty and he lost me.' Perce shook his head in wonder, and they turned to look ahead again.

After he had thought awhile Perce said, 'We better get over to Largo by tomorrow if we're gonna get into that rodeo. They's gonna be a crowd trying to sign up for that one.'

'We'll drive down in the morning,' Gay said.

'I'll have to see about gettin' me some stock.'

'We'll get there early tomorrow; you'll get stock if you come in early.'

'Like to win some money,' Perce said. 'I just wish I get me a good horse down there.'

'They be glad to fix you up, Perce. You're known pretty good around there now. They'll fix you up with some good stock,' Gay said. Perce was one of the best bronc riders, and the rodeos liked to have it known he would appear.

Then there was silence. Gay had to hold the gear-shift lever in high or it would slip out into neutral when they hit bumps. The transmission fork was worn out, he knew, and the front tyres were going too. He dropped one hand to his pants pocket and felt the four silver dollars he had from the ten Roslyn had given him when they had left her days ago.

As though he had read Gay's mind, Perce said, 'Roslyn would've liked it up here. She'd liked to have seen that antelope, I bet.' Perce grinned as both of them usually did at Roslyn's eastern surprise at everything they did and saw and said.

'Yeah,' Gay said, 'she likes to see things.' Through the corners of his eyes he watched the younger man, who was looking ahead with a little grin on his face. 'She's a damned good sport, old Roslyn,' Gay said.

'Sure is,' Perce Howland said. And Gay watched him for any sign of guile, but there was only a look of glad appreciation. 'First woman like that I ever met,' the younger man said.

'They's more,' Gay said. 'Some of them eastern women fool you sometimes. They got education but they're good sports. And damn good *women* too, some of them.'

There was a silence. Then the younger man asked, 'You get to know a lot of them? Eastern women?'

'Ah, I get one once in a while,' Gay said.

'Only educated women I ever know, they was back home near Teachers College. Students. Y'know,' he said, warming to the memory, 'I used to think, hell, education's everything. But when I saw the husbands some of them got married to – schoolteachers and everything, why I don't give them much credit. And they just as soon climb on a man as tell him good morning. I was teachin' them to ride for a while near home.'

'Just because a woman's educated don't mean much. Woman's a woman,' Gay said. The image of his wife came into his mind. For a moment he wondered if she was still living with the same man he had beaten up when he discovered them together in a parked car six years ago.

'You divorced?' Perce asked.

'No. I never bothered with it,' Gay said. It always surprised him how Perce said just what was on his mind sometimes. 'How'd you know I was thinkin' of that?' he asked, grinning with embarrassment. But he was too curious to keep silent.

'Hell, I didn't know,' Perce said.

'You're always doin' that. I think of somethin' and you go ahead and say it.'

'That's funny,' Perce said.

They rode on in silence. They were nearing the middle of the desert, where they would turn east. Gay was driving faster now because he wanted to get to the rendezvous and sit quietly waiting for the plane to appear. He held on to the gear-shift lever and felt it trying to spring out of high and into neutral. It would have to be fixed. The time was coming fast when he would need about fifty dollars or have to sell the truck, because it would be useless without repairs. Without a truck and without a horse he would be down to what was in his pocket.

Perce spoke out of the silence. 'If I don't win Saturday I'm gonna have to do somethin' for money.'

'Goddam, you always say what's in my mind.'

Perce laughed. His face looked very young and pink. 'Why?'

'I was just now thinkin',' Gay said, 'what I'm gonna do for money.'

'Well, Roslyn give you some,' Perce said.

He said it innocently, and Gay knew it was innocent, and yet he felt angry blood moving into his neck. Something had happened in these five weeks, and Gay did not know for sure what it was. Roslyn had taken to calling Perce cute, and now and again she would bend over and kiss him on the back of the neck when he was sitting in the living-room chair, drinking with them.

Not that that meant anything in itself, because he'd known eastern women before who'd do something like that and it was just their way. Especially college graduate divorced women. What he wondered at was Perce's way of hardly even noticing what she did to him. Sometimes it was like he'd already had her and could ignore her, the way a man will who knows he's boss. But then Gay thought it might just be that he really wasn't interested, or maybe that he was keeping cool in deference to Gay.

Again Gay felt a terrible longing to earn money working. He sensed the bottom of his life falling if it turned out Roslyn had really been loving this boy beside him. It had happened to him once before with his wife, but this frightened him more and he did not know exactly why. Not that he couldn't do without Roslyn. There wasn't anybody or anything he couldn't do without. She was about his age and full of laughter that was not laughter and gaiety that was not gaiety and adventurousness that was laboured, and he knew all this perfectly well even as he laughed with her and was high with her in the bars and rodeos. He had only lived once, and that was when he had had his house and his wife and his children. He knew the difference, but you never kept anything, and he had never particularly thought about keeping anything or losing anything. He had been all his life like Perce Howland, sitting beside him now, a man moving on or ready to. It was only when he discovered his wife with a stranger that he knew he had had a stake to which he had been pleasurably tethered. He had not seen her or his children for years and only rarely thought about any of them. Any more than his father had thought of him very much after the day he had gotten on his pony, when he was fourteen, to go to town from the ranch, and had kept going into Montana and stayed there for three years. He lived in this country as his father did, and it was the same endless range wherever he went, and it connected him sufficiently with his father and his wife and his children. All might turn up sometime in some town or at some rodeo, where he might happen to look over his shoulder and see his daughter or one of his sons, or they might never turn up. He had neither left anyone nor not-left as long as they were all alive on these ranges, for everything here was always beyond the farthest shot of vision and far away, and mostly he had worked alone or with one or two men, between distant mountains anyway.

In the distance now he could see the shimmering wall of the heat waves rising from the clay flatland they wanted to get to. Now they were approaching closer, and it opened to them beyond the heat waves, and they could see once again how vast it was, a prehistoric lake bed thirty miles long by seventeen miles wide, couched between the two mountain ranges. It was a flat, beige waste without grass or bush or stone, where a man might drive a car at a hundred miles an hour with his hands off the wheel and never hit anything at all. They drove in silence. The truck stopped bouncing as the tyres rolled over harder ground where there were fewer sage clumps. The waves of heat were dense before them, nearly touchable. Now the truck rolled smoothly and they were on the clay lake bed, and when they had gone a few hundred yards on to it Gay pulled up and shut off the engine. The air was still in a dead, sunlit silence. When he opened his door he could hear a squeak in the hinge he had never noticed before. When they walked around they could hear their shirts rasping against their backs and the brush of a sleeve against their trousers.

They stood on the clay ground, which was as hard as concrete, and turned to look the way they had come. They looked back toward the mountains at whose feet they had camped and slept, and scanned their ridges for Guido's plane. It was too early for him, and they made themselves busy, taking the gas drum off the truck and setting it a few yards away on the ground, because they would want the truck bed clear when the time came to run the horses down. Then they climbed up and sat inside the tyres with their necks against the tyre beads and their legs hanging over.

Perce said, 'I sure hope they's five up in there.'

'Guido saw five, he said.'

'He said he wasn't sure if one wasn't only a colt,' Perce said.

Gay let himself keep silent. He felt he was going to argue with Perce. He watched Perce through the corners of his eyes, saw the flat, blond cheeks and the strong, lean neck, and there was something tricky about Perce now. 'How long you think you'll be stayin' around here, Perce?' he asked.

They were both watching the distant ridges for a sign of the plane.

'Don't know,' Perce said and spat over the side of the truck. 'I'm gettin' a little tired of this, though.'

'Well, it's better than wages, Perce.'

'Hell, yes. Anything's better than wages.'

Gay's eyes crinkled. 'You're a real misfit, boy.'

'That suits me fine,' Perce said. They often had this conversation and savoured it. 'Better than workin' for some goddam cow outfit buckarooin' so somebody else can buy gas for his Cadillac.'

'Damn right,' Gay said.

'Hell, Gay, you are the most misfitted man I ever saw and you done all right.'

'I got no complaints,' Gay said.

'I don't want nothin' and I don't want to want nothin'.'

'That's the way, boy.'

Gay felt closer to him again and he was glad for it. He kept his eyes on the ridges far away. The sun felt good on his shoulders. 'I think he's havin' trouble with them sumbitches up there.'

Perce stared out at the ridges. 'Ain't two hours yet.' Then he turned to Gay. 'These mountains must be cleaned out by now, ain't they?'

'Just about,' Gay said. 'Just a couple small herds left. Can't do much more around here.'

'What you goin' to do when you got these cleaned out?'

'Might go north, I think. Supposed to be some big herds in around Thighbone Mountain and that range up in there.'

'How far's that?'

'North about a hundred miles. If I can get Guido interested.'

Perce smiled. 'He don't like movin' around much, does he?'

'He's just misfitted like the rest of us,' Gay said. 'He don't want nothin'.' Then he added, 'They wanted him for an airline pilot flyin' up into Montana and back. Good pay too.'

'Wouldn't do it, huh?'

'Not Guido,' Gay said, grinning. 'Might not like some of the passengers, he told them.'

Both men laughed, and Perce shook his head in admiration of Guido. Then he said, 'They wanted me take over the ridin' academy up home. I thought about that. Two hundred a month and board. Easy work too. You don't hardly have to ride at all. Just stand around and see the customers get satisfied and put them girls off and on.'

He fell silent. Gay knew the rest. It was the same story always. It brought him closer to Perce, and it was what he had liked about Perce in the first place. Perce didn't like wages either. He had come on Perce in a bar where the boy was buying drinks for everybody with his rodeo winnings, and his hair still clotted with blood from a bucking horse's kick an hour earlier. Roslyn had offered to get a doctor for him and he had said, 'Thank you kindly. But I ain't bad hurt. If you're bad hurt you gonna die and the doctor can't do nothin', and if you ain't bad hurt you get better anyway without no doctor.'

Now it suddenly came upon Gay that Perce had known Roslyn before they had met in the bar. He stared at the boy's profile. 'Want to come up north with me if I go?' he asked.

Perce thought a moment. 'Think I'll stay around here. Not much rodeoin' up north.'

'I might find a pilot up there, maybe. And Roslyn drive us up in her car.'

Perce turned to him, a little surprised. 'Would she go up there?'

'Sure. She's a damn good sport,' Gay said. He watched Perce's eyes, which had turned interested and warm.

Perce said, 'Well, maybe; except to tell you the truth, Gay, I never feel comfortable takin' these horses for chicken feed.'

'Somebody's goin' to take them if we don't.'

'I know,' Perce said. He turned to watch the far ridges again. 'Just seems to me they belong up there.'

'They ain't doin' nothin' up there but eatin' out good cattle range. The cow outfits shoot them down if they see them.'

'I know,' Perce said.

'They don't even bother takin' them to slaughter. They just rot up there if the cow outfits get to them.'

'I know,' Perce said.

There was silence. Neither bug nor lizard nor rabbit moved on the great basin around them, and the sun warmed their necks and their thighs. Gay said, 'I'd as soon sell them for riding horses but they ain't big enough, except for a kid. And the freight on them's more than they're worth. You saw them – they ain't nothin' but skinny horses.'

'I just don't know if I'd want to see like a hundred of them goin' for chicken feed, though. I don't mind like five or six, but a hundred's a lot of horses. I don't know.'

Gay thought. 'Well, if it ain't this it's wages. Around here anyway.' He was speaking of himself and explaining himself.

'I'd just as soon ride buckin' horses and make out that way,

Gay.' Perce turned to him. 'Although I might go up north with
you. I don't know.'

'Roslyn wouldn't come out here at first,' Gay said, 'but soon
as she saw what they looked like she stopped complainin' about it.
You didn't hear her complainin' about it.'

'I ain't complainin', Gay. I just don't know. Seems to me God
put them up there and they belong up there. But I'm doin' it and
I guess I'd go on doin' it. I don't know.'

'Sounds to me like the newspapers. They want their steaks,
them people in town, but they don't want castration or branding
or cleanin' wild horses off the ranges.'

'Hell, man, I castrated more bulls than I got hairs on my head,'
Perce said.

'I better get the glasses,' Gay said and slid out of the tyre in
which he had been lounging and off the truck. He went to the cab
and reached in and brought out a pair of binoculars, blew on the
lenses, mounted the truck, and sat on a tyre with his elbows resting on his knees. He put the glasses to his eyes and focused them.
The mountains came up close with their pocked blue hides. He
found the pass through which he believed the plane would come
and studied its slopes and scanned the air above it. Anger was still
warming him. 'God put them up there!' Why, Christ, God put
everything everywhere. Did that mean you couldn't eat chickens,
for instance, or beef? His dislike for Perce was flowing into him
again.

They heard the shotgun off in the sky somewhere and they
stopped moving. Gay narrowed his eyes and held the binoculars
perfectly still.

'See anything?' Perce asked.

'He's still in the pass, I guess,' Gay said.

They sat still, watching the sky over the pass. The moments
went by. The sun was making them perspire now, and Gay wiped
his wet eyebrows with the back of one hand. They heard the shotgun again from the general sky. Gay spoke without lowering the
glasses. 'He's probably blasting them out of some corner.'

Perce quickly arched out of his tyre. 'I see him,' he said quickly.
'I see him glintin', I see the plane.'

It angered Gay that Perce had seen the plane first without glasses. In the glasses Gay could see it clearly now. It was flying out of the pass, circling back, and disappearing into the pass again. 'He's got them in the pass now. Just goin' back in for them.'

'Can you see them?' Perce asked.

'He ain't got them in the clear yet. He just went back in for them.'

Now through his glasses he could see moving specks on the ground where the pass opened on to the desert table. 'I see them,' he said. He counted, moving his lips. 'One, two, three, four. Four and a colt.'

'We gonna take the colt?' Perce asked.

'Hell, can't take the mare without the colt.'

Perce said nothing. Then Gay handed him the glasses. 'Take a look.'

Gay slid off the truck bed and went forward to the cab and opened its door. His dog lay shivering on the floor under the pedals. He snapped his fingers, and she warily got up and leaped down to the ground and stood there quivering, as she always did when wild horses were coming. He watched her sit and wet the ground, and how she moved with such care and concern and fear, sniffing the ground and moving her head in slow motion and setting her paws down as though the ground had hidden explosives everywhere. He left her there and climbed on to the truck and sat on a tyre beside Perce, who was still looking through the glasses.

'He's divin' down on them. God, they sure can run!'

'Let's have a look,' Gay said and reached out, and Perce handed him the glasses, saying, 'They're comin' on fast.'

Gay watched the horses in the glasses. The plane was starting down toward them from the arc of its climb. They swerved as the roaring motor came down over them, lifted their heads, and galloped faster. They had been running now for over an hour and would slow down when the plane had to climb after a dive and the motor's noise grew quieter. As Guido climbed again Gay and Perce heard a shot, distant and harmless, and the shot sped the horses on again as the plane took time to bank and turn. Then, as they slowed, the plane returned over them, diving down over their backs, and their heads shot up again and they galloped until the engine's roar receded over them. The sky was clear and lightly blue, and only the little plane swung back and forth across the desert like the glinting tip of a magic wand, and the horses came on toward the vast stripped clay bed where the truck was parked.

The two men on the truck exchanged the glasses from time to time. Now they sat upright on the tyres, waiting for the horses to reach the edge of the lake bed, when Guido would land the plane and they would take off with the truck. And now the horses stopped.

'They see the heat waves,' Gay said, looking through the glasses. He could see the horses trotting with raised, alarmed heads along the edge of the barren lake bed, which they feared because the heat waves rose from it like liquid in the air and yet their nostrils did not smell water, and they dared not move ahead on to unknowable territory. The plane dived down on them, and they scattered but would not go forward on to the lake bed from the cooler, sage-dotted desert behind them. Now the plane banked high in the air and circled out behind them over the desert and banked again and came down within yards of the ground and roared in behind them almost at the height of their heads, and as it passed over them, rising, the men on the truck could hear the shotgun. Now the horses leaped forward on to the lake bed, all scattered and heading in different directions, and they were only trotting, exploring the ground under their feet and the strange, superheated air in their nostrils. Gradually, as the plane wound around the sky to dive again, they closed ranks and slowly galloped shoulder to shoulder out on to the borderless lake bed. The colt galloped a length behind with its nose nearly touching the mare's long silky tail.

'That's a big mare,' Perce said. His eyes were still dreamy and his face was calm, but his skin had reddened.

'She's a bigger mare than usual up here, ya,' Gay said.

Both men watched the little herd now, even as they got to their feet on the truck. There was the big mare, as large as any full-grown horse, and both of them downed their surprise at the sight of her. They knew the mustang herds lived in total isolation and that inbreeding had reduced them to the size of large ponies. The herd swerved now and they saw the stallion. He was smaller than the mare but still larger than any Gay had brought down before. The other two horses were small, the way mustangs ought to be.

The plane was coming down for a landing now. Gay and Perce Howland moved to the forward edge of the truck's bed where a strap of white webbing was strung at hip height between two stanchions stuck into sockets at the corners of the truck. They drew another web strap from one stanchion to the other and stood inside the two. Perce tied the back strap to his stanchion. Then they turned around inside their harnesses and each reached into a tyre behind him and drew out a coil of rope whose end hung in a loop. They glanced out on the lake bed and saw Guido taxiing toward them, and they stood waiting for him. He cut the engine twenty yards from the truck and leaped out of the open cockpit before the plane had halted. He lashed the tail of the plane to a rope that was attached to a spike driven into the clay and trotted over to the truck, lifting his goggles off and stuffing them into his torn jacket pocket. Perce and Gay called out laughingly to him, but he seemed hardly to have seen them. His face was puffed with preoccupation. He jumped into the cab of the truck, and the collie dog jumped in after him and sat on the floor, quivering. He started the truck and roared ahead across the flat clay into the watery waves of heat.

They could see the herd standing still in a small clot of dots more than two miles off. The truck rolled smoothly, and in the cab Guido glanced at the speedometer and saw it was past sixty. He had to be careful not to turn over and he dropped back to fifty-five. Gay, on the right front corner of the truck bed, and Perce Howland on the left, pulled their hats down to their eyebrows and hefted the looped ropes, which the wind was threatening to coil and foul in their palms. Guido knew that Gay Langland was a good roper and that Perce was unsure, so he headed for the herd's left in order to come up to them on Gay's side of the truck if he could. This whole method – the truck, the tyres, the ropes, and the plane – was Guido's invention, and once again he felt the joy of having thought of it all. He drove with both heavy hands on the wheel and his left foot ready over the brake pedal. He reached for the shift lever to feel if it was going to spring out of gear and into neutral, but it felt tight, and if they did not hit a bump he could rely on it. The herd had started to walk but stopped again now, and the horses were looking at the truck, ears raised, necks stretched up and forward. Guido smiled a little. They looked silly to him standing there, but he knew and pitied them their ignorance.

The wind smashed against the faces of Perce and Gay standing on the truck bed. The brims of their hats flowed up and back from a low point in front, and their faces were dark red. They saw the horses watching their approach at a standstill. And as they roared closer and closer they saw that this herd was beautiful.

Perce Howland turned his head to Gay, who glanced at him at the same time. There had been much rain this spring, and this herd must have found good pasture. They were well rounded and shining. The mare was almost black, and the stallion and the two others were deep brown. The colt was curly-coated and had a grey sheen. The stallion dipped his head suddenly and turned his back on the truck and galloped. The others turned and clattered after him, with the colt running alongside the mare. Guido pressed down on the gas and the truck surged forward, whining. They were a few yards behind the animals now and they could see the bottoms of their hoofs, fresh hoofs that had never been shod. They could see the full manes flying and the thick and long black tails that would hang down to their fetlocks when they were still.

The truck was coming abreast of the mare now, and beside her the others galloped with only a loud ticking noise on the clay. It was a gently tacking clatter for they were light-footed and unshod. They were slim-legged and wet after running almost two hours in this alarm, but as the truck drew alongside the mare and Gay began twirling his loop above his head the whole herd wheeled away to the right, and Guido jammed the gas peddle down and swung with them, but they kept galloping in a circle, and he did not have the speed to keep abreast of them so he slowed down and fell behind them a few yards until they would straighten out and move ahead again. And they wheeled like circus horses, slower now, for they were at the edge of their strength, and suddenly Guido saw a breadth between the stallion and the two browns and he sped in between, cutting the mare off at the left with her colt. Now the horses stretched, the clatter quickened. Their hind legs flew straight back and their necks stretched low and forward. Gay whirled his loop over his head, and the truck came up alongside the stallion, whose lungs were hoarsely screaming with exhaustion, and Gay flung the noose. It fell on the stallion's head, and with a whipping of the lead Gay made it fall over his neck. The horse swerved away to the right and stretched the rope until the tyre was pulled off the truck bed and dragged along the hard clay. The three men watched from the slowing truck as the stallion, with startled eyes, pulled the giant tyre for a few yards, then leaped up with his forelegs in the air and came down facing the tyre and trying to back away from it. Then he stood still, heaving, his hind legs dancing in an arc from right to left and back again as he shook his head in the remorseless noose.

As soon as he was sure the stallion was secure Guido scanned the lake bed and without stopping turned sharply left toward the mare and the colt, which were trotting idly together by themselves. The two browns were already disappearing toward the north, but Guido knew they would halt soon because they were tired, while the mare might continue to the edge of the lake bed and back into her familiar hills where the truck could not follow. He straightened the truck and jammed down the gas pedal. In a minute he was straight on behind her, and he drew up on her left side because the colt was running on her right. She was very heavy, he saw, and he wondered now if she was a mustang at all. As he drove alongside her his eyes ran across her flanks, seeking out a brand, but she seemed unmarked. Then through his right window he saw the loop flying out and down over her head, and he saw her head fly up, and then she fell back. He turned to the right, braking with his left boot, and he saw her dragging a tyre and coming to a halt, with the free colt watching her and trotting very close beside her. Then he headed straight ahead across the flat toward two specks, which rapidly enlarged until they became the two browns, which were at a standstill and watching the oncoming truck. He came in between them, and as they galloped Perce on the left roped one, and Gay roped the other almost at the same time. And Guido leaned his head out of his window and yelled up at Perce, who was on the truck bed on his side. 'Good boy!' he hollered, and Perce let himself return an excited grin, although there seemed to be some trouble in his eyes.

Guido made an easy half circle and headed back to the mare and the colt, and in a few minutes he slowed to a halt some twenty yards away and got out of the cab. The dog remained sitting on the floor of the cab, her body shaking all over.

The three men approached the mare. She had never seen a man, and her eyes were wide in fear. Her rib cage stretched and collapsed very rapidly, and there was a trickle of blood coming out of her nostrils. She had a heavy dark brown mane, and her tail nearly touched the ground. The colt with dumb eyes shifted about on its silly bent legs, trying to keep the mare between itself and the men, and the mare kept shifting her rump to shield the colt from them.

They wanted now to move the noose higher up on the mare's neck because it had fallen on her from the rear and was tight around the middle of her neck, where it could choke her if she kept pulling against the weight of the tyre. They had learned from previous forays that they could not leave a horse tied that way without the danger of suffocation, and they wanted them alive until they could bring a larger truck from Bowie and load them on it.

Gay was the best roper so Perce and Guido stood by as he twirled a noose over his head, then let it fall open softly, just behind the forefeet of the mare. They waited for a moment, then approached her, and she backed a step. Then Gay pulled sharply on the rope, and her forefeet were tied together. Then with another rope Gay lass'd her hind feet, and she swayed and fell to the ground on her side. Her body swelled and contracted, but she seemed resigned. The colt stretched its nose to her tail and stood there as the men came to the mare and spoke quietly to her, and

Guido bent down and opened the noose and slipped it up under her jaw. They inspected her for a brand, but she was clean.

'Never see a horse that size up here,' Gay said to Guido.

Guido stood there looking down at the great mare.

Perce said, 'Maybe wild horses was all big once,' and he looked to Guido for confirmation.

Guido bent and sat on his heels and opened the mare's mouth, and the other two looked in with him. 'She's fifteen if she's a day,' Gay said, and to Perce he said, 'She wouldn't be around much longer anyway.'

'Ya, she's old,' Perce agreed, and his eyes were filled with thought.

Guido stood up, and the three went back to the truck. Perce hopped up and sat on the truck bed with his legs dangling, and Gay sat in the cab with Guido. They drove across the lake bed to the stallion and stopped, and the three of them walked toward him.

'Ain't a bad-lookin' horse,' Perce said.

They stood inspecting the horse for a moment. He was standing still now, heaving for breath and bleeding from the nostrils. His head was down, holding the rope taut, and he was looking at them with his deep brown eyes that were like the lenses of enormous binoculars. Gay got his rope ready in his hand. 'He ain't nothin' but a misfit,' he said, 'except for some kid. You couldn't run cattle with him, and he's too small for a riding horse.'

'He is small,' Perce conceded. 'Got a nice neck, though.'

'Oh, they're nice-*lookin*' horses, some of them,' Guido said. 'What the hell you goin' to do with them, though? Cost more to ship them anywhere than they'd bring.'

Gay twirled the loop over his head, and they spread out around the stallion. 'They're just old misfit horses, that's all,' he said, and he flung the rope behind the stallion's forelegs, and the horse backed a step, and he drew the rope and the noose bit into the horse's lower legs, drawing them together, and the horse swayed but would not fall.

'Take hold,' Gay called to Perce, who ran around the horse and grabbed on to the rope and held it taut. Then Gay went back to the truck, got another rope, returned to the rear of the horse, and looped the hind legs. But the stallion would not fall.

Guido stepped closer to push him over, but the horse swung his head and showed his teeth, and Guido stepped back. 'Pull on it!' Guido yelled to Gay and Perce, and they pulled on their ropes to trip the stallion, but he righted himself and stood there bound by the head to the tyre and his feet by the two ropes the men held. Then Guido hurried over to Perce and took the rope from him and walked with it toward the rear of the horse and pulled hard. The stallion's forefeet slipped back, and he came down on his knees and his nose struck the clay ground and he snorted as he struck, but he would not topple over and stayed there on his knees as though he were bowing to something, with his nose propping up his head against the ground and his sharp bursts of breath blowing up dust in little clouds under his nostrils.

Now Guido gave the rope back to young Perce Howland, who held it taut, and he came up alongside the stallion's neck and laid his hands on the side of the neck and pushed, and the horse fell over on to his flank and lay there; and, like the mare, when he felt the ground against his body he seemed to let himself out, and for the first time his eyes blinked and his breath came now in sighs and no longer fiercely. Guido shifted the noose up under the jaw, and they opened the ropes around the hoofs, and when the horse felt his legs free he first raised his head curiously and then clattered up and stood there looking at them, from one to the other, blood dripping from his nostrils and a stain of deep red on both dusty knees.

For a moment the three men stood watching him to be sure he was tightly noosed around the neck. Only the clacking of the truck's engine sounded on the enormous floor between the mountains, and the wheezing inhale of the horse and his blowing out of air. Then the men moved without hurrying to the truck, and Gay stored his two extra ropes behind the seat of the cab and got behind the wheel with Guido beside him, and Perce climbed on to the back of the truck and lay down facing the sky, his palms under his head.

Gay headed the truck south toward where they knew the plane

was, although it was still beyond their vision. Guido was slowly catching his breath, and now he lighted a cigarette, puffed it, and rubbed his left hand into his bare scalp. He sat gazing out the windshield and the side window. 'I'm sleepy,' he said.

'What you reckon?' Gay asked.

'What you?' Guido said. He had dust in his throat, and his voice sounded high and almost girlish.

'That mare might be six hundred pounds.'

'I'd say about that, Gay,' Guido agreed.

'About four hundred apiece for the browns and a little more for the stallion.'

'That's about the way I figured.'

'What's that come to?'

Guido thought. 'Nineteen hundred, maybe two thousand,' he said.

They fell silent, figuring the money. Two thousand pounds at six cents a pound came to a hundred and twenty dollars. The colt might make it a few dollars more, but not much. Figuring the gas for the plane and the truck, and twelve dollars for their groceries, they came to the figure of a hundred dollars for the three of them. Guido would get forty-five dollars, since he had used his plane, and Gay would get thirty-five including the use of his truck, and Perce Howland, if he agreed, as he undoubtedly would, would have the remaining twenty.

They fell silent after they had said the figures, and Gay drove in thought. Then he said, 'We should've watered them the last time. They can pick up a lot of weight if you let them water.'

'Yeah, let's be sure to do that,' Guido said.

They knew they would as likely as not forget to water the horses before they unloaded them at the dealer's lot in Bowie. They would be in a hurry to unload and to be free of the horses, and only later, as they were doing now, would they remind themselves that by letting the horses drink their fill they could pick up another fifteen or twenty dollars in added weight. They were not thinking of the money any more, once they had figured it, and if Perce were to object to his smaller share they would both hand him a five-or ten-dollar bill or more if he wanted it.

Gay stopped the truck beside the plane at the edge of the lake bed. The tethered horses were far away now, except for the mare and her colt, which stood in clear view less than half a mile off. Guido opened his door and said to Gay, 'See you in town. Let's get the other truck tomorrow morning.'

'Perce wants to go over to Largo and sign up for the rodeo tomorrow,' Gay said. 'Tell ya – we'll go in and get the truck and come back here this afternoon maybe. Maybe we bring them in tonight.'

'All right, if you want to. I'll see you boys tomorrow,' Guido said, and he got out and stopped for a moment to talk to Perce.

'Perce?' he said. Perce propped himself up on one elbow and looked down at him. He looked very sleepy. Guido smiled. 'You sleeping?'

Perce's eyelids almost seemed swollen, and his face was indrawn and troubled. 'I was about to,' he said.

Guido let the reprimand pass. 'We figure about a hundred dollars clear. Twenty all right for you?'

'Ya, twenty's all right,' Perce said, blinking heavily. He hardly seemed to be listening.

'See you in town,' Guido said and turned and waddled off to the plane, where Gay was already standing with his hands on the propeller blade. Guido got in, and Gay swung the blade down and the engine started immediately. Guido waved to Gay and Perce, who raised one hand slightly from the truck bed. Guido gunned the plane, and it trundled off and into the sky, and the two men on the ground watched as it flew toward the mountains and away.

Gay returned to the truck, and as he started to climb in behind the wheel he looked at Perce, who was still propped up on one elbow, and he said, 'Twenty all right?' And he said this because he thought Perce looked hurt.

'Heh? Ya, twenty's all right,' Perce answered. Then he let himself down from the truck bed, and Gay got behind the wheel. Perce stood beside the truck and wet the ground while Gay waited for him. Then Perce got into the cab, and they drove off.

The mare and her colt stood between them and the sage desert towards which they were heading. Perce stared out the window at the mare, and he saw that she was watching them apprehensively but not in real alarm, and the colt was lying upright on the clay, its head nodding slightly as though it would soon fall asleep. Perce looked long at the colt as they approached, and he thought about how it waited there beside the mare, unbound and free to go off, and he said to Gay, 'Ever hear of a colt leave a mare?'

'Not that young a colt,' Gay said. 'He ain't goin' nowhere.' And he glanced to look at Perce.

They passed the mare and colt and left them behind, and Perce laid his head back and closed his eyes. His tobacco swelled out his left cheek, and he let it soak there.

Now the truck left the clay lake bed, and it pitched and rolled on the sage desert. They would return to their camp and pick up their bedrolls and cooking implements and then drive to the road, which was almost fifteen miles beyond the camp across the desert.

'Think I'll go back to Roslyn's tonight,' Gay said.

'Okay,' Perce said and did not open his eyes.

'We can pick them up in the morning and then take you down to Largo.'

'Okay,' Perce said.

Gay thought about Roslyn. She would probably razz them about all the work they had done for a few dollars, saying they were too dumb to figure in their labour time and other hidden expenses. To hear her, sometimes they hadn't made any profit at all. 'Roslyn goin' to feel sorry for the colt,' Gay said, 'so might as well not mention it.'

Perce opened his eyes, and with his head resting on the back of the seat he looked out the window at the mountains. 'Hell, she feeds that dog of hers canned dogfood, doesn't she?'

Gay felt closer to Perce again and he smiled. 'Sure does.'

'Well, what's she think is in the can?'

'She knows what's in the can.'

'There's wild horses in the can,' Perce said, almost to himself.

They drove in silence for a while. Then Perce said, 'That's what beats me.'

After a few moments Gay said, 'You comin' back to Roslyn's with me or you gonna stay in town?'

'I'd just as soon go back with you.'

'Okay,' Gay said. He felt good about going into her cabin now. There would be her books on the shelves he had built for her, and they would have some drinks, and Perce would fall asleep on the couch, and they would go into the bedroom together. He liked to come back to her after he had worked, more than when he had only driven her here and there or just stayed around her place. He liked his own money in his pocket. And he tried harder to visualize how it would be with her, and he thought of himself being forty-six soon, and then nearing fifty. She would go back East one day, he knew, maybe this year, maybe next. He wondered again when he would begin turning grey and how he would look with grey hair, and he set his jaw against the picture of himself grey and an old man.

Perce spoke, sitting up in his seat. 'I want to phone my mother. Damn, I haven't called her all year.' He stared out the window at the mountains. He had the memory of how the colt looked, and he wished it would be gone when they returned in the morning. Then he said, 'I got to get to Largo tomorrow and register.'

'We'll go,' Gay said.

'I could use a good win,' he said. He thought of five hundred dollars now, and of the many times he had won five hundred dollars. 'You know something, Gay?' he said.

'Huh?'

'I'm never goin' to amount to a damn thing.' Then he laughed. He was hungry, and he laughed without restraint for a moment and then laid his head back and closed his eyes.

'I told you that first time I met you, didn't I?' Gay grinned. He felt the mood coming on for some drinks at Roslyn's.

Then Perce spoke. 'That colt won't bring two dollars anyway. What you say we just left him there?'

'Why, you know what he'd do?' Gay said. 'He'd just follow the truck right into town.'

'I guess he would at that,' Perce said. He spat a stream of juice out the window.

They reached the camp in twenty minutes and loaded the gasoline drum on to three bedrolls and the aluminium grub box in the truck and drove on towards Bowie. After they had driven for fifteen minutes without speaking, Gay said he wanted to go north very soon for the hundreds of horses that were supposed to be in the mountains there. But Perce Howland had fallen fast asleep beside him. Gay wanted to talk about that expedition because as they neared Bowie he began to visualize Roslyn razzing them again, and it was clear to him that he had somehow failed to settle anything for himself; he had put in three days for thirty-five dollars, and there would be no way to explain it so it made sense, and it would be embarrassing. And yet he knew that it had all been the way it ought to be even if he could never explain it to her or anyone else. He reached out and nudged Perce, who opened his eyes and lolled his head over to face him. 'You comin' up to Thighbone with me, ain't you?'

'Okay,' Perce said and went back to sleep.

Gay felt more peaceful now that the younger man would not be leaving him. He drove in contentment.

The sun shone hot on the beige plain all day. Neither fly nor bug nor snake ventured out on the waste to molest the four horses tethered there, or the colt. They had run nearly two hours at a gallop, and as the afternoon settled upon them they pawed the hard ground for water, but there was none. Toward evening the wind came up, and they backed into it and faced the mountains from which they had come. From time to time the stallion caught the smell of the pastures up there, and he started to walk toward the vaulted fields in which he had grazed; but the tyre bent his neck around, and after a few steps he would turn to face it and leap into the air with his forelegs striking at the sky, and then he would come down and be still again.

With the deep blue darkness the wind blew faster, tossing their manes and flinging their long tails in between their legs. The cold of night raised the colt on to its legs, and it stood close to the mare for warmth. Facing the southern range, five horses blinked under the green glow of the risen moon, and they closed their eyes and slept. The colt settled again on the hard ground and lay under the mare.

In the high hollows of the mountains the grass they had cropped this morning straightened in the darkness. On the lusher swards, which were still damp with the rains of spring, their hoofprints had begun to disappear. When the first pink glow of another morning lit the sky the colt stood up, and as it had always done at dawn it walked waywardly for water. The mare shifted and her bone hoofs ticked the clay. The colt turned its head and returned to her and stood at her side with vacant eye, its nostrils sniffing the warming air.

[*1957*]

Glimpse at a Jockey

IT's like this saloon, it's the best in New York, right? You can't even sit down in the can here without a hundred-dollar bill in each ear, look over there at that grey-hair loafer with the broad, getting himself loaded to put the wife out of his mind and for what? So he can make it with that Sue he paid anyway. I love them all. I bequeath myself to this world, life, the whole skam.

I'm happy here talking to you. Why is that? Who knows why you cross the bridge to some people and not to others? I'm absolutely happy right now. They underrate the whole nature of loyalty between men, it's different than with a woman, the kind of challenge. I'd win sometimes and be ashamed because the friggin' horse had me bobbling around coming over the finish line, instead of stylish. I could get down closer to the horse than any son of a bitch ordinarily, but sometimes you draw some broken-legged horse and you bump in like a trussed flounder on a no-spring truck. You ride for the other jocks, for their admiration, the style. My last race I went through the fence in Argentina, wired, screwed, and welded twenty-two bones, and after three months in the hospital the flowers stopped. A jock is like a movie star, the whole skam's night and day, the broads drooling your name printed on your friggin' forehead. Nothin'. Except two guys, mostly Virgil, that loyal son of a bitch, I'd die for the bastard.

Who understands that any more? I went to see this Doctor Hapic last year, what a sweet old starch, the greatest according to what you hear. And I lay down on the broken-down old couch and he looks around in the bins and comes up with a racing form! I figure I'm in for homosexuality because that's the hinge if men move you so much, and here's old Al diggin' me for a line on the sixth race, askin' me who's an honest bookie and all. I put in three hours with him, he cancelled one appointment after another, and when I left he charged me for half an hour! But how the hell do I know who's goin' to win? Even when I was riding I didn't know. Chrissake, the horse didn't know! Why can't they leave it alone, I mean the analysing? Everybody I know who went come out a friggin' judge. I admit it, the whole skam is pistils and stamens, all right I surrender. But Jesus, give me room, let me die laughing if I'm goin' to die. I'm ready. If I slide off a snowbank under a cab outside there I'll cheer death. I love her, my wife, married eighteen years, and my kids, but you draw a line somewhere, someplace, before there's no room left for the chalk down in the corner. The men are scared, did you see it where you been around? They keep makin' little teeny marks but they can't draw the line. Nobody knows any more where he begins or ends, it's like they pied the maps and put Chicago in Latvia. They don't allow nobody to die for loyalty any more, there's nothin' in it to steal.

What the hell do I know, ignorant, accordion-pleated mind that I have, but I know style in anything. The great thing is not winning, it's riding the friggin' horse nobody else could stay on to. That's the bastard you want to ride. Where the other jocks look and know the horse wants to kill you. That's when the flag stretches out and your corpuscles start laughing. Once I went to see my father.

I never told this to anybody, and you know how much I talk. Honest, I never told this. I made this television thing, interviewing ugly authors about their books, the line was that a jockey could actually read words, and it went over big till I threw myself in the Jag and drove to Mexico, I couldn't stand it. I'm all for stealing but not pickpocketing, these authors weren't any goddam good authors, but every week you got to make over them like it's Man O'War did the mile in nothin' pissing all the way and a blind jock on top. Anyway the station gets this letter from Duluth asking if I was born in Frankfort, Kentucky, and my mother's name is so and so, and if I was all them things he's probably my old man. This silly old handwriting like he wrote it on a tractor. So I throw myself into a plane and drive up to the door and he's a house painter.

I just wanted to see, you know? I wanted to lay my both eyes on him. And there he was, about seventy or a hundred. He left when I was one. I never saw him. Now I'd always dreamed of him like he was a high roller or some kind of elegant thief or maybe a Kentucky Rousseau or somebody stylish with broads, and left to seek his fortune. Some goddam thing interesting. But there he is, a house painter. And lives in the nigger section. I'm the last of the holdouts, I can't stand them. But there's this one next door, a real nice guy, and his wife was nice too. You could see they loved him. And I'm standing there. What did I come for? Who is he? Who am I if he's my father? But the crazy thing is I knew I belonged to him. It's like you said, I'm the son of my father. I knew it even if he was a total stranger. I just wanted to do something for him. Anything. I was ready to lay down my life for him. After all, who knows the situation? Maybe my old lady drove him out. Who knows the inside of the outside? So I ask him what do you want?

I'll get you anything, I said, that is within my means, although I was loaded, it was after the Derby. He was small too, although not as small as me. I'm so small I'm almost un-American, but he was small too, and he says, The grass in the back yard gets so high and thick I can't push the mower through it. So if I had one of them mowers with an engine on it.

So I grab the phone and they send over a truckload of all the kinds. And he was all afternoon goin' over each one and finally he picks out one with a motor bigger than this friggin' table, and I buy it for him. I had to leave to make the plane back because I promised Virgil I'd be in San Pedro to guard some broad he had to leave there a whole night, so I go into the back yard to say good-bye. And he wouldn't even turn the motor off so we could talk quietly. And I left him enjoying himself, joggling around that yard behind that friggin' mower.

Christ, how did I get so drunk! Those two broads across there have been lookin' at us. What do you say? What's the difference what they look like, they're all the same, I love 'em all.

[*1962*]

The Prophecy

NOT all, but some winters in those parts are almost unendurable. A fog settles into the old Dutch valley toward the end of November and never really goes away until April. Some nights it suddenly appears on the ridge tops, leaving the lowlands clear, and no one knows why it moves about, but it does, sometimes settling around a particular house for days at a time and nowhere else. Then it goes away and reappears around another house. And some winters the sun never properly comes out for two months at a time. A greyness like water drowns all the views, and the trees drip all day when their branches are not covered with creaking ice.

At the start of winter there is always hope, of course, that it will be a decent one. But when, day after day and week after week, the same monotonous wind sucks the heat out of the house, and there is never even a momentary break in the iron sky, the old people first and then everyone else gradually change their temperaments. There are unaccountable arguments in the supermarkets and at the gas station, lifelong enmities are started, people decide to move away and do, forever, and there is always a rash of unnecessary road accidents. People break arms, hitting trees whose locations they know by heart; there are always one or two who get run over by their own cars rolling back down the driveways; and decisions are made out of desperation, which permanently change the course of many lives.

Toward the end of December of such a winter Stowey Rummel decided to supervise personally the hanging of his architectural drawings and the display of his models for a permanent exhibition of his work in a new Florida university whose campus he had designed a few years before. He was in his mid-fifties at this time, long past the establishment of his name and the wish to be lionized yet once again, and it was almost a decade since he had sworn off lecturing. There was never a doubt any more how his structures would be received; it was always the same unqualified success now. He could no longer build anything, whether a private residence in his Pennsylvania county or a church in Brazil, without its being obvious that he had done it, and while here and there he was taken to task for repeating the same airy technique, they were such fanciful and sometimes even playful buildings that after a time the public's sense of recognition overwhelmed any dispute as to their other values. Stowey Rummel was internationally famous, a crafter of a genuine Americana in foreign eyes, an original designer whose inventive childishness with steel and concrete was made even more believably sincere by his personality.

He had lived for almost thirty years in this same stone farmhouse with the same wife, a remarkably childish thing in itself; he rose at half-past six every morning, made himself some French coffee, had his corn flakes and more coffee, smoked four cigarettes while reading last Sunday's *Herald Tribune* and yesterday's *Pittsburgh Gazette,* then put on his high-topped farmer's shoes and walked under a vine bower to his workshop. This was an enormously long building whose walls were made of rocks, some of them brought home from every continent during his six years as an oil geologist. The debris of his other careers was piled everywhere; a stack of wire cages for mice from his time as a geneticist and a microscope lying on its side on the window sill; vertical steel columns wired for support to the open ceiling beams with spidery steel cantilevers jutting out into the air; masonry constructions on the floor from the time he was inventing his disastrous fireplace, whose smoke would pass through a whole house, visible all the way up through wire gratings on each floor. His files, desk, drafting-board, and a high stool formed the only clean island in the chaos. Everywhere else his ideas lay or hung in visible form – his models, drawings, ten-foot canvases in monochromes from his painting days – and underfoot a windfall of broken-backed books that looked as though their insides had been ransacked by a maniac. Bicycle gear sets he had once used as the basis of a design for the Camden Cycle Company plant hung up on a rope in one corner, and over his desk, next to several old and dusty hats, was a clean pair of roller skates, which he occasionally used up and down in front of his house. He worked standing, with his left hand in his pocket, as though he were merely stopping for a moment, sketching with the surprised stare of one who was watching another person's hand. Sometimes he would grunt softly to some invisible onlooker beside him; sometimes he would look stern and moralistic as his pencil did what he disapproved. It all seemed – if one could have peeked in at him through one of his windows – as though this broken-nosed man with the muscular arms and wrestler's neck was merely the caretaker trying his hand at the boss's work. This air of disengagement carried over to his apparent attitude toward his things, and people often mistook it for boredom in him or a surrender to repetitious routine. But he was not bored at all; he had found his style quite early in his career, and he thought it quite wonderful that the world admired it, and he could not imagine why he should alter it. There are, after all, fortunate souls who hear everything but know how to listen only to what is good for them, and Stowey was, as things go, a fortunate man.

He left his home the day after New Year's, wearing a mackinaw and sheepskin mittens and without a hat. He would wear this same costume in Florida, despite his wife Cleota's reminders over the past five days that he must take some cool clothes with him. But he was too busy to hear what she was saying. So they parted when she was in an impatient humour. When he was bent over behind the wheel of the station wagon, feeling in his trouser cuffs for the ignition key he had dropped a moment before, she came out of the house with an enormous Rumanian shawl over her head, which she had bought in that country during one of their trips abroad, and handed him a clean handkerchief through the window. Having found the key under his shoe, he started the engine, and while it warmed up he turned to her standing there in the dripping fog and said, 'Defrost the refrigerator.'

He saw the surprise in her face and laughed as though it were the funniest expression he had ever seen. He kept on laughing until she started laughing with him. He had a deep voice, which was full of good food she had cooked, and good humour; an explosive laugh that always carried everything before it. He would settle himself into his seat to laugh. Whenever he laughed it was all he was doing. And she was made to fall in love with him again, there in the rutted dirt driveway, standing in the cold fog, mad as she was at his going away when he really didn't have to, mad at their both having got older in a life that seemed to have taken no more than a week to go by. She was forty-nine at this time, a lanky woman of breeding, with an austere, narrow face that had the distinction of a steeple or some architecture designed long ago for a stubborn sort of prayer. Her eyebrows were definite and heavy and formed two lines moving upward toward a high forehead and a great head of brown hair that fell to her shoulders. There was an air of blindness in her grey eyes, the startled-horse look that ultimately comes to some women who are born at the end of an ancestral line long since divorced from moneymaking, which, besides, has kept its estate intact. She was personally sloppy, and when she had colds would blow her nose in the same handkerchief all day and keep it, soaking wet, dangling from her waist, and when she gardened she would eat dinner with dirt on her calves. But just when she seemed to have sunk into some depravity of peasanthood she would disappear and come down bathed, brushed, and taking deep breaths of air, and even with her broken nails her hands would come to rest on a table or a leaf with a thoughtless delicacy, a grace of history, so to speak, and for an instant one saw how ferociously proud she was and adamant on certain questions of personal value. She even spoke differently when she was clean, and she was clean now for his departure, and her voice clear and rather sharp.

'Now drive carefully, for God's sake!' she called, trying to attain a half-humorous resentment at his departure. But he did not notice and was already backing the car down to the road, saying 'Toot-toot!' to the stump of a tree as he passed it, the same stump that had impaled the car of many a guest in the past thirty years and that he refused to have removed. She stood clutching her shawl around her shoulders until he had swung the car on to the road. Then, when he had it pointed down the hill, he stopped to gaze at her through the window. She had begun to turn back toward the house, but his look caught her and she stood still, waiting there for what his expression indicated would be a serious word of farewell. He looked at her out of himself, she thought, as he did only for an instant at a time, the look that always surprised her even now, when his uncombable hair was yellowing a little and his breath came hard through his nicotine-choked lungs, the look of the gaunt youth she had suddenly found herself staring at in the Louvre on a Thursday once. Now she kept herself protectively ready to laugh again, and sure enough he pointed at her with his index finger and said 'Toot!' once more and roared off into the fog, his foot evidently surprising him with the suddenness with which it pressed the accelerator, just as his hand did when he worked. She walked back to the house and entered, feeling herself returning, sensing some kind of opportunity in the empty building. There is a death in all partings, she knew, and promptly put it out of her mind.

She enjoyed great parties when she would sit up talking and dancing and drinking all night, but it always seemed to her that being alone, especially alone in her house, was the most real part of life. Now she could let out the three parakeets without fear they would be stepped on or that Stowey would let them out one of the doors; she could dust the plants, then break off suddenly and pick up an old novel and read from the middle on; improvise cha-chas on the harp; and finally, the best part of all, simply sit at the plank table in the kitchen with a bottle of wine and the newspapers, reading the ads as well as the news, registering nothing on her mind but letting her soul suspend itself above all wishing and desire. She did this now, comfortably aware of the mist running down the windows, of the silence outside, of the dark afternoon it was getting to be.

She fell asleep leaning on her hand, hearing the house creaking as though it were living a private life of its own these two hundred years, hearing the birds rustling in their cages and the occasional whirring of wings as one of them landed on the table and walked across the newspaper to perch in the crook of her arm.

Every few minutes she would waken for a moment to review things: Stowey, yes, was on his way south, and the two boys were away in school, and nothing was burning on the stove, and Lucretia was coming for dinner and bringing three guests of hers. Then she fell asleep again as suddenly as a person with fever, and when she awoke it was dark outside and the clarity was back in her eyes. She stood up, smoothing her hair down, straightening her clothes, feeling a thankfulness for the enveloping darkness outside, and, above everything else, for the absence of the need to answer, to respond, to be aware even of Stowey coming in or going out, and yet, now that she was beginning to cook, she glimpsed a future without him, a future alone like this, and the pain made her head writhe, and in a moment she found it hard to wait for Lucretia to come with her guests.

She went into the living room and turned on three lamps, then back into the kitchen, where she turned on the ceiling light and the switch that lit the floods on the barn, illuminating the driveway. She knew she was feeling afraid and inwardly laughed at herself. They were both so young, after all, so unready for any final parting. How could it have been thirty years already? she wondered. But yes, nineteen plus thirty was forty-nine, and she was forty-nine and she had been married at nineteen. She stood still over the leg of lamb, rubbing herbs into it, quite suddenly conscious of a nausea in her stomach and a feeling of wrath, a sensation of violence that started her shivering. She heard the back door opening and immediately went through the pantry toward it, knowing it must be Alice.

The old woman met her, having already entered, and was unhooking her yellow slicker with her stiff white fingers. 'Something's wrong with my phone,' she said, proving at once that she had come with a purpose and not to intrude.

'What do you want to do?' Cleota asked, not moving from the centre of the pantry, her position barring the way to the kitchen door. Her anger astounded even her; she would never have dared bar the way if Stowey were here, and she thrilled at her aggressiveness toward his old sister.

'I'd better call the company, hadn't I?' Alice asked, already indicating in her tone that she recognized the outlandish barrier and was not prepared to go out at once.

'Well, you can certainly use the phone,' Cleota said and turned her back on the old woman and went to her leg of lamb on the table.

Alice, wearing calf-height rubber boots and a fisherman's drooping-brim rubber hat, got to the phone and held it away from her ear, blinking papery eyelids and avidly inspecting the kitchen as she waited for the operator to come on. Beside the instrument – between it and a flour canister – stood a Fiji mask, a carved, elongated face. She turned it absent-mindedly.

'*Please* don't, Alice!'

The old lady turned in such a quick shock that her deep-brimmed hat slid and remained sideways on her head. Cleota, her face swollen with feeling, bent to the oven and put in the meat.

'It was facing toward the wall a little,' Alice started to explain.

Cleota stood erect, her cheeks red now. The house was hit by a slap of wind, a push that shuddered it. 'I *have* asked you not to touch my things, Alice. I'm having guests and I've a lot to do. So will you please do what you have to and let me get on with it!'

She went to the refrigerator, opened it, and stood half bent over, looking into it, trying to concentrate on what she had thought to take from it.

The old lady put down the phone. 'Yours is out too, I guess.'

Cleota did not answer, remaining before the open refrigerator, unable to think.

For a moment they stood there waiting, one for the other, as they had waited at odd moments since Alice had moved into the house down the road nine years before. Now the old woman hooked up her slicker, her watery eyes glancing hungrily about the kitchen as though for some new detail she might not have seen before. She had no thought to ask what the matter was, not because she clearly knew but because she took for granted she was hated by this woman with a reasonless hatred that nothing could ever dissolve. In her autobiography, which she wrote at every day in her kitchen and in good weather under the apple tree behind her house, she was developing the concept of human types, unchangeable personalities created by a primeval spirit, each of which had the function of testing others who were equally unchangeable. Cleota, in her book, was the Eternally Dissatisfied. She did not blame Cleota for her personality; indeed she pitied her and knew that nothing she could say or do would ever mitigate her need for an opponent, an enemy. Cleota, like so many other perversely incomprehensible phenomena, was Necessary.

Alice dawdled at the pantry door. She would not leave in too much of a hurry. She had a right, she felt, to have been invited tonight; certainly she would have been if Stowe had been at home. Besides she was hungry, having neglected her lunch today, and the few morsels she did eat would hardly matter to the dinner that was to be served. And if there were to be any men here, they would certainly be – as they always were – interested in her views, as so many of her brother's guests had told him after they had met her.

She reached the back door and turned back to her sister-in-law. 'Good night,' she said. The first tremors of her hurt quavered the words and stiffened Cleota, who barely glanced at her to return the farewell. Alice grasped the doorknob. She felt the question rising to her mouth and tried to escape before it came out, but it was too late. She heard herself asking, 'Who are you having?'

The ladle in Cleota's hand struck the stove and slid along the floor. 'I can't have this, Alice. You know exactly what I am talking about, so there is nothing more to say about it.'

The old lady shook her head, just once, turned the knob and went out, softly closing the door behind her.

Cleota picked up the ladle and stood there shaking. Once again the house was no longer hers. The indignity of the visit made her clench her teeth; Alice knew perfectly well that if her phone was out, then theirs was too, since they were on the same line. She had come simply, purely, to demonstrate that she had the freedom of the premises, to show once again that whatever else he may have become and whomever he might have married, Stowey was her baby brother first.

Cleota, who did not believe in a definite god, looked toward the ceiling despite herself, with a longing for an ear that would hear, and whispered, 'Why doesn't she die?' Alice was seventy-three, after all, and was nothing any longer but a smell, a pair of watery eyes, and, above all, a coiled power secreted in that house down the road which Stowe had bought for her when her husband had died. She felt now, as she often did, that the old woman lived on only to laugh secretly at her. She knew how unreasonable this idea was; the woman survived falls on the ice, broken hips, and cold and pneumonia last winter because she wanted to live for her own sake, but this stubborn refusal to succumb was somehow obscene to Cleota, quite as though the woman had something illicit in her unabashed craving for a life that would never end.

Cleota went to the Fiji mask and turned it as it had been before, as though this would cancel out Alice's having moved it. She touched the hard brown wood, and her finger rested on a rough spot under the lower lip. This had always felt like a wart and made the image seem alive, and the touching of the spot recalled her father's hands on it when he gave it to her. As foolish a man as he had been, he had known how to disappear from the lives of those he could not help. She felt a rising pride in her father now; with his own bizarre dignity he had assembled his lunatic expeditions, read the wrong books, learned outmoded anthropological theories, sailed to the unmeaningful islands, spent years studying tribes that had been categorized many times before, and had succeeded only in cluttering the homes of his children with the bric-à-brac of the South Seas. Now, however, now that he could never return, she sensed in his career a certain hidden purpose, which she felt he must have secretly followed. It had been his will to declare himself even in his inanity, and to keep on declaring himself until the idiotic end, his ankle caught in a rope and his bald head in the water, discovered hanging over the side of his sloop off San Francisco harbour. How strange it was that this fool had slowly taken on – for many besides herself – an air of respect! And it was not wrong that this should be, she thought. He had had a passion, and that, she felt now, was everything.

Returning to her stove, she saw that she was separated from herself as her father had not been from himself. The gaunt image of Stowey appeared before her, enraging her mind; why could she not *have* him! They were like two planets circling each other, held in their orbits by an invisible force that forbade their juncture, the force coming out of those two watery eyes, those clawed white fingers, that put-on stupidity, that selfish arrogance which sat in the house down the road, grinning and enthroned. A burst of wind against the house reminded her that guests would be here. She turned her mind to the food and sought once more the soft suspension of all desire. One of the parakeets flew up from the floor and perched on her wrist. She stopped working and moved it to her lips and kissed its glistening head, and as always it bowed and plucked at her flesh with its talons.

To Cleota it was faintly ill-mannered to ask biographical data of a guest. What people did for a living, whether they were married or divorced, had mistresses or lovers, had been to jail or Princeton or in one of the wars – the ordinary pegs on which to drape the growing tapestry of an evening's conversation did not exist for her mind. Until she was sixteen she had not met, or at least had not had to cope with, anyone whose background and attitudes were different from her own. Her uncles, aunts, and cousins had all been of a piece and of a place, even if they had gone all over the world to live, and it was – or seemed – quite the same for the other girls who attended her schools. Her life had taken her, at Stowe's side, into many countries, the *palazzos* of financiers, the hovels of artists, the Harlems of the world, the apartments of *nouveau riches* and university trustees, and the furnished rooms of doped musicians, but rich or poor, famous or infamous, genius or dilettante, they were all greeted and listened to with her same blind stare, her inattention to details, her total absence of discrimination. She seemed not to realize that people ordinarily judged others; not that she liked everyone equally, but so long as they were in some way amusing, or sincere, or something at least definite, she was happy to have them in her house. What did arouse her was to be put upon – or ever to be told what to think or to feel. It was simply an absurdity that anyone should impose on anyone else. Beyond this prohibition, which her manner made it unnecessary to enforce very often, she was not troubled by people. Unexpectedly, however, she did not disapprove of moralists. It was simply that moralizing for them was, or must surely be, somehow necessary, just as some people hated the outdoors and others never ate peppery food. There were things, of course, of which she disapproved, and she often appeared to verge on moral indignation, as toward people being denied passports by the government or being kept out of restaurants because they were coloured. But it soon became clear she was not speaking of any moral situation; it was simply that her sense of her own person had been inflamed by the idea of some blind, general will being imposed upon an individual. And then it was not indignation she felt so much as bewilderment, an incomprehension similar to her father's when he travelled around the world three different times at his own expense to present petitions to the League of Nations protesting the oppression of various tribes, one of which had come close to eating him, and failed to get any response.

Lucretia had called this morning and among other things had said that John Trudeau had stopped by the night before on his way to New York, and when the two women had decided to have dinner together Trudeau was inevitably included, along with another guest of Lucretia's, a Madame something who was also visiting her. Cleota had known Trudeau and especially his wife Betty until last year, when he quit his job teaching at Pemmerton School in Banock, a few miles from her house, and went to live in Baltimore. She had been less impressed with him than with his wife, a tall young beauty, yet sensible. Some six years ago their wedding party had spilled over into the Rummel house, and Cleota still connected Trudeau with that evening, when with Betty at his side he seemed a promising, deeply serious fellow who she hoped would become the poet he had set his heart on being.

There had seemed to be a touching faith between them, like hers in Stowe when young. They had had four children and lived poorly in an unremodelled farmhouse near the school, and Cleota had often dropped in there in the hope she could draw them out of a deepening seclusion, which gave her the feeling that they were perhaps ashamed of their poverty. She had made sure to invite them whenever there was anything going at her house, and they had come more often than not, but toward the end of their years here she could not help seeing that they were cool to each other and that Trudeau had gotten grey quite suddenly, and she could not tell why their failure had left her feeling an angry frustration, especially when they had never been close friends.

So she was not entirely surprised to see Trudeau tonight with a girl who was not his wife, but that it should be a girl like this! He was still a handsome man in a conventional way, tall, white-haired at the temples, a rather long face with a Byronic nose, but, she thought now, somewhat on the weak side overall. She saw now that she had met his face on many a sailing boat long ago, the perpetual sportsmen who remained Princeton boys forever. How had she misjudged him so? Yet he still had something serious, some suffering in his eyes, which she fancied looked at her now with a tinge of nervous shame, whose cause she quickly concluded was the physical appearance of this girl who obviously was his mistress.

All through dinner Cleota could neither look at her directly nor take her eyes from her profile. The girl hardly spoke but stared over the others' heads in seeming judgement upon the not brilliant conversation, straining her brows, which were pencilled nearly into her hair, blinking her enormous brown eyes whose lids were blackened like a ballerina's in a witches' dance. She wore a black sweater and a black felt skirt, both tightened over enormous breasts and weighty but well-made thighs, and her shoes were spike-heeled and black too. There was no make-up on her olive skin, not even lipstick. Her arms jangled with bracelets and her name was Eve Saint Bleu. Trudeau, incredibly, called her 'Saint' and from time to time tried to draw her into the talk, but she would only turn her morose eyes toward him instead of the walls and windows. At each of his slavish attempts to engage the girl, Cleota would turn quickly to hear what remark would fall from Saint's full lips, to witness Saint when she might leave off with what to Cleota was an incredibly rude attempt to appear bored and disapproving of everything. Or was she merely as stupid as she looked? After twenty minutes of this silent sparring Cleota refused any further interest in Saint and did what she always did with people in her house – left out whoever did not appeal to her and attended to those who did.

She had always liked Lucretia, her friend since their school-days, and Madame. . . . 'I don't think I heard your name, Madame,' she said to the woman who sat across the table from her, eating the lamb in large chunks and chewing with a full mouth.

'Lhevine. Manisette-Lhevine. Ish shpelled with an aish,' the lady said, trying to swallow at the same time.

Cleota laughed at her attempt and liked this ugly woman who was so small she had to sit on a cushion at the table. She had the face of a man, the skin of a mulatto, with a blob of a nose that seemed to have been deboned, it hung so unsupported and un-shaped. Her eyes were black like her kinky hair, which was bobbed high and showed her manly ears, which stuck out from her head. She had a large mouth and well-filled teeth. Her hands were bulb-knuckled and veined, and when she laughed, which she did often, deep creases cut parentheses into her tight cheeks. She had asked permission to remove the jacket of her grey suit, exposing her skinny, muscular arms, which sprouted from a sleeveless blouse like the twisted branches of an old apple tree. Cleota, as though to compensate Madame for the sensuous form of her other guests, kept placing fresh slices of bread and meat before her alone as they talked.

'I want Madame to do you,' Lucretia said, and only now Cleota recalled her having mentioned on the phone that this woman told fortunes. An oddly suspended smile was hanging on Lucretia's face as Cleota turned to her. Lucretia sat there as though she were going to brazen out an embarrassing but true confession, for she had always been a severely practical, scientifically minded woman with no patience whatsoever for any kind of mysticism. During the first years of her marriage she had even returned to school for her master's degree in bacteriology and had worked in laboratories until the children came. She knew exactly how many calories, proteins, and carbohydrates there were in every food, used pressure cookers to preserve the vitamins, kept instruments in her kitchen with which she could predict humidity and weather, and dealt with everyone, including her own children, with a well-scrubbed avoidance of sentimentality and muddle.

But there she sat, not half as embarrassed as Cleota thought she would surely be at having admitted this intense interest in fortune telling, and Cleota could not absorb such a violent contradiction of her old friend's character, and for a moment her mouth went from a smile to a serious expression as she wondered if she were the victim of a joke.

'She's wonderful, Cleota,' Lucretia insisted. 'I haven't told her anything about you, but you wait and see what she finds out.'

Quite suddenly Saint spoke. 'I had an aunt who did that.' It was her first remark unprompted by a question from Trudeau, and everyone turned to her, waiting for more. And she momentarily looked so eager to tell them something, her supercilious air gone, that she seemed merely a shy girl who had been intimidated to find herself in Stowe Rummel's actual house. Trudeau relaxed and smiled for the first time and encouraged her with happier eyes to go on. She opened her lips to speak.

'Your aunt didn't do *this*, dear,' Madame Lhevine cut her off, grinning across the table at her with clear resentment and giving the table one significant pat.

Saint looked hurt, and Trudeau put a hand on her thigh under the table and said, 'Honey. . . .' But Madame Lhevine was going on now to Cleota, to whom she looked with softened eyes, as though she shared a secret understanding with her alone. 'There's no need to do you,' she said.

'Why not?' Cleota blushed.

'You're there already.'

Cleota laughed high. 'Where?'

'Where it all begins,' Madame said, and her persistent calm, absurd to Cleota at first, gave her an authority that now caused all to watch her every movement.

Cleota's high, hawking laugh burst from her; it was followed by a sip of red wine and a wondering glance at Lucretia, for it suddenly swept in upon her that to have become so intensely involved with this woman her long-time friend must be in some great personal trouble. But she quickly turned back to Madame Lhevine.

'I'm not laughing at you, Madame,' she said, busying her hands with sweeping crumbs toward herself. 'It's just that I don't know where *anything* begins. Or ends.' She laughed again, blushing. 'Or anything at all.'

Madame Lhevine's eyes did not stir. 'I know that, dear,' she said.

A blow seemed to have struck Cleota from somewhere; she felt herself pierced by the fantastic but oddly kind eyes of the fortune-teller. A new need for this woman's attention and even for her care pressed upon Cleota, who suddenly felt herself lonely. She lowered her gaze to the last crumbs, saying, 'I suppose it's just as real as anything else, though.'

'Neither more nor less,' Madame Lhevine said with the quiet joy of those who believe and are saved.

Cleota could not sit there any longer. 'I'll get some coffee,' she said and went out into the kitchen.

Her hand unaccountably shook as she held the kettle under the faucet. Her cheeks were hot. The faces in the living room revolved before her until Lucretia's expression hung in her mind, the close-set eyes so strangely eager for Cleota to accept Madame Lhevine. All at once it was obvious to her that Lucretia and her husband had broken.

She stared at the flame, still, quiet. Bud Trassel was home only week-ends this year not because he had to be travelling all over the state on business. They were effectually separated.

This knowledge was like something sliding out of her that she

had not known was in her at all. How could she have been so
blind to what was so obvious! She felt frightened. Her kitchen
itself began to seem strange. What else, she wondered, was lying
in her mind, unknown to her? Again she thought of Lucretia's
new, almost lascivious manner tonight, the same Lucretia who
had always sat with one leg entwined about the other, always
blushing before she ever dared to laugh! And now so ...
immoral. But what had she done or said that was immoral? It was
all silly!

A coldness spread through her body, and she glanced toward
the pantry to see if the door had opened. She sensed Alice outside, listened, but it was quiet out there. Still, it was not beneath
Stowe's sister to peek through the windows. She strode to the
back door and opened it brusquely, already infuriated. No one
was there. The swift wind was wracking the trees, and through
their waving branches her eyes caught a distant, unaccustomed
light. She stopped moving, tracing the geography of the roads in
her mind until she decided it was Joseph's house, a surprise since
he and his wife rarely came up in winter, although he did alone
sometimes, to write. Had she known she would have called him
tonight.

Already there was a smile on her face as she returned to the
stove, thinking of Joseph confronting Madame Lhevine. 'A
fortune-*what*?' he would ask, poker-faced – or some such half-
joke that would make her laugh with embarrassment. There was
always something on the verge of the inappropriate about what
he said, on the verge of ... of the truth. She went to the phone
and held it absently to her ear, waiting for the tone. And still, she
thought, visualizing this man, he is also a believer. So many Jews
were, she thought for the first time. And his image came strongly
to her mind as she stared at the mask beside the phone – he was
like her father that way, he had some torturing statement in him
that was always seeming to come out but never quite did. Like
Stowe too! Now she became aware of the receiver's silence and
put it down in pique, half blaming Alice for having damaged it
somehow. When she turned back to the stove Lucretia walked in
and stood without speaking in the middle of the kitchen, slump-

ing her long, wide-shouldered body on to one hip. And Cleota saw the willed smile on her shy face.

'Is it upsetting you?' Lucretia's voice was deep; she always seemed to imitate a man when she had to perform a duty.

'No!' Cleota laughed, surprised at her own sharpness. And instantly the feeling came over her that for some reason she was being got at by Lucretia tonight – she had brought the fortune-teller for a reason. What? If only they would both leave! Now, before this dreadful intimacy thickened! It had never been like this, not even in their beds at school when they had talked into the nights – from the beginning there had been an unspoken agreement to leave truly private matters untouched. It had been not a relation through words, but something like the silent passage of light from sun to moon, as when Lucretia had let her hair grow after Cleota stopped cutting hers, or took to wearing rings when Cleota returned with some for herself from Mexico. Facing her lifelong friend now, seeing the oddly broken smile on her face – was it a cynical smile? – she felt the fear of one who has wielded the power of example without having known it and must now deal with the revolt of the unwittingly oppressed. It flashed through her mind that Lucretia had moved to the country only because she had, and would never, never straighten out the chaos of her house because it was only an imitation of this house, and that her chains of projects – starting her shrub nursery, then designing shoes, now breeding horses – were not the good and natural blossoms of her joyous energy, as she always tried to imply, but abortive distractions in a life without a form, a life, Cleota saw now, that had been shaded by her own and Stowe's. Cleota stared at the seemingly guilty and dangerous eyes, sensing – what she had always known! – that a disaster had been spreading roots through her friend's life this last thirty years and now had burst it apart.

Lucretia took a swallow of her drink and said, 'Bud's left me, Cleota,' and smiled.

Cleota's spine quivered at her prophecy come true. She cocked her head like a dog that has been summoned and does not know whether to approach or flee. 'When?' she asked, merely to fill the silence until she could think what to say.

'I don't know when. He's been on his way a long time, I guess.' And now she raised her arms, put them around Cleota's neck, and – much the taller – rested her head awkwardly on Cleota's shoulders. In a moment Cleota pressed her lightly away, and they looked at one another, changed.

'Are you divorcing?' she asked Lucretia. How dreamily unfeeling that embrace had been!

'Yes,' Lucretia said, red-faced but grinning.

'Is it another – ?'

'No,' Lucretia cut her off. 'At least I don't think there's anybody else.' And, glancing at the pot, she said, 'Coffee'll be cold, won't it?'

The coffee? Cleota only now remembered why she had come into the kitchen. She got the cups down and set them on the tray.

'It won't be much of an adjustment anyway,' Lucretia said, behind her.

'You don't seem very upset. Are you?' Cleota turned to her, picked up the tray, thinking that she had never before asked anyone such absurdly personal questions. Some dangerously obscene thing had invaded her person, she felt, and her house, and it must be stopped. And yet Lucretia appeared not to notice. It suddenly seemed ages ago since Stowe had been here.

'I've been miserable for a long time, Clee,' Lucretia answered.

'I didn't know.'

'Yes.'

They stood in the middle of the kitchen under the hanging bulb, looking at each other.

'He's actually moved out?'

'Yes.'

'What are you going to do?'

'Look for a job, I guess. I think I've had it up here anyway.'

'Oh,' Cleota said.

'I'm glad I could tell you alone. Without Stowe.'

'Really? Why?'

'He likes Bud so.' Lucretia laughed dryly. 'I'd feel ashamed to tell him.'

'Oh, Stowe won't mind. I mean,' she corrected, 'he's never surprised at anything.' She laughed at Stowe's childish insulation of mind, his somehow irritating ignorance of people's relations, and said, '*You* know – ' and broke off when Lucretia smiled as though celebrating Stowe's trouble-blind charm.

Cleota picked up the loaded tray. 'Have you known her long? Madame?'

'Only since yesterday. She came up to buy the horses. She has a place near Harrisburg or somewhere. She's fabulous, Clee. Let her do you.'

Lucretia's persistence again pressed down upon Cleota, like some sort of need for her complicity. Trudeau walked in, bowing a little to both women to apologize for interrupting them. 'We'll have to leave, Cleota.'

He gripped her hand, which she offered him under the tray, and held it under some terrific pressure, which only leaving her house would evidently alleviate. She felt she could not ask him what the matter was because it was obviously the girl's insisting he must take her away even without coffee. Cleota reddened at his embarrassment, telling him, 'It was nice to see you again, John. I think the driveway light is still on.'

Trudeau nodded thankfully for her unquestioning farewell, but his honour seemed to forbid him to turn away too soon from the openly bewildered look in her face.

'Tell Stowe I left my best,' he said, letting go of her hand.

'Yes.'

Now he turned away, a slight shift in his eyes confessing to her that his life was misery. The three entered the living-room together.

Saint was already in her coat, a black pile, and wore a black gauze veil over her head. She was looking out at the driveway through the pane in the door and turned to Trudeau, who immediately got his coat and joined her. She glanced once at Cleota, who had hardly time to put the tray on the table when both of them were gone.

'Well!' She laughed, blushing but relieved. 'What happened?'

'She got mad at me,' Madame Lhevine said.

'Why?' Cleota asked, still tingling from Saint's hatred of her. What a weird night it was! From out of nowhere a strange girl comes to hate her! And yet everything seemed to be somehow in order and as it had to be, all around her the broken cliffs of people's lives sliding so deftly into the sea.

'Her aunt *couldn't* have been a gypsy. A gypsy is a gypsy, not somebody you just call a gypsy. I told her her aunt was not a gypsy.'

'Oh,' Cleota said, her eyes very wide as she tried to understand what was so serious about Madame Lhevine's point. 'Are you a gypsy?' she asked innocently.

'Me? No, I'm Jewish.'

Lucretia nodded in confirmation. Evidently she also thought these identities important. Cleota felt that the two of them had the secret of some closed world, which gave them some assurance, some belonging sense. She swallowed whisky. Madame lit a cigarette and squinted her eyes in the smoke. Lucretia looked at the table and played with a match. A moment passed in total silence. Cleota realized that she was now supposed to ask Madame to tell her fortune. It was, she began to feel, a matter of their dignity that she ask. To refuse to ask would be to question their authenticity. And a feeling rose in Cleota again that she was being put upon, pressured toward a discipleship of some vague sort.

'I can't understand John,' she said to Lucretia. 'Do you?'

'It's just sex,' Lucretia said, implying a surfeit of experience that Cleota knew she did not have. Or did she?

'But that girl,' Cleota said, 'she's not very pretty, is she?'

Lucretia was strangely excited and suddenly reached across what seemed like half the room to drag a small table over to herself with a pack of cigarettes on it. 'What's pretty got to do with sex?' she said.

"Well, I don't understand it. He must have his reasons, but his wife is much more beautiful than this one.'

Cleota was perfectly aware that Lucretia was playing toward Madame Lhevine, acting out some new familiarity with degradation, but she still could not help feeling on the outside, looking in at an underwater world. *The* world? She prayed Stowe had forgotten something and would suddenly walk in.

Madame Lhevine spoke with certainty, an elder who was used to waiting for the issue to be joined before moving in to resolve it along the right lines. 'The spirit doesn't always love what the person loves,' she said.

Oh, how true that was! Cleota sensed a stirring in her own depths, a delight in the quickening of her own mind.

'It's a difficult thing,' Madame went on. 'Not many people know how to listen to the inner voice. Everything distracts us. Even though we know it's the only thing that can guide us.'

She squinted into the ash tray and truly listened as Cleota spoke. 'But how can one hear? Or know what to believe? One senses so many things.'

'How do you know your body? Your hands feel it, your eyes see it every day in the mirror. It is practice, that's all. Every day we inspect our bodies, do we not? But how often do we set time aside to inspect our souls? To listen to what it can tell us? Hardly ever. People,' she said with some protest now, 'scoff at such things, but they accept that one cannot sit down at a piano and play the first time. Even though it is much more difficult, and re-quires much more technique, to hear one's own inner voice. And to understand its signs – this is even more difficult. But one can do it. I promise you.'

With enormous relief Cleota saw that Madame Lhevine was serious and not a fool.

'She's marvellous,' Lucretia said, without any reserve now that she saw the impression made on Cleota.

'I don't tell fortunes,' Madame went on, 'because there is really no future in the vulgar sense.'

How kind she was! How her certainty even loaned her a love-liness now! To have lost touch with oneself, Cleota thought, was what made women seem unattractive. 'I don't understand that,' Cleota said, 'about the future.'

'Perhaps you would tell me more about what you don't under-stand,' Madame said.

Cleota was reached by this invitation; she felt understood suddenly, for she did want to speak of her idea of the future. She settled more comfortably in her chair and sought her thoughts. 'I don't really know. I suppose I never used to think about it at all, but – well, I suppose when one gets to a certain point, and there's more behind than ahead, it just somehow . . . doesn't seem to have been quite worth it. I don't mean,' she added quickly, for she noted that Lucretia seemed oddly gratified with this implication of her failure, 'I don't say that I've had a bad time of it, really. I haven't. It's really got nothing to do – my idea – with happiness or unhappiness. It's more that you . . . you wonder if it wasn't all a little too' – she laughed, blushing – 'small.' And before Madame could speak she added without any emphasis, 'I suppose when the children aren't around any more one thinks of that.' It struck her that she would never have shown such doubt with Stowe around, and she felt freed by his absence.

'It's more than the children not being around,' Lucretia said.

'It's that too,' Madame reminded Lucretia. 'We must not underestimate the physical, but' – she turned back to Cleota – 'it is also the climax inside.'

Cleota waited. She felt she was being perceived, but not any longer by a merely curious mind. Madame, she felt, was seeing something within her with which the world climax was connected.

'One sees that there will be no ecstasy,' Madame Lhevine said. 'and that is when the crisis comes. It comes, you might say, when we see the future too clearly, and we see that it is a plain, an endless plain, and not what we had thought – a mountain with a glory at the top.'

'Oh, I never thought of any glory.'

'I am not speaking of accomplishment. I am speaking of oneness. The glory is only the moment when we are at one.'

Death burst into Cleota's mind, the complete sense of a dying; not any particular person, not herself, but some unidentifiable person lying dead. Then her oneness would be in her, and a glory, a beneficent peace.

A quick joyousness raised her to her feet and she went to the sideboard and got a new bottle of whisky and returned to the table and, without asking, poured. Then she looked across at Madame Lhevine, her face flushed.

'What do you do?' she asked, forbearing to say 'now'. She did not want to impute any formal routine to Madame, any cheap ritual. Some truth was closing in, some singular announcement, which, she felt, must not be spoiled.

'If you wish, you can simply put your hands on the table.'

Stowe would laugh; her father would have looked at the ceiling and stalked out of the room. She raised her hands, and when she set them on the table it felt as though they had been thrust into a cold wind. Now Madame's hands glided and came to rest with her middle fingers touching Cleota's. They were old hands, much older than Madame's face. The four hands looked like separate living animals facing one another on the table.

Cleota awaited her next instruction, but there was none. She raised her eyes to Madame's.

The woman's great age struck her anew. Her cheeks seemed to have sunk, she looked Slavic now, her skin cracked like milk skim, the veins in her eyeballs twisted like a map of jungle rivers.

'Look in my eyes, please,' Madame Lhevine said.

Cleota shuddered. 'I am,' she said. Was it possible the woman had gone blind? Looking more sharply, Cleota saw in fact that Madame was not seeing, that her gaze had died, gone within. It was too appropriate, and for a moment she thought to break off, but a feeling came that she would lose by mocking; whatever her distrust, she felt she must continue to look into these black eyes if she ever was to hope again for a connexion to herself.

Now Madame Lhevine lifted her hands and patted Cleota's and breathed. Cleota put her hands back in her lap. Madame Lhevine blinked at nothing, seeming to be putting together what she had heard or seen.

'Is there an older woman – ?' Madame broke off. 'Is there an old woman?' she corrected.

'My husband's sister. She lives nearby.'

'Oh.' Madame raised her chin. She seemed to be steeling herself. 'She will live longer than he.'

A tremor shook Cleota's head; she looked stupidly at Madame Lhevine, her mind shocked by the picture of Stowe in his casket and Alice standing over it, while she must wait forever by herself in a corner, a stranger again. It seemed to her she had always had this picture in her head and the only news was that now someone else had seen it too.

Cleota was agonized by the relief she felt at the image of Alice's outliving Stowe. Simply, it wiped out her entire life with him. She had met him first in the gallery with Alice at his side, the air between them thickened by a too dense, too heavy communication. She had never broken into it herself, never stood alone in the centre of his vision. Thirty years vanished, nullified. She was now where she had come in, with nothing to show.

'I'm sorry I had to –' Madame broke off as she laid her hand on Cleota's. The touch brought Cleota back to the room and an awareness of Alice hovering somewhere near the house. Anger puffed her eyelids. What Madame and Lucretia saw was the furious look that was sweeping up into her face.

A car, driven fast, squealed to a halt in the driveway. The three women turned together toward the door, hearing the approaching footsteps outside, the steps of a man. Cleota went toward it as the knocking began and opened it.

'Joseph!' she almost shouted.

The young man threw up his hands in mock fright. 'What'd I do?' he called.

Cleota laughed. 'Come in!'

Now he entered, grinning at her and speaking the drollery that had always served best between them. 'Am I too late?'

'For what?' Cleota heard the girlish crack in her voice.

'Whatever it is,' he said, taking off his zipper jacket and tossing it to a chair. 'I mean it's late and I didn't want to wake you.'

'We're obviously awake,' she taunted him, feeling a new cruelty torn loose within her.

He felt hung up, facing the other two women, and so he shouted, 'I mean will I be in the way if I come in for a few minutes because I'm not ready to go to sleep yet and I thought it would be nice to say hello! Is what I mean!'

Lucretia also laughed. There was something aboriginal about him, in her opinion, as she had once told Cleota.

'So hello!' he said and drew a chair up to the table, combed his fingers through his thick brown hair, and lit a cigar.

'Have you had dinner?' Cleota asked.

'I ate once at five and again at nine,' he said. Cleota seemed oddly charged up. He did not know if it was because he was intruding or because he was very welcome as the only man.

He glanced toward Madame Lhevine, who gave him a nodding smile, and only now did Cleota realize, and she introduced them.

'How long will you stay up here?'

'I don't know. Few days.' He drank what she put before him. 'How's Stowey?'

'Oh, all right,' and she gave a quick, deprecating laugh. This had always given him a smoky sense of an understanding with her, about what precisely he did not know. But now she added seriously, 'He's having a show in Florida.'

'Oh, that's nice.'

She laughed again.

'Well, I meant it!' he protested.

Her face turned instantly grave. 'I know you did.'

To Madame Lhevine and Lucretia he said, 'Between us it's always a battle of half-wits.'

The women's laughter relieved him; he was some ten years younger than Cleota and Lucretia, a rolling-gaited, hands-in-pockets novelist whose vast inexperience with women had given him a curiosity about them so intense as to approach understanding. With women, he usually found himself behind any one of various masks, depending on the situation; at the moment it was that of the raffish youth, the younger poet, perhaps, for it was never possible to arrive – especially before Cleota – as himself. She was, he always sensed, an unhappy woman who perhaps did not even know her unhappiness; she therefore sought something, some sensuous reassurance, which he could distract her from by simulating this carefree artist's bantering. Not that Cleota herself attracted him; that she was a wife was enough to place her in a vaguely sacred area. Unless he should strike out toward another sort of life and character for himself, a life, as he visualized it, of truthful relations – which is to say, personal relations of a confessional sort. But somewhere in his mind he knew that real truths only came out of disaster, and he would do his best to avoid disaster in all the departments of his life. He had to, he felt, out of decency. For the true terror of living in a false position was that the love of others became attached to it and so would be betrayed if one were to strike for the truth. And treason to others – to Joseph Kersh – was the ultimate destruction, worse even than treason to himself, living with a wife he could not love.

By the time he was seated at the table he was already chafing at the boyish role Cleota had thrust upon him these six or seven years of their acquaintance. He made his manner grave and seemingly even troubled, and since, as the only man present, attention was centred on him for the moment and he had to speak, he looked directly into Lucretia's eyes and asked, 'How's your husband?'

Lucretia lowered her gaze to her cigarette and, tapping it impatiently, she said, 'He's all right.'

He heard her door clap shut. Women discovered alone, he believed, must have been talking about sex. He had believed this since his childhood, when his mother's bridge parties had always gone from screaming hilarity to matronly silence as soon as he appeared. He knew then, as he knew now, that there was something illicit here, something prohibited in the air. Knowing was no problem to him; it was admitting that he knew. For it tore at his sense of good, of right, and of the proper nature of things that wives should betray the smallest contempt for their husbands. And yet, he felt, contempt was around this table now. And he was dismayed that this flattered him and gave him a joyous feeling of fitness. 'Just a half,' he said to Cleota, who was pouring more whisky into his glass. 'I've got to get to sleep soon.'

'Oh, don't go!' she said strongly, and he saw that she was flushed with whisky. 'Are you writing up here?'

'No.' Gratified, he saw how she was waiting for serious news of him. Lucretia too was curious. 'I'm just worrying.'

'*You?*'

'Why not?' he asked, genuinely surprised.

'Just that you seem to do everything you want to do.'

Her admiration, he believed, was for some strength she seemed to think he had, and he accepted with pleasure. But a distant alarm was ringing for him tonight; something intimate was happening here, and he should not have come.

'I don't know,' he answered Cleota. 'Maybe I do do what I want to. The trouble is I don't know I'm doing it.' And he resolved, in the name of some distant truthfulness, to reveal a little of his own bewilderment. 'I really go from moment to moment, despite appearances. I don't know what I'm doing any more than anybody else.'

'Ah, but you do know,' said Madame Lhevine, narrowing her eyes. He looked at her with surprise. 'I have read your books. You do know. Within yourself you know.'

He found himself liking this ugly woman. Her tone reminded him of his mother's when she would look at him after he had knocked over a vase and say, 'You will be a great man.'

'You follow your spirit, Mr Kersh,' she went on, 'so it is not necessary to know anything more.'

'I suppose I do,' he said, 'but it would save a lot of trouble if I could believe it.'

'But I'm sure you understand,' Madame pressed on, 'that the sense you have of not knowing is what makes your art. When an artist knows what he is doing he can no longer do it, don't you think?'

This so matched the licence Joseph secretly claimed for himself, and the blessed freedom from responsibility he longed for, that he could not in good conscience accept it. 'Well, I wouldn't go that far,' he said. 'It's romantic to think an artist is unconscious.' And now he broadened his shoulders and his right hand closed in a fist. 'A work of art must work, like a good machine – '

'But a machine made by a blind man,' Madame said in an experienced tone.

'I deny that,' he said, shaking his head, helpless to dam up this flood of certainty. 'I have to think through a form before I can write. I have to engineer a structure. I have to know what I am doing.'

'Of course,' Madame cut in, 'but at a certain point you must know nothing and allow yourself only your feelings. In fact, that is my only – my only reservation about your work.'

'What?' he asked. He did not like her. Women ought not to criticize. She was repulsively ugly, like a dwarf.

'They are a bit overconstructed,' she said. 'I hope you will not think me presumptuous, but I do have that feeling even though I admire enormously what you say.'

He hoped that the heat he felt rising in his face would be attributed to the whisky. Crossing his knees suddenly, he knocked the table against Madame and quickly set it back in place, laughing. 'I'm sorry, I didn't mean to cripple you.'

He saw, with near shock, that Cleota was openly staring at him – with admiration. It was most noticeable. Why was Stowe gone, alone?

Lucretia was deep in thought, looking at the ash tray and tapping her cigarette on it. 'But really, Joe' – she faced him with her overpuzzled look 'don't you think that people are really much more disoriented than you portray them? I mean – '

'My characters are pretty disoriented, Lucretia,' he said and made Cleota laugh.

'No, seriously; your people always seem to *learn* something,' she complained.

'Don't you think people learn?' he asked and wondered what they were secretly arguing about. There was, in fact, something dense about Lucretia, he had always thought. The first time he had met her she had just come from mating two horses and was feverish with her success, and it had seemed so clear that she had had a sexual interest in the procedure herself, yet was unaware of it, and this had given her a dull quality in his eyes – a musky one too, however.

'Of course they learn,' she said – and it was clear she was matching intellects with him, which a woman ought not to do, he felt – 'but they learn geometry and the necessary dates. Not . . .' She sought the word, and Madame supplied it.

'Not spirit.'

'Yes!' Lucretia agreed but deferred to Madame to continue.

'I'm sure you agree,' said Madame, 'that essentially the spirit is formed quite early. Actually it knows all it will ever know from the beginning.'

'Then what's the point in living?'

'Because we must live. That is all.'

'I wouldn't call that much of a point,' Joseph said.

'Maybe there isn't much of a point,' Cleota suddenly put in.

Joseph turned to her, struck by her sad gravity. He wondered whether Stowe had any idea she was so hopeless. But he checked himself – she was only talking and being her usual tolerant self. That was what he could never understand – she and Stowe could feel deeply about some issue and yet be perfectly friendly with people who stood for everything they opposed. Life to them was some kind of game, whereas one ought to believe something to the point of suffering for it. He wished he could find a way of leaving now instead of sitting here with these three crocked lunks arguing about spirits!

'Although I do think we learn,' Cleota went on, with an open glance of support for Joseph. 'I don't know if we learn only what we unconsciously knew before, or whether it's all continuously new, but I think we learn.'

How admirably direct she was! Joseph caught this flower she had surprisingly tossed him and with it charged against the other two women. 'What always gets me is how people will scoff at science and conscious wisdom and the whole rational approach to life, but when they go to the more "profound" places, like Mexico or Sicily or some other spiritual-type country, they never forget to take their typhoid shots!'

The mocking voices of Madame Lhevine and Lucretia were in the air, and he reddened with anger. Lucretia yelled, 'That's got nothing to do with – '

'It's only the exact point! If you believe something you have to live by it or it's just talk! You can't say we don't learn and then blithely accept the fruits of what we've learned. That's – it's – ' He wanted to say, 'Lying.'

'Oh, now, Joe,' Lucretia drawled, looking at him with toleration – he sounded like her husband proving to her on engineering principles that she was not unhappy – 'what we're talking about is simply not on that *plane*. You're ten years behind the times. Nobody's underrating science and conscious wisdom; it's simply that it doesn't provide an inner aim, a point to live for. It still leaves man essentially alone.'

'Except that the only people I ever met who feel part of an international, a world community are scientists. They're the only ones who aren't alone.'

'Now, Joe, really – what does a sentence like that *mean*?'

He was furious. 'It means that they don't live for themselves only, they live in the service of a greater thing.'

'*What*, for heaven's sake?'

'What? The alleviation of human pain and the wiping out of human poverty.'

'We can't all be wiping out poverty, Joseph. What do *we* do? We're simply not talking about the same things.' She turned to Cleota. 'Do you sense the difference, Clee?'

'Of course there's a difference,' Cleota said, her eyes avoiding Lucretia's, 'but why can't you both be right?' And she glanced at Joseph for confirmation of this, to him, total absurdity.

'I don't care about being right,' he said quietly now. But his hopes for Cleota had again subsided; she was a total mystery to him. Nothing ever came to an issue for her. The idea came sharply to his mind that every time he came here it was an anticlimax. This was why he always left feeling he had wasted his time – they were people who simply lived in an oblong hum and did not strive for some apotheosis, some climax in life, either a great accomplishment or a discovery or any blast of light and sound that would fling them into a new speed, a further orbit.

Yet, inexplicably, when he had been fired from the university for his refusal to disavow the Left-wing youth, she had gone on for months indignantly talking about it, phoning to see how he was, and for a while even spoke of living abroad to protest the oppressive American atmosphere.

Madame and Lucretia evidently felt he had been put down

successfully, and the ugly woman allowed him a kind look and said, 'It doesn't matter anyway – you are a very good writer.'

This outstretching of a finger instead of a whole hand made Joseph and Cleota laugh, and he said, 'I'm not knocking intuition.' Cleota laughed louder, but he had meant this as a compromise with Madame and said to Cleota, 'Wait a minute, I'm making up to her,' and Cleota laughed louder still. His abruptness always entertained her, but it was something more now; in his passion for his ideas, ideas she understood but did not find irreplaceable, she sensed a fleshed connexion with an outside force, an unseen imperative directing his life. He *had* to say what he said, believe what he believed, was helpless to compromise, and this spoke a dedication not different from love in him.

She drank three inches of whisky straight, observing a bright stain of green moonlight through the wet windows over her guests' heads. A planetary silence seemed to surround the continuing argument; she felt herself floating away. Her only alarm was that the talk was dying and they would all soon leave. She poured whisky for Joseph, who was pounding the table with his open hand. 'I am not knocking intuition,' he was saying again, 'I work with it, I make my living by it.' Out of nowhere an idea hit him. 'I'll tell you something, Madame Lhevine. I come from a long line of superstitious idiots. I once had an aunt, see, and she told fortunes – '

Cleota exploded, throwing her hands up in the air and turning from the table doubled over by laughter. Lucretia first smiled, trying to resist for Madame's sake, but she caught the infection, and then Madame herself unwillingly joined, and Joseph, smiling stupidly, looked at the three women laughing hysterically around him, asking, 'What? What!' but no one was able to answer, until he too was carried into the waves; and, as always happens in such cases, one of them had only to look at the other to begin insanely laughing all over again. And when they had quieted enough for him to be heard he explained to Cleota, 'But she did. In fact, she was part gypsy!'

At this Cleota screamed, and she and Lucretia bent across the table, grasping each other's arms, gasping and laughing with their faces hidden by their shoulders, and Madame kept slapping the table and shaking her head and going, 'Ho, ho, ho.'

Joseph, without understanding what it was all about, could not help feeling their hysteria was at his expense. His soberness returned before theirs, and he sat patiently smiling, on the verge of feeling the fool, and lit his cigar and took a drink, waiting for them to come to.

At last Cleota explained with kindness that Saint had said precisely the same things, and that. . . . But now it was hard to reconstruct the earlier situation, especially Madame's resentment at the girl's presumptuous claim of an aunt who could do what Madame did – at least it could not be explained, Cleota realized, without characterizing Madame Lhevine as being extremely jealous and even petty about her talent for fortune-telling; and, besides, Cleota was aware that Madame was not happy with the title of fortune-teller and yet she did not know what else to call her without invoking words like spiritualist or seer or whatever – words that embarrassed Cleota and might in the bargain again offend the lady. The net of the explanation was a muddle, a confusion which confirmed in Joseph his recurring notion that the Rummels were in fact trivial and their minds disoriented, while for Cleota her inability to conclusively describe Madame left her – however hilariously amused she still appeared – with the feeling that Madame was perhaps a fraud. This was not at all a distasteful idea to Cleota; it was simply Madame's character. What did disturb her under her flushed smile, and prevented her from detaining Madame, who now said it was getting late, was the thought of being left alone. The image surged up of Stowe lying dead in his casket, and it stiffened her a little toward Lucretia as she helped her into her coat, quite as though Lucretia had borne her this prophecy in part, carrying it from her own blasted home where nothing ever went right.

Cleota returned from the driveway and removed her Rumanian shawl and poured herself a new drink, still enjoying the exhilaration that follows helpless laughter, the physical cleanliness and strength that it leaves behind in healthy people, and at the same time her eyes had the indrawn look that the discomposing news had left there, and Joseph watched her, bewildered by her double mood.

Without asking him she handed him a drink, and they faced each other at the fire, which she had just fanned to life. 'I'll go soon,' he said. 'I have to work tomorrow.'

He saw that she was drunk, much drunker than she had seemed with the other two women present. In one continuous motion she sat down and let her knees spread apart, staring over his head. Then she leaned over heavily and set her drink on the floor between her feet and fell back into the chair again, blowing out air and turning her face toward the fire. Her breathing was still deep, and her hands hung limply from the arms of the wicker chair. Her seeming abandon was not a sign of sensuousness to him at first. He thought she was even indicating such trust in him that she need not look composed.

Drunken women made Joseph nervous. He spoke, trying for their customary bantering tone. 'Now what was *that* all about?' he asked, grinning.

She did not answer, seemed hardly to have heard. Her staring eyes suggested some vast preoccupation and finally a despair that he had never before seen in her. An engagement, a moment of personal confrontation, seemed to be approaching, and to ward it off Joseph said, 'I did have an aunt like that. She read my palm that night before I left home for college and predicted I'd flunk out after one semester.'

He had hardly started his remark when it sounded to him like chatter unworthy of the moment. And now Cleota turned her head, still resting on the rim of the chair's back, and looked at him. With a shock he felt the challenge in her eyes. She was looking at him as a man, and for the first time. Her challenge kept growing in him, and to throw her off he lazily put his arm over the back of his chair and turned to the fire as though he too were preoccupied with other thoughts. Was it possible? Cleota Rummel?

'Do you remember John Trudeau?' she asked.

He turned to her, relieved; it would be gossip after all. 'I think so. That tall guy used to teach up at – '

'Why – do you know why – ?' She broke off, her face drawn together in mystification. She was seeing past him and around him, staring. 'Why do they all end in sex?'

He was relieved at the genuinely questioning note; she was not being coy. He damned his evil mind of a moment before. 'What do you mean?' he asked.

'He has a perfectly beautiful wife. Those children too. He was here tonight. With a girl. A perfectly ghastly girl.' And once again she demanded of him, as though he must certainly know, being a man, 'Do you know why that is happening? To everybody?'

Her driving need for an answer pierced him because the question was his obsession these days. It seemed very strange she had reached into him and had grasped precisely what bewildered him.

'It seems to me,' she went on, 'that almost everyone I know is going crazy. There doesn't seem to be any other subject any more. Any other *thing* – ' She broke off again and drew in a long breath and wiped a strand of hair out of her eyes. Then she turned back to the fire, unable for the moment to continue looking at Joseph's resolute face. She wanted to weep, to laugh, to dance – anything but to sit here at this disadvantage. For an instant she remembered the warmth in Madame Lhevine's eyes, the feeling she was being enfolded by one more powerful, and she longed desperately to be taken up and held.

Her tone of supplication told Joseph that he was moving into a false position, for he dared not betray his own feelings of bewilderment. If they were both at a loss they would join in their miseries, and he could not, on even larger grounds, declare himself dumbfounded by life. 'I know what you mean,' he said, careful to direct his mournful tone toward unspecified others and away from himself and Cleota. 'I see it myself all the time.'

She looked at him from the fire. 'Do you?' she asked, demanding he go on.

'I don't know the answer,' he said and only glanced at her with this. 'I guess it's that there is no larger aim in life any more. Everything has become personal relations and nothing more.'

The blurred sensuousness drained out of her eyes, and she seemed alert to him again. 'Is there something more?'

'Sure. That is, there might be.'

'What?'

'Well . . . ' he felt like a schoolboy, having to say that the welfare of mankind, the fight for justice, caring for the oppressed, were the something more. But as he began to evoke these thoughts their irrelevancy choked off his words, their distance from the suffering he saw in this woman lying back in the wicker chair with her knees fallen outward and the drink at her feet. She was lusting for a truth beyond what he possessed, yet he had to go on. 'It's a law of history. When a society no longer knows its aims, when it's no longer dominated by the struggle to get food and safety, the private life is all there is. And we are all anarchists at heart when there is no great aim. So we jump into each other's beds.' God, what a fraud all ideas were – all anyone wanted was love!

'Joseph,' she began, her voice very soft, her eyes on the fire, 'why is it happening?'

He felt her proposal stretching out its wings, testing the air. He finished his drink and stood up. 'I'll go, Cleota,' he said.

She looked up at him, blinking lazily. 'That woman said Stowe would die before his sister.'

He could not speak; her belief in the prophecy shocked and persuaded him. He saw Stowe dead. He reached down and pressed his hand on hers awkwardly. 'You can't believe that nonsense, can you?'

'Why are you going?' she asked.

Her simplicity terrified him. 'I'll have one more drink,' he said and got the bottle and set it on the floor beside his chair and sat again, taking as long as he could with the business. And again he damned his suspicious mind – she was simply frightened for Stowe, for God's sake! He would stay until she either fell asleep or came out of her fright.

Through the warm haze that surrounded her she saw that Joseph had suddenly come to life. How young he really was! His hair was not even greying, his skin was tight, and there was no judgement coming to her from him, no orders, no husband's impatience; her body felt new and unknown. 'A larger aim,' she said, her words muffled.

'What?' he asked.

She stood up and thrust her fingers into her hair and, breathing deeply, walked to the door. He sat still, watching her. She stopped at the pane and looked out through the mist, like a prisoner, he thought. He took a long swallow of his drink, resolved to leave. She stood there ten yards away with her hands in her hair, and he admired the angled backthrust of her torso secreted in her gay woollen dress. He saw her in bed, but all he could feel was her suffering. And then Stowe would return sometime, and the three of them in this room? The weedy morass of that scene shuddered him.

Moments went by and she did not turn from the door. She was waiting for him, he saw. Goddam! Why had he stayed? He saw that he had acted falsely, a role, the protector's part. Beneath his character and hers, beneath their very powers of speech, was the anarchy of need, the lust for oblivion and its comfort. He sat there reddening with shame at having misled her, his manhood spurious to him and thought itself a pretence.

She turned to him, still at the door, lowering her arms. The amateurishness of her seduction pained him for her sake as she stood there openly staring at him. 'Don't you like me?'

'Sure I do.'

Her brows came together densely as she walked to him and stood over him, her hands hanging at her sides, her head thrust forward a little, and as she spoke her open hands turned ever so slightly toward him. 'What's the matter with you?'

He stood up and faced her, unable to speak at the sight of the animal fury in her face.

'What's the matter with you?' she screamed.

'Good night,' he said, walking around her toward the door.

'What did you stay for?' she screamed at his back.

She came toward him unsteadily, a smile of mockery spreading on her face. She could feel, almost touch, his trembling, and she clenched her teeth together with the wish to tear with them.

She felt her hands opening and closing and an amazing strength across her back. 'You . . . ! You . . . !'

She stood up close to him, saw his eyes widening with surprise and fear. The taste of her stomach came into her mouth; her disgust for him and his broken promise brought tears to her eyes. But he did not move a hand to her; he was pitiless, like Stowe when he stared through her toward Alice, and like Alice moving in and out of this house. She wept.

Joseph touched her shoulder with his hand and instantly saw Stowe's laughing face before him. She neither accepted his touch nor rejected it. As though he had no importance for her any more. So he raised the immense weight of his arms and held her. The stairs to the second floor were a few yards away; he would almost have to carry her. She would be half conscious on the pillow; toward dawn the countryside from the bedroom window would be littered with hair, with bones, with the remnants of his search for an order in his life. Holding her to him, he feared her offering was an accusation of his complicity, a sign of their equal pointlessness. But he tightened his arms around her to squash out of her any inkling she might have of his unwillingness to share her world's derangement.

She encircled his waist and pressed her body against him. To love! To know nothing but love!

He took hold of her head and turned her face up to forestall the next moment. Her eyes were shut and tears were squeezing out of their corners, her skin hot in his hands. Cleota! Cleota Rummel! But without love? he thought, without even desire? He once again saw Stowe in this room, saw himself bantering with him, discussing, felt Stowe's bumbling warmth. How easy to ruin a man! From tomorrow on he could ruin Stowe with their usual handshake and the clap on the back. The power to destroy shaped itself in his mind like a rising rocket, astounding him with its frightfulness and its beauty, an automatic force given to him like a brand-new character, a new power that would somehow finish a struggle against the meaninglessness of life, joining him at his ease with that sightless legion riding the trains and driving the cars and filling the restaurants, a power to breathe

the evil in the world and thus at last to love life. She pressed her lips against his throat, surprisingly soft lips. Disastrous contempt if he should try to leave her now, but to take her upstairs – his practical mind saw the engineering that would entail. A willed concussion of skeletons. He knew it was not virtue loosening his embrace but an older lust for a high heart uncondemned, a niggardly ambition it seemed to him now as he summoned his powers to say, 'Good night, Cleota,' and in such a tone as would convince her that he did not dislike her in his arms.

She opened her eyes. God, he thought, she could kill! 'Whaz a matter with you?' she asked him.

'Nothing's the matter with me,' he said, dropping his hands to his sides but blushing.

'What?' She swayed, peering at him through bewildered eyes, genuinely asking, 'What'd you stay for?'

A good question, he thought, damning his naïveté. 'I thought you didn't want to be alone,' he said.

'Yez. You don't like me. I'm old. Older and older.'

He reached out his hand to her, afraid she would fall, and she slapped it away, sending herself stumbling sideways, banging against the wall, where she held herself upright, her hair fallen over half her face. 'Whaz a matter with all of you? All of you and all of you!' She was sobbing but seemed not to know it. 'And if he dies before she does? Doesn't someone have to . . . have to win before the end?' She bent over, thrusting out her hands in a strangely theatrical gesture of supplication – how awkward she had become! How false all gracefulness is! And dredging up her arms from near the floor, her fingers wide, she called, weeping, a furious grimace stretching the two tendons of her throat, 'Don't you have to win before it's over? Before . . . it's *overrrr*!'

He could not stop the tears in his eyes. 'Yes,' he whispered. The attempt to speak loosened some muscle in his stomach, and he fled weeping from the house.

The thumping resounded through his dreamless sleep. Boom, boom, boom. He opened his eyes. Boom. Again. He got out of bed and staggered. The whisky, he thought. He was dizzy and held on to the window sill. The booming sounded again below. He pulled up the shade. The sun! A clear day at last! The sun was just starting to come up at the far edges of the valley. The booming sounded again below. He pulled the window up and started to lean out but his head hit the screen. Now he saw Cleota's car in the road before the house, parked askew as though it had been left there in an emergency. The booming noise went on, now violently. He called out, 'Yes!' then ran to the bed as though it were a dream and he could go back to sleep now that he had realized it.

But it was truly dawn and the noise was a knocking on his door, a dreadful emergency knocking. He called out 'Yes!' again and got into his pants, which were lying on the floor, and struggled into his shirt and ran down the stairs barefoot and opened the door.

She was standing there, morning-fresh except for the exhaustion in her eyes. But her hair was brushed and she stood tall, herself again, if one did not know that she had never looked so frightened, so pleadingly at anyone in all her life. Suddenly he thought her beautiful with the sparkling air around her head. He was still passing up through the webs of his sleep, and she was part dream standing there in his doorway in a fox-collared coat of deep, rich brown, looking at him as though she had sprung from the grass without a history except that of earth and the immense trees on the road behind her. He reached out his hand, and she took it and stepped into the hallway. He was freezing in the icy breeze and started to close the door, but she held it and looked desperately up at him, wanting back what she had given him.

'I beg your pardon for last night,' she said.

It was entirely askew to her; he was standing there trying to keep his eyes open, obviously undisturbed, she felt, by what she had done. Obviously, she saw now, he had had many women, and her coming here now was idiotically naïve to him. She felt such shame at her naïveté that she turned abruptly and pulled open the partly closed door, but he caught her arm and turned her to him.

'Cleota . . .'

Drawing her to him, he caught a scent of cherries in her hair.

The sheer presence of her body in his house astounded him. Only now was he drunk. He lowered his lips to her but was stopped by the surprise in her eyes, a surprise that had something stiff-necked about it, a resistance, a propriety he would have to overcome, and suddenly he felt he wanted to.

His hesitation, like respect, moved her; but he was unnecessary to her now that she could feel his demand. Raising her hand, she tenderly touched his chest, relieved that he wanted her a little. They were accomplices now and she could trust his silence. She straightened before him, and a smile softened her face as she recognized his open need.

He saw a little of her old stance returning, her self-respect, but it was no longer necessary to obey it. He kissed her cheek. But she was less beautiful to him now that her despair was going; she was Cleota again, well-brushed, clear-eyed, and profoundly unapproachable.

'Take care of yourself,' he said, meaninglessly, except for the brittle-shelled tone, the bantering voice they both knew so well. But how alive their simulation had become, how much more interesting it was now, this propriety, than it used to be!

'Would you like breakfast?' she asked.

Safe and sound, as on a shore they had finally reached, he said he had to go back to sleep for a while yet.

'Come later then,' she said warmly, deeply satisfied.

'Okay.'

She went down to her car and got in and drove away with a wave of one hand through the window, already slipping out of her coat with the other. She will be digging in her garden soon, he thought.

He did not go to her later. He lay in bed until the late morning, castigating himself for a coward at one moment, at the next wondering if he ought to be proud that he had been loyal to himself – and, as it turned out, to her as well.

But it never left the back of his mind that every claim to virtue is at least a little false; for was it virtue he had proved, or only fear? Or both! He wanted very much to believe that life could have a virtuous centre where conscience might lie down with sensuality in peace, for otherwise everything but sexual advantage was a fraud. He heard her voice again. 'What's the matter with you!' It rang. But was there really nothing truthful in her morning voice just now, so civilized and reserved, inviting him to breakfast? Once again good order reigned in this countryside. He smiled at a thought – she would probably welcome Stowey more warmly now that she had glimpsed a conquest. He was glad for her. So maybe some good had come of the evening. God! What a ring of fire there always is around the truth!

He lay a long time listening to the silence in his loveless house.

Alice died toward the end of May, falling asleep in her rocker as she looked at the valley view while waiting for dinner-time. Joseph heard of it only accidentally, when he returned after settling his divorce. He had put his house up for sale and discovered he had no key to the front door to give the real-estate agent. He removed the lock and took it to the hardware store to have a key fitted, and the clerk mentioned the old lady's funeral. He wanted to ask how Stowe was but caught himself. He returned with the key, installed the lock and closed the place, got into his car and drove off. Before he could think he found himself on the road to the Rummel house. He had not seen Stowe since some time before his trip to Florida, nor had he seen Cleota since the morning after her fortune was told.

Realizing he was on their road, he reduced speed. In this fine weather they might be outside and would look up and see him passing. But what, after all, had he to be ashamed of? He resolutely resumed speed, aware now that it was Stowe he would rather not face. Unless, he thought – was this possible too? – Stowe was dead?

The car travelled the long turn that straightened on to a view of the Rummel house. Stowe and Cleota were walking idly on the road, he with a stick knocking the heads off daisies and peering into the weeds every few yards, she at his side watching, breathing – Joseph could already see – her breaths of fitness and staring now and then at the newly green valley beyond Stowe's head. They both turned, hearing the car, and, recognizing it, stood still and tall. Stowe, seeing Joseph through the window, nodded, looked at him, as he had the first time they had met many years ago, with cool and perceptive eyes. Joseph nodded back, angered by his friend's coolness but smiling, and to both of them said, 'How are you?'

'Very well,' Cleota said.

Only now could he look directly at her and, strengthened by Stowe's unjust condemnation, he dared hold her in his gaze. She was afraid of him!

'Selling out?' Stowe asked with noticeable contempt.

It dawned that Stowe was condemning him for the divorce; he had always admired Joseph's wife. Only now Joseph realized how correct his estimate of them had been – they were an old-fashioned family underneath, and Stowe despised those who, at the last moment, did not abide by the laws of decency.

'I'm trying to sell it,' Joseph said, relaxing in his seat. 'But I'll probably be by again before long. Maybe I'll drop in.'

Stowe barely nodded.

' 'Bye,' Joseph said. But this time Stowe simply looked at him.

'Have a good summer,' Joseph said, turning to Cleota, and he saw, with surprise, that now she was observing him as a stranger, as Stowe was doing. They were joined.

He drove off past them, laughter rising in his heart, a joy at having seen good order closing back over chaos like an ocean that has swallowed a wreck. And he took a deep breath of May, glancing out the side window at the countryside, which seemed now never to have been cold and wet and unendurably dark through so many months.

When his car had gone and it was silent on the road, Stowe swung his stick and clipped a daisy. For a few yards neither spoke, and then he blew his nose and said, 'He's not much.'

'No,' she said, 'I suppose he isn't.'

'There was always some sneakiness in him, something like that.'

'Yes,' she said and took his arm and they walked together past his sister's empty house. She kissed his shoulder, and he looked at her, grinning and surprised, for she did not make such displays.

He grunted, quite pleased, and she held him tighter, feeling the sun on her back like a blessing, aware once again of Stowe's deep reliability, and her own. Thank God, she thought, for good sense! Joseph, she remembered, had wanted her very much that morning in his hallway. And she walked in silence, cherishing a rapture, the clear heart of those whose doors are made to hold against the winds of the world.

'Still,' she felt the need to say, 'it's rather a shame about them.'

He shrugged and bent over to part the roadside weeds, reached in and brought out a young toad whose squeaks made him laugh. And suddenly he tossed it to her. She shrieked, reddening with anger, but then she laughed. And as sometimes happened with them, they just stood face to face, laughing down at each other with an enormous heartiness.

[*1961*]

Fame

SEVEN hundred and fifty thousand dollars – minus the ten-percent commission, that left him six hundred and seventy-five thousand spread over ten years. Coming out of his agent's building on to Madison Avenue, he almost smiled at this slight resentment he felt at having to pay Billy the seventy-five thousand. A gaunt, good-looking woman smiled back at him as she passed; he did not turn, fearing she would stop and begin the conversation that by now was unbearable for him. 'I only wanted to tell you that it's really the wisest and funniest play I think I've ever . . .' He kept close to the storefronts as he walked, resolving once again to develop some gracious set of replies to these people who, after all – at least some of them – were sincere. But he knew he would always stand there like an oaf, for some reason ashamed and yet happy.

A rope of pearls lay on black velvet in the window of a jewellery store; he paused. My God, he thought, I could buy that! I could buy the whole window maybe. Even the store! The pearls were suddenly worthless. In the glass he saw his hound's eyes, his round, sad face and narrow beard, his sloping shoulders and wrinkled corduroy lapels; for the King of Broadway, he thought, you still look like a failure. He moved on a few steps, and a hand grasped his forearm with annoying proprietary strength and turned him to an immense chest, a yachtsman's sunburned face with a chic, narrow-brimmed hat on top.

'You wouldn't be Meyer Berkowitz?'

'No. I look like him though.'

The man blushed under his tan, looked offended, and walked away.

Meyer Berkowitz approached the corner of Fiftieth Street, feeling the fear of retaliation. What do I want them to do, hate me? On the corner he paused to study his watch. It was only a quarter to six and the dinner was for seven-fifteen. He tried to remember if there was a movie house in the neighbourhood. But there wouldn't be time for a whole movie unless he happened to come in at the beginning. Still, he could afford to pay for half a movie. He turned west on Fiftieth. A couple stared at him as he passed. His eye fell on a rack of magazines next to the corner news-stand. The edge of *Look* showed under *Life,* and he wondered again at all the airplanes, kitchen tables, dentists' offices, and trains where people would be staring at his face on the cover. He thought of shaving his beard. But then, he thought, they won't recognize me. He smiled, I am hooked. So be hooked, he muttered and, straightening up, he resolved to admit to the next interloper that he was in fact Meyer Berkowitz and happy to meet his public. On a rising tide of honesty he remembered the years in the Burnside Memorial Chapel, sitting beside the mummified dead, his notebooks spread on the cork floor as he constructed play after play, and the mirror in the men's room where he would look at his morose eyes, wondering when and if they would ever seem as unique as his secret fate kept promising they would someday be. On Fifth Avenue, so clean, grey, and rich, he headed downtown, his hands clasped behind his back. Two blocks west, two blocks to the right of his shoulder, the housemen in two theatres were preparing to turn the lights on over his name; the casts of two plays were at home checking their watches; in all, maybe thirty-five people, including the stage managers and assistants, had been joined together by him, their lives changed and in a sense commanded by his words. And in his heart, in a hollowed-out place, stood a question mark, was it possible to write another play? Thankfully he thought of his wealth again, subtracted ten per cent commission from the movie purchase price of *I See You* and divided the remainder over ten years, and angrily swept all the dollars out of his head. A cabdriver slowed down beside him and waved and yelled, 'Hey, Meyer!' and the two passengers were leaning forward to see him. The cab was keeping pace with him, so he lifted his left hand a few inches in a cripped wave – like a prizefighter, it occurred to him. An unexplainable disgust pressed him toward a sign overhanging the sidewalk a few yards ahead.

He had a vague recollection of eating in Lee Fong's years ago with Billy, who had been trying unsuccessfully to get him a TV assignment ('Meyer, if you would only follow a plot line . . . '). It would probably be empty at this hour and it wasn't elegant. He pushed open the bright-red lacquered door and thankfully saw that the bar was empty and sat on a stool. Two girls were alone in the restaurant part, talking over tea-cups. The bartender took his order without any sign of recognizing him. He settled both arms on the bar, purposefully relaxing. The Scotch and soda arrived. He drank, examining his face, which was segmented by the bottles in front of the mirror. Cleanly and like a soft blow on his shoulder the realization struck him that it was getting harder and harder to remember talking to anyone as he used to last year and all his life before his plays had opened, before he had come on view. Even now in this empty restaurant he was already expecting a stranger's voice behind him, and half wanting it. Crummy. A longing rose up in him to face someone with his mind on something else; someone who would not show that charged, distorted pressure in the eyes which, he knew, meant that they were seeing his printed face superimposed over his real one. Again he watched himself in the mirror behind the bar: Meyer the Morose, Sam Ugly, but a millionaire with plays running in five countries. Setting his drink down, he noticed the soiled frayed cuffs of his once-tan corduroy jacket, and the shirt cuff sticking out with the button off. With a distant feeling of alarm he realized that he was meeting his director and producer and their wives at the Pavillon and that these clothes, to which he had never given any thought, would set him off as a character who went around like a bum when he had two hits running.

Thank God anyway that he had never married! To come home to the old wife with this printed new face – not good. But now, how would he ever know whether a woman was looking at him or 'Meyer Berkowitz' in full colour on the magazine cover? Strange – in the long Memorial Chapel nights he had envisaged roomfuls of girls pouring over him when his plays succeeded, and now it was almost inconceivable to make a real connexion with any woman he knew. He summoned up their faces, and in each he saw calculation, that look of achievement. It was exhausting him, the whole thing. Months had gone by since he had so much as made a note. What he needed was an apartment in Besonhurst or the upper Bronx somewhere, among people who . . . But they would know him in the Bronx. He sipped his second drink. His stomach was empty and the alcohol went straight to the backs of his eyes and he felt himself lifted up and hanging restfully by the neck over the bar.

The bartender, a thin man with a narrow moustache and only faint signs of Chinese features, stood before him. 'I beggin' you pardon. Excuse me?'

Meyer Berkowitz raised his eyes and before the bartender could speak, he said, 'I'm Meyer Berkowitz.'

'Ha!' The bartender pointed into his face with a long fingernail. 'I know. I recognizin' you! On *Today Show*, right?'

'Right.'

The bartender now looked over Meyer's head toward someone behind him and, pointing at Meyer, nodded wildly. Then, for some reason whispering into Meyer's ear, he said, 'The boss invite you to havin' something on the house.'

Meyer turned around and saw a Chinese with sunglasses on standing beside the cash register, bowing and gesturing lavishly toward the expanse of the bar. Meyer smiled, nodded with aristocratic graciousness as he had seen people do in movies, turned back to the bartender and ordered another Scotch, and quickly finished the one in his hand. How fine people really were! How they loved their artists! Shit, man, this is the greatest country in the world.

He stirred the gift Scotch, whose ice cubes seemed just a little clearer than the ones he had paid for. How come his refrigerator never made such clear ice cubes? Vaguely he heard people entering the restaurant behind him. With no warning he was suddenly aware that three or four couples were at the bar alongside him and that in the restaurant part the white linen tablecoths were now alive with moving hands, plates, cigars. He held his watch up to his eyes. The undrunk part of his brain read the time. He'd finish this drink and amble over to the Pavillon. If he only had a pin for his shirt cuff . . .

'Excuse me . . .'

He turned on the stool and faced a small man with very fair skin, wearing a grey-checked overcoat and a grey hat and highly polished black shoes. He was a short, round man, and Meyer realized that he himself was the same size and even the same age, just about, and he was not sure suddenly that he could ever again write a play.

The short man had a manner, it was clear, the stance of a certain amount of money. There was money in his pause and the fit of his coat and certain ineffable condescension in his blue eyes, and Meyer imagined his wife, also short, wrapped in mink, waiting a few feet away in the crowd at the bar, with the same smug look.

After the pause, during which Meyer said nothing, the short man asked, 'Are you Meyer Berkowitz?'

'That's right,' Meyer said, and the alcohol made him sigh for air.

'You don't remember me?' the short man said, a tiny curl of smile on the left edge of his pink mouth.

Meyer sobered. Nothing in the round face stuck to any part of his memory, and yet he knew he was not all this drunk. 'I'm afraid not. Who are you?'

'You don't remember me?' the short man asked with genuine surprise.

'Well, who are you?'

The man glanced off, not so much embarrassed as unused to explaining his identity; but, swallowing his pride, he looked back at Meyer and said, 'You don't remember Bernie Gelfand?'

Whatever suspicion Meyer felt was swept away. Clearly he had known this man somewhere, sometime. He felt the debt of the forgetter. 'Bernie Gelfand. I'm awfully sorry, but I can't recall where. Where did I know you?'

'I sat next to you in English four years! DeWitt Clinton!'

Meyer's brain had long ago drawn a blind down on all his high-school years. But the name Gelfand did rustle the fallen leaves at the back of his mind. 'I remember your name, ya, I think I do.'

'Oh, come on, guy, you don't remember Bernie Gelfand with the curly red hair?' With which he raised his grey felt hat to reveal a bald scalp. But no irony showed in his eyes, which were transported back to his famous, blazing hair and to the seat he had had next to Meyer Berkowitz in high school. He put his hat back on again.

'Forgive me,' Meyer said, 'I have a terrible memory. I remember your name though.'

Gelfand, obviously put out, perhaps even angered but still trying to smile, and certainly full of intense sentimental interest, said, 'We were best friends.'

Meyer laid a beseeching hand on Gelfand's grey coat sleeve. 'I'm not doubting you, I just can't place you for the moment. I mean, I believe you.' He laughed.

Gelfand seemed assuaged now, nodded, and said, 'You don't look much different, you know? I mean, except for the beard, I'd know you in a minute.'

'Yeah, well ...' Meyer said, but still feeling he had offended he obediently asked, 'What do you do?' preparing for a long tale of success.

Gelfand clearly enjoyed this question, and he lifted his eyebrows to a proud peak. 'I'm in shoulder pads,' he said.

A laugh began to bubble up in Meyer's stomach; Gelfand's coat was in fact stiffly padded at the shoulders. But in an instant he remembered that there was a shoulder-pad industry, and the importance which Gelfand attached to his profession killed the faintest smile on Meyer's face. 'Really,' he said with appropriate solemnity.

'Oh, yes. I'm General Manager, head of everything up to the Mississippi.'

'Don't say. Well, that's wonderful.' Meyer felt great relief. It would have been awful if Gelfand had been a failure – or in charge of New England only. 'I'm glad you've done so well.'

Gelfand glanced off to one side, letting his achievement sink deeply into Meyer's mind. When he looked again at Meyer he could not quite keep his eyes from the frayed cuffs of the corduroy jacket and the limp shirt cuff hanging out. 'What do *you* do?' he asked.

Meyer looked into his drink. Nothing occurred to him. He touched his finger against the mahogany bar and still nothing came to him through his shock. His resentment was clamouring in his head; he recognized it and greeted it. Then he looked directly at Gelfand, who in the pause had grown a look of benevolent pity. 'I'm a writer,' Meyer said and watched for the publicity-distorted freeze to grip Gelfand's eyeballs.

'That so!' Gelfand said, amused. 'What kind of writing you do?'

If I really had any style, Meyer thought, I would shrug and say I write part-time poems after I get home from the post office, and we could leave Bernie to enjoy his dinner. On the other hand, I do not work in the post office, and there must be some way to shake this monkey off and get back to where I can talk to people again as if I were real. 'I write plays,' he said to Gelfand.

'That so!' Gelfand smiled, his amusement enlarging toward open condescension. 'Anything I would have . . . heard of?'

'Well, as a matter of fact, one of them is down the street.'

'Really? On *Broadway*?' Gelfand's face split into its parts; his mouth still kept its smile, but his eyes showed a certain wild alarm. His head, suddenly, was on straighter, his neck drawn back.

'I wrote *I See You*,' Meyer said and tasted slime on his tongue.

Gelfand's mouth opened. His skin reddened.

'And *Mostly Florence*.'

The two smash hits seemed to open before Gelfand's face like bursting flags. His finger lifted toward Meyer's chest. 'Are you . . . *Meyer Berkowitz*?' he whispered.

'Yes.'

Gelfand held out his hand tentatively. 'Well, I'm very happy to meet you,' he said with utter formality.

Meyer saw distance locking into place between them, and in the instant wished he could take Gelfand in his arms and wipe out the poor man's metaphysical awe, smother his defeat, and somehow retract this very hateful pleasure which he knew now he could not part with any more. He shook Gelfand's hand and then covered it with his left hand.

'Really,' Gelfand went on, withdrawing his hand as though it had already presumed too much, 'I ... I've enjoyed your – excuse me.' Meyer's heavy cheeks stirred vaguely toward a smile.

Gelfand closed his coat and quickly turned about and hurried to the little crowd waiting for tables near the red entrance door. He took the arm of a short woman in a mink wrap and turned her toward the door. She seemed surprised as he hurried her out of sight and into the street.

[*1966*]

Fitter's Night

By four in the afternoon it was almost dark in winter, and this January was one of the coldest on record, so that the night shift filing through the turnstiles at the Navy Yard entrance was sombre, huddling in zipper jackets and pulling down earflaps, shifting from foot to foot as the Marine guards inspected each tin lunchbox in turn and compared the photographs on identity cards with the squint-eyed, blue-nosed faces that passed through. The former grocery clerks, salesmen, unemployed, students, and the mysteriously incapacitated young men whom the Army and Navy did not want; the elderly skilled machinists come out of retirement, the former truckdrivers, elevator operators, masons, disbarred lawyers, and a few would-be poets, poured off the buses in the blue light of late afternoon and waited their turn at the end of the lines leading to the fresh-faced Marines in the booths, who refused to return their quips and dutifully searched for the bomb and the incendiary pencil under the lettuce-and-tomato sandwiches leaking through the waxed paper, against all reason unscrewing the Thermos bottles to peer in at the coffee. With some ten thousand men arriving for each of the three shifts, the law of averages naturally came into play, and it was inevitable that every few minutes someone would put his Thermos back into his lunchbox and say, 'What's Roosevelt got against hot coffee?' and the Marines would blink and wave the joker into the Yard.

To the naval architects, the engineers, the Yard Master and his staff, the New York Naval Shipyard was not hard to define; in fact, it had hardly changed since its beginnings in the early eighteen hundreds. The vast dry docks facing the bay were backed by a maze of crooked and curving streets lined with one-storey brick machine shops and storehouses. In dark Victorian offices papers were still speared on sharp steel points and filing cabinets were of dark oak. Ships of war were never exactly the same, whatever anybody said, and the smith was still in a doorway hammering one-of-a-kind iron fittings, the sparks falling against his floor-length leather apron; steel bow-plates were still sighted by eye regardless of the carefully mapped curves of the drawing, and when a man was injured a two-wheel pushcart was sent for to bump him along the cobblestones to the infirmary like a side of beef.

It was sure that Someone knew where everything was, and this faith was adopted by every new man. The shipfitter's helper, the burner, the chipper, the welder; painters, carpenters, riggers, drillers, electricians – hundreds of them might spend the first hour of each shift asking one stranger after another where he was supposed to report or what dry dock held the destroyer or carrier he had been working on the night before; and there were not a few who spent entire twelve-hour shifts searching for their particular gangs, but the faith never faltered. Someone must know what was supposed to be happening, if only because damaged ships did limp in under tow from the various oceans and after days, weeks, or sometimes months they did sail out under Brooklyn Bridge, ready once again to fight the enemy. There were naturally a sensitive few who, watching these gallant departures, shook their heads with wonder at the mystery of how these happened to have been repaired, but the vast majority accepted this and even felt that they themselves were somehow responsible. It was like a baseball game with five hundred men playing the outfield at the same time, sweeping in a mob toward the high arching ball, which was caught somewhere in the middle of the crowd, by whom no one knew, except that the game was slowly and quite inconceivably being won.

Tony Calabrese, Shipfitter First Class, was one of that core of men who did know where to report once he came through the turnstile at four in the afternoon. In 'real life', as the phrase went, he had been a steamfitter in Brooklyn and was not confused by mobs, Marines looking into his sandwiches, or the endless waiting around that was normal in a shipyard. Once through the turnstile, his lunchbox tucked under his arm again, his cap on crooked, he leaned into the wind with his broken nose, notifying oncoming men to clear the way, snug inside his pile zipper jacket and woollen shirt, putting down his feet on the outside edges like a bear, bandy-legged, low-crotched, a graduate of skyscraper construction, brewery repairing, and for eight months the City Department of Water Supply, until it was discovered that he had been sending a substitute on Tuesdays, Wednesdays, and Fridays while he went to the track and made some money.

Tony had never until a year and a half ago seen a ship up close and had no interest in ships, any more than he had had in the water supply, breweries, or skyscrapers. Work was a curse, a misfortune that a married man had to bear, like his missing front tooth, knocked out in a misunderstanding with a bookie. There was no mystery what the good life was, and he never lived a day without thinking about it, and more and more hopelessly now that he was past forty; it was being like Sinatra, or Luciano, or even one of the neighbourhood politicians who wore good suits all day and never bent over, kept two apartments, one for the family, the other for the boloney of the moment. He had put his youth into trying for that kind of life and had failed. Driving the bootleggers' trucks over the Canadian border, even a season as Johnny Peaches' bravo and two months collecting for a longshoreman's local, had put him within reach of a spot, a power position from which he might have retired into an office or apartment and worked through telephones and over restaurant tables. But at the last moment something in his make-up had always defeated him, sent him rolling back into the street and a job and a paycheck, where the future was the same never-get-rich routine. He knew he was simply not smart enough. If he were, he wouldn't be working in the Navy Yard.

His face was as round as a frying pan with a hole in it, a comical face now that the nose was flattened, his front tooth gone, and no neck. He had risen to First in a year and a half, partly because the supervisor, old Charley Mudd, liked a good phone number, which Tony could slip him, and also because Tony could read blueprints quickly, weld, chip, burn, and bulldoze a job to its finish when, as happened occasionally, Charley

Mudd had to get a ship back into the war. As Shipfitter First, he was often given difficult and complicated jobs and could call on any of the various trades to come in and burn or weld at his command. But he was not impressed by his standing, when Sinatra could open his mouth and make a grand. More important was that his alliance with Charley Mudd gave him jobs below decks in cold weather and above decks when the sky was clear. If indisposed, he could give Charley Mudd the sign and disappear for the night into a dark corner and a good sleep. But most of the time he enjoyed being on the job, particularly when he was asked how to perform one operation or another by 'shipfitters' who could not compute a right angle or measure in smaller units than halves. His usual way of beginning his instruction was always the same and was expected by anyone who asked his help. He would unroll the blueprint, point to a line or figure, and say, 'Pay 'tention, shithead,' in a voice sludged with the bottom of wine bottles and the Italian cigars he inhaled. No one unable to bear this indignity asked him for help, and those who did knew in advance that they would certainly lose whatever pretensions they thought they had.

But there was another side to Tony, which came out during the waits. Before Pearl Harbour there had been some six thousand men employed in the Yard, and there were now close to sixty thousand. Naturally they would sometimes happen to collect in unmanageable numbers in a single compartment, and the repairs, which had to be done in specific stages, made it impossible for most of them to work and for any to leave. So the waits began; maybe the welder could not begin welding until the chipper finished breaking out the old weld, so he waited, with his helper or partner. The burner could not cut steel until the exhaust hose was brought down by his helper, who could not get hold of one until another burner down the corridor was finished with it, so he waited; a driller could not drill until his point was struck into the steel by the fitter, who was forbidden to strike it until the electricians had removed the electric cables on the other side of the bulkhead through which the hole had to be drilled, so they waited; until the only way out was a crap game or Tony

'enjoying' everybody by doing imitations or picking out somebody to insult and by going into his grin, which, with the open
space in his teeth, collapsed the company in hysteria. After these
bouts of entertainment Tony always became depressed, reminded
again of his real failing, a lack of stern dignity, leadership, force.
Luciano would hardly be clowning around in a cruiser compartment, showing how stupid he could look with a tooth missing.

On this January afternoon, already so dark and the wind biting
at his eyes, Tony Calabrese, going down the old streets of the
Yard, had decided to work below decks tonight, definitely. Even
here in the shelter of the Yard streets the wind was miserable –
what would it be like on a main deck open to the bay? Besides, he
did not want to tire himself this particular shift when he had a
date at half-past four in the morning. He went through his
mental checklist: Dora would meet him at Baldy's for breakfast;
by six a.m. he would be home to change his clothes and take a
shower; coffee with the kids at seven before they went to school,
then maybe a nap till nine or half-past, then pick up Dora and
make the first show at the Fox at ten; by twelve to Dora's room,
bang-bang, and a good sleep till half-past two or three, when he
would stop off at home and put on workclothes, and maybe see
the kids if they got home early, and into the subway for the Yard.
It was a good uncomplicated day in front of him.

Coming out of the end of the street he saw the cold stars over
the harbour, a vast sky stretching out over the bay and beyond
to the sea. Clusters of headlights coursed over Brooklyn Bridge,
the thickening traffic of the homebound who did not know they
were passing over the Yard or the war-broken ships. He picked
his way around stacks of steel plate and tarpaulin-shrouded gear
piled everywhere, and for a moment was caught in the blasting
white glare of the arc lamp focused downward from the top of a
travelling crane; slowly, foot by foot, it rolled along the tracks,
tall as a four-storey building on two straddling legs, its one arm
thrust out against the stars, dangling a dull glinting steel plate
the width of a bus, and led by a fitter hardly taller than its wheels,
who was walking backward between the tracks ahead of it and
pointing off to the right in the incandescent whiteness of its

one eye. As though intelligent, the crane obediently swivelled its great arm, lowering the swaying plate to a spot pointed at by the fitter, whose face Tony could not make out, shaded as it was by the peak of his cap against the downpouring light of the high white eye. Tony circled wide around the descending plate, trusting no cable or crane operator, and passed into the darkness again toward the cruiser beyond, raised in the dry dock, her bow curving high over the roadway on which he walked with his lips pressed together to keep the wind off his teeth. Turning, he moved along her length, head down against the swift river of cold air, welcoming the oncoming clumps of foot-stamping men mounting her along the gangplank – the new shift boarding, the occasional greeting voice still lively in the earliness of the evening. He rocked up the length of the gangplank on to the main deck, with barely a nod passing the young lieutenant in upturned collar who stood hitting his gloved hands together in the tiny temporary guardhouse at the head of the plank. There was the happy smell of burned steel and coffee, the straightforward acridity of the Navy, and the feeling of the hive as he descended a steep stair clogged down its whole length with black welder's cables and four-inch exhaust hoses, the temporary intestine that always followed repair gangs into the patient ships.

His helper, Looey Baldu – where an Italian got a name like Baldu Tony could not understand, unless a Yugoslav had got into the woodpile or they shortened it – Looey was already waiting for him in the passageway, looking twenty-three, dignified and superior, with his high-school education, regulation steel-tipped shoes – which Tony steadfastly refused to wear – and his resolute but defensive greeting.

'Where's Charley Mudd?'

'I didn't see him yet.'

'You blind? There he is.'

Tony walked around the surprised Baldu and into a compartment where Charley Mudd, sixty, and half asleep, sat on three coils of electric cable, his eyes shut and a clipboard starting to slide out of his opening hands. Tony touched the older man's back and bent to talk softly and put in the fix. Charley nodded, his eyes rolling. Tony gave him a grateful pat and came out into the passageway, which was filling with men trying to pass one another in opposite directions while dragging endless lengths of hose, cable, ladders, and bulky toolboxes, everybody looking for somebody else, so that Tony had to raise his voice to Baldu. He always spoke carefully to the high-school graduate, who never caught on the first time but was a good boy although his wife, he said, was Jewish. Baldu was against race prejudism, whatever the hell that meant, and frowned like a judge when talked to as though some kind of veil hung before his face and nothing came through it loud and clear.

'We gonna watertight hatches C-Deck,' Tony said and turned, hands still clenched inside his slit pockets, and walked.

Baldu had had no time to nod and already felt offended, but he followed with peaked eyebrows behind his fitter, keeping close so as not to know the humiliation of being lost again and having to face Tony's scathing ironies implying incessant masturbation.

They descended to C-Deck, a large, open area filled with tiered bunks in which a few sailors lay, some sleeping, others reading or writing letters. Tony was pleased at the nearness of the coffee smell, what with any more than a pound a week almost impossible for civilians to get except at black-market prices. Without looking again at his helper, he unzipped his jacket, stowed his lunchbox on the deck under an empty bunk, took out a blue handkerchief and blew his nose and wiped his teary eyes, removed his cap and scratched his head, and finally sat on his heels and ran his fingers along the slightly raised edge of a hatch opening in the deck, through which could be seen a ladder going down into dimness.

'Let that there cover come to me, Looey.'

Baldu, his full brown-paper lunchbag still in his hand, sprang to the heavy hatch cover lying on the deck and with one hand tried to raise it on its hinges. Unwilling to admit that his strength was not enough or that he had made a mistake, he strained with the one hand, and as Tony regarded him with aggravation and lowering lids he got the hatch cover up on one knee, and only then let his lunchbag down on to the deck and

with two hands finally raised the cover toward Tony, whose both
hands were poised to stop it from falling shut.

'Hold it, hold it right there.'

'Hold it open?'

'Well, what the fuck, you gonna hold it closed? Of course
open. What's a-matta wichoo?'

Tony ran his fingertips along the rubber gasket that ran
around the lip of the cover. Then he took hold of it and let it
close over the hatch. Bending down until his cheek pressed the
cold deck, he squinted to see how closely gasket met steel. Then
he got up, and Looey Baldu stood to face him.

'I'm gonna give you a good job, Looey. Git some chalk, rub
it on the gasket, then git your marks on the deck. Where the chalk
don't show, build it up with some weld, then git a grinder and
tell him smooth it nice till she's nice an' even all around. You
understand?'

'Sure, I'll do it.'

'Just don't get wounded. That's it for tonight, so take it
easy.'

Baldu's expression was nearly fierce as he concentrated
patriotically on the instructions, and now he nodded sternly
and started to step back. Tony grabbed him before he tripped
over the hatch cover behind him, then let him go and without
further remark fled toward the coffee smell.

It was going to be a pretty good night. Dora, whom he had
gotten from Hindu, was a little shorter than he would have liked,
but she had beautiful white skin, especially her breasts, and lived
alone in a room with good heat – no sisters, aunts, mothers,
nothing. And both times she had brought home fresh bread from
Macy's, where she packed nights. Now all he had to do was keep
relaxed through the shift so as not to be sleepy when he met her
for breakfast at Baldy's. Picking his way along a passage toward
the intensifying coffee smell, he felt joyous, and, seeing a drunken
sailor trying to come down a ladder, he put his shoulder under the boy's seat and gently let him down to the deck, then
helped him a few yards along the passage until the boy fell into
a bunk. Then he lifted his legs on to it, turned him over, opened

his pea jacket and shoelaces, and returned to the search for the source of the coffee smell.

He might have known. There was Hindu, standing over an electric brewer tended by two sailors in T-shirts. Hindu was big, but next to him stood a worker who was a head taller, a giant. Tony sauntered over, and Hindu said to the sailors, 'This here's a buddy, how about it?'

A dozen lockers stood against the nearby bulkhead, from one of which a sailor took a clean cup and a five-pound bag of sugar. Tony thanked him as he took the full cup and then moved a foot away as Hindu came over.

'Where you?' Hindu asked.

'C-Deck, watertight hatch cover. Where you?'

'I disappeared. They're still settin' up the windbreak on Main Deck.'

'Fuck that.'

'You know what Washington said when he crossed the Delaware?'

Then both together, 'It's fuckin' cold.'

They drank coffee. Hindu's skin was so dark he was sometimes taken for an Indian; he made up for it by keeping his thick, wavy hair well combed, his blue beard closely shaved, and his big hands clean.

'I gotta make a phone call,' he said quietly, stooping to Tony. 'I left her bawlin'. Jesus, I passed him comin' up the stairs.'

'Ta hell you stay so long?'

'I coun' help myself.' His eyes softened, his mouth worked in pleasurable agony. 'She's dri'n' me crazy. We even wen' faw walk.'

'You crazy?'

'I coun' help it. If you seen her you drop dead. Byoodiful. I mean it. I'm goin' crazy. I passed him comin' up the stairs, I swear!'

'You'll end up fuckin' a grave, Hindu.'

'She touches me, I die. I die, Tony.' Hindu shut his eyes and shook his head, memorializing.

Activity behind them turned them about. The big worker, his

coffee finished, was pulling on a chain that ran through a set of pulleys hooked to a beam overhead, and a gigantic electric motor was rising up off the deck. Tony, Hindu, and the two sailors watched the massive rigger easily raise the slung motor until it reached the pulleys and could be raised no farther, and three inches yet to go before it could be slid on to a platform suspended from the deck overhead. The rigger drew his gauntlets up tighter, set himself underneath the motor with his hands up under it, and, with knees bent, pushed. The motor rose incredibly until its feet were a fraction above the platform; the rigger pushed and got it hung. Then he came out from under, stood behind it, and shoved it fully on to the platform where it belonged. His face was flushed, and, expanded by the effort, he looked bigger than ever. Slipping off his gauntlets, he looked down to the sailors, who were still sitting on the deck.

'Anybody ever read *Oliver Wiswell*?'

'No.'

'You ought to. Gives you a whole new perspective on the American Revolution. You know, there's a school that doesn't think the Revolution was necessary.'

Tony was already walking, and Hindu followed slightly behind, asking into his ear, 'Maybe I could hang wichoo tonight, Tony. Okay? I ask Cholly, okay?'

'Go ahead.'

Hindu patted Tony's back thankfully and hurried up a ladder. Tony looked at his pocket watch. Five o'clock. He had chopped an hour. It was too early to take a nap. A sense of danger struck him, and he looked ahead up the passage, but there was only a coloured worker he did not know fooling with a chipping gun that would not receive its chisel. He turned the other way in time to see a captain and a man in a felt hat and overcoat approaching with blueprints half unrolled in their hands. He caught sight of a chipping-gun air hose, which he followed into a compartment on hands and knees. The two brass went by, and he stood up and walked out of the compartment.

It was turning into one of the slow nights when the clock never moved. The coffee had sharpened him even more, so a nap was out of the question. He moved along passageways at a purposeful pace, up ladders and down, looking for guys he might know, but the ship was not being worked much tonight; why, he did not know and did not care. Probably there was a hurry-up on the two destroyers that had come in last night. One had a bow blasted off, and the other had floated in from the bay listing hard to one side. The poor bastards on the destroyers, with no room to move, and some of those kids seasick in bad weather. The worst was when the British ships came in. Good he wasn't on one of those bastards, with the cockroaches so bad you couldn't sit down, let alone stretch out, and their marines a lot of faggos. That was hard to believe the first time he saw it – like last summer with that British cruiser, the captain pacing the deck day and night and the ship in dry dock. A real jerked-off Englishman with a monocle and a moustache and a crushed cap, and a little riding crop in his hands clasped behind his back, scowling at everybody and refusing to go off duty even in dry dock. And piping whistles blowing every few hours to bring the marines on deck for rifle drill, that bunch of fags screaming through the passageways, goosing each other, and pimples all over their faces. Christ, he hated the English the way they kicked Italy around, sneering. And those stupid officers, in July, walking around in thick blue hairy uniforms, sweating like pigs all over their eyeglasses. You could tell a U.S. ship blindfolded, the smell of coffee and cleanliness, and ice water anywhere you looked. Of course they said the British gunners were better, but who was winning the war, for Christ's sake? Without us they'd have to pack it in and salute the fuckin' Germans. The French had a good ship, that captured *Richelieu,* what panelling in the ward room, like a fuckin' palace, but something was wrong with the guns, they said, and couldn't hit nothin'.

He found himself in the engine room and looked up through the barrel-like darkness, up and up through the belly of the ship. There was, he knew, a cable passage where he could lie down. Somebody he could barely see high above in the darkness was showering sparks from a welding arc spread too far from the steel, but he pulled up his collar and climbed ladders, moved along the catwalks until he came to a low door which he opened, went into a hole lined with electric cables, and lay down with his hands clasped under his head. The welding buzz was all he could hear now. Footsteps would sound on the steel catwalks and give good warning.

Not tired, he closed his eyes to screw the government. Even here in the dark he was making money every minute – every second. With this week's check he would probably have nearly two thousand in his account and a hundred and twenty or so in the account Margaret knew about. Jesus, what a dumb woman! Dumb, dumb, dumb. But a good mother, that's for sure. But why not, with only two kids, what else she got to do? He would never sleep with her again and could barely remember the sight of her body. In fact, for the thousandth time in his life, he realized that he had never seen his wife naked, which was as it should be. You could fill a lake with the tears she had shed these fifteen years – an ocean. Good.

He stoked his anger at his wife, the resentment that held his life together. It was his cause, his agony, and his delight to let his mind go and imagine what she must feel, not being touched for eleven – no, twelve, yes, it was twelve last spring – years. This spring it would be thirteen, then fourteen, then twenty, and into her grave without his hand on her. Never, never would he give in. On the bed, when he did sleep at home, with his back to her, he stretched into good sleep, and sometimes her wordless sobs behind him were like a soft rain on the roof that made him snug. She had asked for it. He had warned her at the time. He might look funny, but Tony Calabrese was not funny for real. To allow himself to break, to put his hand on her ever again, he would have to forgive what she had done to him. And now, lying in the cable passage with his eyes closed, he went over what she had done, and as always happened when he reached for these memories, the darling face of the boloney formed in his darkness, Patty Moran, with genuine red hair, breasts without a crease under them, and lips pink as lipstick. Oh, Jesus! He shook his head in the dark, and where was she now? He did not dare hate his grandfather; the old man was like a storm or an animal that did only what it was supposed to do. He let himself remember what had become for him like a movie whose end he knew and dreaded to see once more, and yet wanted to. It was the only time in his life that had not been random, when each day that had passed in those few months had changed his position and finally sealed him up forever.

From the day he was born, it seemed to him, his mother had kept warning him to watch out for Grampa. If he stole, hit, lied, tore good pants, got in cop trouble, the same promise was made – if Grampa ever came to America he would settle each and every one of Tony's crimes in a day long, maybe week long beating combined with an authoritative spiritual thundering that would straighten out Tony for the rest of his life. For Grampa was gigantic, a sport in the diminutive family, a throwback to some giants of old whose wit and ferocity had made them lords in Calabria, chiefs among the rocks, commanders of fishing boats, capos of the mines. Even his cowed father relied on the absent, never-seen old man for authority and spent every free hour away from work on the BMT tracks, playing checkers with his cronies, rather than chastise his sons. Grampa would come one day and settle them all, straighten them out, and besides, if he did come, he would bring his money. He owned fishing boats, the star of the whole family, a rich man who had made it, astoundingly, without ever leaving Calabria, which meant again that he was wily and merciless, brave and just.

The part that was usually hard to remember was hard to remember again, and Tony opened his eyes in the cable passage until, yes, he remembered. How he had ever gotten mixed up with Margaret in the first place, a mewly girl, big-eyed but otherwise blanketed bodily, bodiless, shy, and frightened. It was because he had just come out of the Tombs, and this time Mama was not to be fooled with. She was a fury now as he walked into the tenement, unwilling to listen to the old promises or to be distracted by all his oaths of innocence and frame-up. And this time fate began to step in, that invisible presence entered Tony's life, the Story; his tight time began when nothing was any longer random, and every day changed what he was and what he had to do.

A letter had arrived that nobody could read. They sat around the table, Mama and Papa and Aunt Celia from next door, and Frank and Salvatore, his married cousins. Tony slowly traced the Italian script, speaking it aloud so that Papa could mouth the words and penetrate the underlying thought, which was unbelievable, a marvel that chilled them all. Grampa had sold his holdings, now that Grandma was dead, and was sailing for America for a visit, or, if he approved, to stay the rest of his life.

The cable passage seemed to illuminate with the lightning flashes of the preparations for the arrival – the house scrubbed, walls painted, furniture shined, chairs fixed, and the blackmail begun. Mama, seeing the face of her son and the hope and avidity in his eyes, sat him down in the kitchen. I am going to tell Grampa everything what you done, Tony. Everything. Unless you do what I say. You marry Margaret.

Margaret was a year older than Tony. Somehow, he could not imagine how, now that he knew her, he had come to rest on her stoop from time to time, mainly when just out of jail, when momentarily the strain of bargaining for life and a spot was too much, those moments when, like madness, a vision of respectability overwhelmed him with a quick longing for the clean and untroubled existence. She was like a nervous pony at his approach, and easy to calm. It was the time he was driving booze trucks over the Canadian border for Harry Ox, the last of the Twenties, and out of jail it was sweet to spend a half-hour staring at the street with Margaret, like a clam thrown up by the moiling sea for a moment. He had been in his first gunfight near Albany and was scared. And this was the first time he had said he would like to take her to the movies. In all the years he had known her the thought had never crossed his mind to make a date. Home that night, he already heard his mother talking about Margaret's family. The skein was folding over him, and he did not resist. He did not decide either. He let it come without touching it, let it drape over him like a net. They were engaged, and nobody had used the word even, but whenever he saw Margaret she acted as though she had been waiting for him, as though he had been missing, and he let it happen, walked a certain way with her in the street, touching her elbow with his fingertips, and never took her into the joints, and watched his language. Benign were the smiles in her house the few times he appeared, but he could never stay long for the boredom, the thickness of the plot to strangle his life.

His life was Patty Moran by this time. Once across her threshold over Ox's saloon, everything he saw nearly blinded him. He had started out with her at three o'clock in the morning in the back of Ox's borrowed Buick, her ankle ripping the corded rope off the back of the front seat, and the expanse of her thigh across the space between the back and front seats was painted in cream across his brain forever. He walked around the neighbourhood dazed, a wire going from the back of his head to her hard soft belly. She was not even Harry Ox's girl but a disposable one among several, and Tony started out knowing that and each day climbed an agonizing stairway to a vision of her dearness, almost but not quite imagining her marriageable. The thought of other men with her was enough to bring his fist down on a table even if he was sitting alone. His nose had not yet been broken; he was small but quick-looking, sturdy and black-eyed. She finally convinced him there was nobody else, she adored his face, his body, his stolen jokes. And in the same two or three months he was taking Margaret to the movies. He even kissed her now and then. Why? Why! Grampa was coming as soon as he could clear up his affairs, and what had begun with Margaret as a purposeless yet pleasant pastime had taken on leverage in that it kept Mama pleased and quiet and would guarantee his respectability in Grampa's eyes – long enough anyway, to get his inheritance.

No word of inheritance was written in the old man's letters, but it was first imagined, then somehow confirmed, that Tony would get it. And when he did it was off-to-Buffalo, him and the boloney, maybe even get married someplace where nobody knew her and they'd make out seriously together. And best of all, Mama knew nothing of the boloney. Nowadays she was treating Tony like the head of the house. He had taken a job longshore, was good as gold, and sat home many an evening listening to the tock-tick.

The final letter came. Tony read it alone in the bathroom first and announced that Grampa was coming on the tenth although the letter said the ninth. On the morning of the ninth Tony said he had to get dressed up because, instead of working, he was going to scout around for a good present for Grampa's arrival tomorrow. Congratulated, kissed, waved off, he rounded the block to Ox's and borrowed three hundred dollars and took a cab to the Manhattan pier.

The man in truth was gigantic. Tony's first glimpse was this green-suited, oddly young old man, a thick black tie at his throat, a black fedora held by a porter beside him, while down the gangway he himself was carrying on his back a small but heavy trunk. Tony understood at once – the money was in the trunk. On the pier Tony tipped the porter for carrying the furry hat, and kissed his six-foot grandfather once he had set the trunk down. Tony shook his hand and felt the power in it, hard as a bannister. The old man took one handle of the trunk and Tony the other, and in the cab Tony made his proposal. Before rushing home, why not let him show him New York?

Fine. But first Tony wanted to Americanize the clothes; people would get the wrong impression, seeing such a green immigrant suit and the heavy brogans. Grampa allowed it, standing there ravished by the bills Tony peeled off for the new suit, new shoes, and an American tie. Now they toured the town, sinking deeper and deeper into it as Tony graded the joints from the middle-class ones uptown to his hangouts near Canal Street, until the old man was kissing his grandson two and three times an hour and stood up cheering the Minsky girls who bent over the runway toward his upturned face. Tony, at four in the morning, carried the trunk up the stairs of the tenement on his own back, feeling the dead weight inside; then back down and carried Grampa on his back and laid him in his own bed and himself on the floor. He had all he could do to keep from rushing over to Patty Moran to tell her he was in like Flynn, the old man loved him like a son, and they might begin by opening a joint together someplace like in Queens. But he kept discipline and slept quickly, his face under the old man's hand hanging over the edge of the mattress.

In the cable passage, staring at the dark, he could not clearly recall his wedding, any more than he had been able to an hour after the ceremony. It was something he was doing and not doing. Grampa had emerged from the bedroom with Tony under his armpit; and, seeing her father, Mama's face lengthened out as though God or the dead had walked in, especially since she had just finished getting dressed up to meet his boat. The shouting and crying and kissing lasted until afternoon, Grampa's pleasure with his manly grandson gathering the complicated force of a new mission in his life, a proof of his own grandeur at being able to hand on a patrimony to a good man of his blood, a man of style besides.

Papa nodded an uncertain assent, one eye glancing toward the trunk, but as evening came Mama, Tony saw, was showing two thoughts in her tiny brown eyes, and after the third meal of the day, with the table cleaned off and the old man blinking drowsily, she laid two open hands on the table, smiled deferentially, and said Tony had been in and out of jails since he was twelve.

Grampa woke up.

Tony was hanging with bootleggers, refused until the last couple of months to hold a regular job, and now he was staying with an Irish whore when he had engaged himself to Margaret, the daughter of a good Calabrian family down the block, a girl as pure as a dove, beautiful, sincere, whose reputation was being mangled every day Tony avoided talk of a marriage date. The girl's brothers were growing restive, her father had gotten the look of blood in his eye. Margaret alone could save Tony from the electric chair, which was waiting for him as sure as God had sent Jesus, for he was a boy who would lie as quickly as spit, the proof being his obvious attempt to hoodwink Grampa with a night on the town before any of the family could get to him with the true facts.

It took twenty minutes to convince Grampa; he had had to stare at Tony for a long time as though through a telescope that would not adjust. Tony downed his fury, defended his life, denied everything, promised everything, brought out the new alarm clock he had bought for the house out of his own money, and at last sat facing Grampa, dying in his chair as the old man levelled his judgement. Tony, you will marry this fine girl or none of my money goes to you. Not the fruit of my labour to a gangster, no, not to a criminal who will die young in the electric chair. Marry the girl and yes, definitely, I give you what I have.

First days, then weeks – then was it months? – passed after the wedding, but the money failed to be mentioned again. Tony worked the piers dutifully now, and when he did see Patty Moran it was at odd hours only, on his way toward the shape-up or on days when it rained and deck work was called off. He would duck into the doorway next to Ox's saloon and fly up the stairs and live for half an hour, then home again to wait; he dared not simply confront the old man with the question of his reward, knowing that he was being watched for deficiencies. On Sundays he walked like a husband with Margaret, spent the afternoons with the family, and acted happy. The old man was never again as close and trusting and comradely as on that first night off the boat, but neither was he hostile. He was watching, Tony saw, to make sure.

And Tony would make him sure. The only problem was what to do in his apartment once he was alone with Margaret. He had never really hated her and he had never liked her. It was like being alone with an accident, that was all. He spoke to her rarely and quietly, listened to her gossip about the day's events, and read his newspaper. He did not expect her to suddenly stand up in the movies and run out crying, some two months after the wedding, or to come home from work one spring evening and find Grampa sitting in the living room with Margaret, looking at him silently as he came through the door.

You don't touch your wife?

Tony could not move from the threshold or lie, suddenly. The old man had short, bristly grey hair that stood up like wire, and he was back to his Italian brogans, a kick from which could make a mule inhale. Margaret dared only glance at Tony, but he saw now that the dove had her beak in his belly and was not going to let go.

You think I'm mentally defective, Tony? A man with spit in the corners of his mouth? Cross-eyed? What do you think I am?

The first new demonstration was, again, at the movies. Grampa sat behind them. After a few minutes Margaret turned her head to him and said, He don't put his arm around me, see?

Put your arm around her.

Tony put his arm around her.

Then after a few more minutes she turned to Grampa. He's only touching the seat, see?

Grampa took hold of Tony's hand and laid it on Margaret's shoulder.

Again, one night, Grampa was waiting for him with Margaret. Okay – he was breaking into English now and then by this time – Okay, I'm going to sleep on the couch.

Tony had never slept in bed with her. He was afraid of Grampa because he knew he could never bring himself to raise a hand to him, and he knew that Grampa could knock him around; but it was not the physical harm, it was the sin he had been committing over and over again of trying to con the old man, whose opinion of him was falling every day, until one day, he foresaw, Grampa would pack up and take the trunk back to Calabria and good-bye. Grampa was no longer astounded by New York, and he still owned his house in Italy, and Tony visualized that house, ready at all times for occupancy, and he was afraid.

He went into the bedroom with Margaret. She snivelled on the pillow beside him. It was still light outside, the early blue of a spring evening. Tony listened for a sound of Grampa through the closed door, but nothing came through. He reached and found her hip and slid up her nightgown. She was soft, too soft, but she was holding her breath. He stretched his neck and rested his mouth on her shoulder. She was breathing at the top of her chest, near her throat, not daring to lay her hand on him, her face upthrust as though praying. He smoothed her hip waiting for his tension, and nothing was happening to him until, until she began to weep, not withdrawing herself but pressed against him.

weeping. His hatred mounted on the disappointed, tattletale sound she was sending into the other room, and suddenly he felt himself hardening and he got to his knees before her, pushed her on to her back and saw her face in the dim light from the window, her eyes shut and spinning out grey teardrops. She opened her eyes then and looked terrified, as though she wanted to call it off and beg his pardon, and he covered her with a baring of his teeth, digging his face into the mattress as though rocks were falling on him from the sky.

'Tony?'

He sat up in the darkness, listening.

'Hey, Tony.'

Somebody was half whispering, half calling from outside the cable hole. Tony waited, uncomprehending. Margaret's teardrops were still in his eyes, Grampa was sitting out in the living room. Suddenly he placed the voice. Baldu.

He crawled out on to the catwalk. His helper was dimly lit by a yellow bulb yards away. 'Looey?'

Baldu, startled, jerked around, and hurried back to him on the catwalk, emergency in his eyes. 'Charley Mudd's lookin' for you.'

'Wha' for?'

'I don't know, he's lookin' high and low. You better come.'

This was rare. Charley never bothered him once he had given the assignment for the shift. Tony hurried down the circular iron stairway, imagining some invasion of brass, a swarm of braid and overcoated men from the Master's office. Last summer they had suddenly halted work to ask for volunteers to burn an opening in the bow of a cruiser that had been towed in from the Pacific; her forward compartments had been sealed against the water that a torpedo had poured into her, trapping nine sailors inside. Tony had refused to face those floating corpses or the bloody water that would surely come rushing out.

In the morning he had seen the blood on the sheets, and Grampa was gone.

On B-Deck, scratching his back under his mackinaw and black sweater, Charley Mudd, alarmingly wide awake and alert, was talking to a Protestant with an overcoat on and no hat, a blond engineer he looked like, from some office. Charley reached out to Tony when he came up and held on to him, and even before Charley began to speak Tony knew there was no way out because the Protestant was looking at Tony with a certain relief in his eyes.

'Here he is. Look, Tony, they got some kind of accident on the North River, some destroyer. So grab a gang and take gas and sledges and see what you can do, will you?'

'Wha' kinda accident, Charley?'

'I don't know. The rails for the depth charges got bent. It ain't much, but they gotta go by four to meet a convoy. This man'll take you to the truck. Step on it, get a gang.'

'How do I heat iron? Must be zero outside.'

'They got a convoy waiting on the river. Do your best, that's all. Take a sledge and plenty of gas. Go ahead.'

Tony saw that Charley was performing for the engineer and he could not spoil his relationship. He found Hindu, sent Baldu for his lunch from under the sailor's bunk, and, cursing the Navy, Margaret, winter, and his life, emerged on to the main deck and felt the whip of a wind made of ice. Followed by Hindu, who struggled with a cylinder of acetylene gas held up at the rear end by Baldu, Tony stamped down the gangplank to the open pickup truck at its foot. A sailor was behind the wheel, racing the engine to keep the heater going hot. He sent Hindu and Baldu back for two more cylinders just in case and extra tips for the burner and one more sledge and a crowbar and sat inside the cab, holding his hands, which were not yet cold, under the heater's blast.

'What happened?' he asked the sailor.

'Don't ask me, I'm only driving. I'm stationed right here in the Yard.'

Forever covering his tracks, Tony asked how long the driver had been waiting, but it had been only fifteen minutes so Charley could not have been looking for him too long. Hindu got in beside Tony, who ordered Looey Baldu on to the open back, and they drove along the donkey-engine tracks, through the dark streets, and finally out the gate into Brooklyn.

Baldu huddled with his back against the cab, feeling the wind coming through his knitted skating cap and his skin hardening. He could not bear to sit on the icy truck bed, and his knees were cramping as he sat on his heels. But the pride he felt was enough to break the cold, the realization that now at last he was suffering, striking his blow at Mussolini's throat, sharing the freezing cold of the Murmansk run, where our ships were pushing supplies to the Russians through swarms of submarines. He had driven a meat truck until the war broke out. His marriage, which had happened to fall the day after Pearl Harbour was attacked, continued to ache like a mortal sin even though he kept reminding himself that it had been planned before he knew America would enter the war, and yet it had saved him for a while from the draft, and a punctured eardrum had, on his examination, put him out of action altogether.

He had gone into the Yard at a slight cut in pay if figured on hourly rates, but with a twelve-hour shift and overtime he was ahead. This bothered him, but much less than the atmosphere of confusion in the Yard, for when he really thought back over the five months he had been here he could count on one hand the shifts during which he had exerted himself. Everything was start and stop, go and wait, until he found himself wishing he could dare to go to the Yard Master and tell him that something was terribly wrong. The endless standing around and, worse yet, his having to cover up Tony's naps had turned his working time into a continuous frustration that seemed to be doing something strange to his mind. He had never had so much time to do nothing, and the shifts seemed endless and finally illicit when he, along with the others, had always to watch out for supervisors coming by. It was a lot different than rushing from store to store unloading meat and barely finishing the schedule by the end of the day.

It had never seemed possible to him that he would be thinking so much about sex. He respected and almost worshipped his wife Hilda, and yet now that she was in Florida with her mother for two weeks he was strangely running into one stimulation after another. Suddenly Mrs Curry next door, knowing when he ate breakfast, was taking out her garbage pail at six in the morning with an overcoat on and nothing underneath, and even on very cold mornings stood bent over with the coat open for minutes at a time at the end of the driveway, facing his kitchen window; and every day, every single day now, when he left for work she just happened to be coming out the front door, until he was beginning to wonder if. . . . But that was impossible; a fine married woman like her was most likely unaware of what she was doing, especially with her husband in the Army, fighting Fascism. Blowing on his heavy woollen gloves, he was held by the vision of her bending over and thrust it furiously out of his mind, only to fall still, again remembering a dream he had had in which he was coming into his own bedroom and there on the bed lay his cousin Lucy, all naked, and suddenly he fell on her, tripped on the rug, and woke up. Why should Lucy have gone to bed in his room?

But now Brooklyn Bridge was unwinding from the tailgate of the truck, and how beautiful it was, how fine to be speeding along like this on a mission for the country, and everybody, even Tony, springing to action for the sake of the war effort. Baldu had to take off his cap and rub the circulation back into his scalp, and finally, feeling shivers trembling in his chest, he looked around and discovered a tarpaulin folded in a corner and covered himself. He sat under it in the darkness, blowing on his gloves.

Tony ate three spinach sandwiches out of his box, swallowing them a half at a time, like wet green cookies. Hindu had fallen silent, signalled by Tony's edgy look. The fitter was combative, turtled into his shoulders. As they crossed Chambers Street, the tall office and bank buildings they saw were dark, the people who worked in them at home, warm and smart and snug. Anybody out tonight was either a cop or a jerk; the defroster could not keep up with the cold, and the windshield was glazed over except for a few inches down near the air exhaust. Every curse Tony knew was welling up into his mouth. On deck tonight! And probably no place to hide either, on a ship whose captain and crew were aboard. *Margaret!* Her name, hated, infuriating, her sneaky face, her tattle-tale mouth, swirled through the air in front of him, the mouth of his undoing. For she had made

Grampa so suspicious of him that he still refused to open the trunk until he had evidence Margaret was pregnant, and even when she got big and bigger and could barely waddle from one corner of the small living room to the other, he refused, until the baby was actually born. Grampa had not earned his reputation for nothing – stupid men did not get rich in Calabria, or men who felt themselves above revenge.

As the last days approached and the three-room apartment was prepared for the baby, the old man started acting funny, coming over after dinner ostensibly to sit and talk to Margaret but really to see, as the three of them well knew, that Tony stayed at home. Nights, for a month or so now, he had followed Tony from bar to bar, knocking glasses out of his hand and, in Ox's, sweeping a dozen bottles to the floor behind the bar to teach Ox never again to serve his grandson, until Tony had to sneak into places where he had never hung before. But even so the old man's reputation had preceded him until Tony was a pariah in every saloon between Fourteenth Street and Houston. He gave up at last, deciding to go with the hurricane instead of fighting it, and returned from the piers night after night now, to sit in silence while his wife swelled. With about eight or nine days to go, Grampa, one night, failed to show up. The next night he was missing too, and the next.

One night Tony stopped by to see if some new disaster had budded, like the old man's falling ill and dying before he could hand over the money, but Grampa was well enough. It was only his normally hard-faced, suspicious glare that was gone. Now he merely stole glances at Tony and even seemed to have softened toward him, like a man in remorse. Sensing some kind of victory, Tony felt the return of his original filial warmth, for the old man seemed to be huddling against the approach of some kind of holiness, Tony believed, a supernatural and hallowed hour when not only was his first great-grandchild to be born but his life's accomplishment handed down, and the first shadow of his own death seen. The new atmosphere drew Tony back night after night, and now when he would rise to leave, the old man would lay a hand on Tony's arm as though his strength was in the process of passing from him to a difficult but proud descendant. Even Mama and Papa joined in the silence and deep propriety of these partings.

The pickup truck was turning on the riverfront under the West Side Highway; the sailor bent low to see out of the hand-sized clear space at the bottom of the windshield. Now he slowed and rolled down his window to look at the number on a pier they were passing and quickly shut it again. The cab was instantly refrigerated, a plunge in the temperature that made Hindu groan 'Mamma mia' and pull his earflaps even lower. The night of the birth had been like this, in January too, and he had tried to walk around the hospital block to waste some time and could only get to the corner for the freezing cold. When he returned and walked back into the lobby Mama was running to him and gripping him like a little wrestler, gulping out the double news. It was twins, two boys, both healthy and big, no wonder she had looked so enormous, that poor girl. Tony swam out of the hospital not touching the floor, stroked through the icy wind down Seventh Avenue, and floated up the stairs and found Grampa, and with one look he knew, he knew then, he already knew, for the old man's head seemed to be rolling on a broken neck so frightened was he, so despondent. But Tony held his hand out for the key anyway and kept asking for it until Grampa threw himself on his knees and grasped him around the legs, hawking and coughing and groaning for forgiveness.

The trunk lid opened, Tony saw the brown-paper bundle tied with rope, a package the size of half a mattress and deep as the trunk itself. The rope flew off, the brown paper crackled like splintering wood, and he saw the tied packets – Italian lire, of course, the bills covered with wings, paintings of Mussolini, aero-planes, and zeros, fives, tens, colourful and tumbling under his searching hands. He knew, he already knew, he had known since the day he was born, but he ran back into the living room and asked. It had been an honest mistake. In Calabria, ask anybody there, you could buy or could have bought, once, once you could have bought, that is, a few years ago, until this thing happened with money all over the world, even here in America, ask Roosevelt why he is talking about closing the banks. There is some kind of sickness in the money and why should Italy be an exception, a poor country once you leave Rome. Hold on to it, maybe it will go up again. I myself did not know until two weeks ago I went to the bank to change it, ask your mother. I took the whole bundle to the National City in good faith with joy in my heart, realizing that all your sins were the sins of youth, the exuberance of the young man who grows into a blessing for his parents and grandparents, making all his ancestors famous with his courage and manliness. It comes to seventeen hundred and thirty-nine dollars. In dollars that is what it comes to.

I used to make three hundred driving a truck from Toronto to New York, four days' work, Grampa. Seventeen hundred – you know what seventeen hundred is? Seventeen hundred is like if I bought one good suit and a Buick and I wouldn't have what to buy gas, that's seventeen hundred. Seventeen hundred is like if I buy a grocery store I be out on my ass the first bad week. Seventeen hundred is not like you got a right to come to a man and say go tie that girl around your neck and jump in the river you gonna come up rich. That's not nowhere near that kinda money, not a hundred and fifty miles near that kinda money, and twins you gave me in the bargain. *I GOT TWO TWINS, GRAMPA!*

The red blood washed down off his vision as the truck turned left and into the pier, past the lone light bulb and the night watchman under it listlessly waving a hand and returning to his stove in the shack. Midway down the length of the piershed one big door was open, and the sailor coasted the truck up to it and braked to a halt, the springs squeaking in the cold as the nose dipped.

Tony followed Hindu out and walked past him to the gangplank, which extended into the pier from the destroyer's deck, and walked up, glancing right and left at the full length of the ship. Warm lights burned in her midship compartments, and as he stepped on to the steel deck he concluded that they might be stupid enough to be in the Navy but not that stupid – they were all snuggled away inside and nobody was standing watch on deck. But now he saw his mistake; a sailor with a rifle at his shoulder, knitted blue cap pulled down over his ears and a face shield covering his mouth and chin, the high collar of a storm-coat standing up behind his head, was pacing back and forth from rail to rail on guard.

Tony walked toward him, but the sailor, who looked straight at him on his starboard turn, continued across the deck toward port as though in an automatic trance. Tony waited for the sailor to turn again and come toward him and then stood directly in his path until the sailor bumped into his zipper and leaped in fright.

'I'm from the Yard. Where's the duty officer?'

The sailor's rifle started tilting off his shoulder, and Tony reached out and pushed it back.

'Is it about me?'

'Hah?'

The sailor lowered his woollen mask. His face was young and wan with staring popeyes. 'I'm supposed to go off sea duty. I get seasick. This ship is terrible, I can't hold any food. But now they're telling me I can't get off until we come back again. Are you connected with – '

'I'm from the Navy Yard. There was an accident, right?'

The sailor glanced at Hindu standing a little behind Tony and then at both their costumes and seemed ashamed and worried as he turned away, telling them to wait a minute, and disappeared through a door.

'Wanna look at the rails?' Hindu joked with a carefully shaped mockery of their order, shifting from one foot to the other and leaning down from his height to Tony's ear.

'Fuck the rails. You can't do nutt'n in this weather. They crazy? Feel that wind. Chrissake, it'll go right up your asshole an' put ice in your throat. But keep your mouth shut, I talk to this monkey. What a fuckin' nerve!'

Looey Baldu appeared out of the darkness of the pier, carrying the two sledges. 'Where do you want these, Tony?'

'Up your ass, Looey. Put 'em back on the truck.'

Baldu, astounded, stood there.

Arthur Miller

'You want a taxi? – move!'

Baldu, uncomprehending, turned and stomped down the gang-plank with the sledges.

The door into which the sailor had vanished opened, spilling the temptation of warm yellow light across the deck to Tony's feet, and a tall man emerged, ducking, and buttoning up his long overcoat. The chief petty officer most likely, or maybe even one of the senior lieutenants, although his gangling walk, like a college boy's, and his pants whipping high on his ankles lowered the estimate to ensign. Approaching, he put up his high collar and pulled down his cap and bent over to greet Tony.

'Oh, fine. I'm very much obliged. I'll show you where it is.'

'Wait, wait, just a minute, mister.'

The officer came back the two steps he had taken toward the fantail, an expression of polite curiosity on his pink face. A new gust sent his hand to his visor, and he tilted his head toward New Jersey, from where the wind was pounding at them across the black river.

'You know the temperature on this here deck?'

'What? Oh. I haven't been out for a while. It has gotten very cold. Yes.'

Hindu had stepped back a deferential foot or so, instinctively according Tony the air of rank that a cleared space gives, and now Baldu returned from the truck and halted beside Hindu.

'Could I ask you a little favour?' Tony said, his fists clenched inside his slit pockets, shoulders hunched, eyes squinting against the wind. 'Would you please go inside and tell the captain what kinda temperature you got out here?'

'I'm the captain. Stillwater.'

'You the captain.' Tony stalled while all his previous estimates whirled around in his head. He glanced down at the deck, momentarily helpless. He had never addressed a commanding officer before; the closest he ever came in the Yard was a severe passing nod to one or two in a corridor from time to time. The fact that this one had come out on deck to talk to him must mean that the repair was vital, and Tony found himself losing the normal truculence in his voice.

192

'Could I give yiz some advice, Captain?'

'Certainly. What is it?'

'We can't do nuttn in this here weather. You don't want a botch job, do ya? Whyn't you take her into the Yard, we give you a brand new pair rails, and yiz'll be shipshape for duty.'

The captain half laughed in surprise at the misunderstanding. 'Oh, we couldn't do that. We're joining a convoy at four. Four this morning. I can't delay a convoy.'

The easy absoluteness shot fear into Tony's belly. He glanced past the captain's face groping for a new attack, but the captain was talking again.

'Come, I'll show it to you. Give me that light, Farrow.'

The sick Watch handed him the flashlight and the captain loped off toward the fantail. Tony followed behind. He was trapped. The next time he saw Charley Mudd . . .

The flashlight beam shot out and illuminated the two parallel steel rails, extending several feet out over the water from the deck. Two feet in from the end of the portside rail there was a bend.

'Jesus! What happened?'

'We were out there' – the captain flipped up the light toward the river beyond the slip – 'and a British ship got a little too close trying to line himself up.'

'Them fuckin' British!' Tony exploded, throwing his voice out toward the river where the Englishman must be. Caught by surprise, the captain laughed, but Tony pulled his hands out of his slit pockets and made a pleading gesture, and his face looked serious. 'Why don't somebody tell them to stop fuckin' around or get out of the war!'

The captain, unaccustomed to the type, watched Tony with great expectation and amusement.

'I mean it! They the only ones brings cockroaches into the Navy Yard!'

'Cockroaches? How do –'

'Ax anybody! We get French, Norways, Brazils, but you don't see no cockroaches on them ships. Only the British brings cockroaches.'

The captain shook his head with commiseration, tightening

his smile until it disappeared. 'Some of their ships have been at sea a long, long time, you know.'

Tony felt a small nudge of hope in his heart. 'Uh-huh,' he muttered, frowning with solicitude for the English. Some unforeseen understanding with the captain seemed to loom; the man was taking him so seriously, bothering to explain why there were cockroaches, allowing himself to be diverted even for ten seconds from the problem of the rail, and, more promising than anything else, he seemed to be deferring to Tony's opinion about the possibility of working at all tonight. And better yet, he was even going into it further.

'Some of those English ships have been fighting steadily ten and twelve months down around the Indian Ocean. A ship will get awfully bad that long at sea without an overhaul. Don't you think?'

Tony put gravity into his face, an awful deliberation, and then spoke generously. 'Oh yeah, sure. I was only sayin'. Which I don't blame them, but you can't sit down on their ships.'

Another officer and two more sailors had come out on deck and were watching from a distance as Tony talked to the captain, and he slowly realized that they must all have been waiting hours for him and were now wondering what his opinion was going to be.

With a nod toward the bent rail the captain asked, 'What do you think? Can you straighten it?'

Tony turned to look out at the damaged rail, but his eyes were not seeing clearly. The pleasure and pride of his familiarity with the captain, his sheer irreplaceability on this deck, were shattering his viewpoint. Striving to knit his wits together, he asked the captain if he could have the flashlight for a minute.

'Oh, certainly,' the captain said, handing it to him.

Leaning a little over the edge of the deck, he shone the beam onto the bend of the rail. That pimping, mother-fuckin' Charley Mudd! Look at the chunks of ice in that water – fall in there it's good-bye for ever. In the skyscrapers at his back men tripled their money every wartime day, butchers were cleaning up with meat so scarce, anybody with a truck in good shape could name his price, and here he stood, God's original patsy, Joe Jerk, without a penny to his name that he hadn't grubbed out by the hour with his two hands.

More than a minute had gone by but he refused to give up until an idea came to him, and he kept the light shining on the bend as though studying how to repair it. There had to be a way out. It was the same old shit – the right idea at the right moment had never come to him because he was a dumb bastard and there was no way around it and never would be.

'What do you think?'

What he thought? He thought that Charley Mudd should be strung up by his balls. Turning back to the captain now, he was confronted with the man's face, close to his in order to hear better in the wind. Could it be getting even colder?

'Lemme show you supm, Captain. Which I'm tryin' my best to help you out but this here thing is a son of a bitch. Excuse me. Look.'

He pointed out at the bend in the rail. 'I gotta hit that rail – you understand?'

'Yes?'

'But where I'm gonna stand? It sticks out over the water. You need skyhooks for this. Which is not even the whole story. I gotta get that steel good and hot. With this here wind you got blowin' here I don't even know if I can make it hot enough.'

'Hmm.'

'You understand me? I'm not trying to crap out on ya, but that's the facts.'

He watched the captain, who was blinking at the bend, his brows kinked. He was like a kid, innocent. Out in the dark river foghorns barked, testifying to the weather. Tony saw the sag of disappointment in the captain's face, the sadness coming into it. What the hell was the matter with him? He had a perfect excuse not to have to go to sea and maybe get himself sunk. The German subs were all over the coast of Jersey waiting for these convoys, and here the man had a perfect chance to lay down in a hotel for a couple of days. Tony saw that the young man needed precise help, his feet placed on the road out.

'Captain, listen to me. Please. Lemme give you a piece of advice.'

Expressionless, the captain turned to Tony.

'I sympathize wichoo. But what's the crime if you call in that you can't move tonight? That's not your fault.'

'I have a position in the convoy. I'm due.'

'I know that, Captain, but lemme explain to you. Cut outa here right now, make for the Yard; we puts up a staging and slap in a new rail by tomorrow noon, maybe even by ten o'clock. And you're set.'

'No, no, that's too late. Now see here' – the captain pointed a leather-gloved finger toward the bend – 'you needn't true it up exactly. If you could just straighten it enough to let the cans roll off, that would be enough.'

'Listen, Captain, I would do anything I could do for you, but. . . .' An unbelievable blast of iced wind squeezed Tony's cheeks. The captain steadied himself, tilting his head toward the river again, gripping his visor with one hand and holding his collar tight with the other. Tony had heard him gasp at the new depth of cold. What was the matter with these people? The Navy had a million destroyers – why the hell did they need this one, only this one and on this particular night? 'I'm right, ain't I? They can't hold it against you, can they? If you're unfit for duty you're unfit for duty, right? Who's gonna blame you, which another ship rammed you in the dark? You were in position, weren't you? It was his fault, not yours!'

The captain glanced at him, and in that glance Tony saw the man's disappointment, his judgement of him. He could not help reaching out defensively and touching the captain's arm. 'Listen a minute. Please. Looka me, my situation. I know my regulations. Captain; nobody can blame me either. I'm not supposed to work unsafe conditions. I coulda took one look here and called the Yard and I'd be back there by now below decks someplace, because if you can't do it safe you not supposed to. The only way I can swing this, if I could swing it, is I tie myself up in a rope and hang over the side to hit that rail. Nobody would kick one minute if I said I can't do such a thing. You understand me?'

The captain, his eyes tearing in the wind, his face squeezing tight against the blast of air, waited for his point.

'What I mean, I mean that. . . .' What did he mean? Standing a few inches from the captain's boyish face, he saw for the first time that there was no blame there. No blame and no command either. The man was simply at a loss, in need. And he saw that there was no question of any official blame for the captain either. Suddenly it was as clear and cold as the air freezing them where they stood – that they were both on a par, they were free.

'I'd be very much obliged if you could do it. I see how tough it is, but I'd be very much obliged if you could.'

Tony discovered his glove at his mouth and he was blowing into it to spread heat on his cheeks. The captain had become a small point in his vision. For the first time in his life he had a kind of space around him in which to move freely, the first time, it seemed, that it was entirely up to him with no punishment if he said no, nor even a reward if he said yes. Gain and loss had suddenly collapsed, and what was left standing was a favour asked that would profit nobody. The captain was looking at him, waiting for his answer. He felt shame, not for having hesitated to try, but for a sense of his nakedness. And as he spoke he felt afraid that in fact the repair would turn out to be impossible and he would end by packing up his tools and, unmanned, retreating back to the Yard.

'Man to man, Captain, can I ask you supm?'

'What is it?'

'Which I'm only mentionin'' – he was finding his truculent tone and it was slowly turning ordinary again with this recollection coming on – 'because plenty of times they run to me, "Tony, quick, the ship's gotta go tonight," and I bust my balls. And I come back next day and the ship is sittin' there, and even two weeks more it's still sittin', you understand me?'

'The minute you finish I'll be moving out into the river, don't you worry about that.'

'What about coffee?' Tony asked, striving to give this madness some air of a transaction.

'Much as you like. I'll tell the men to make some fresh. Just tell the Watch whenever you want it.' The captain put out his hand. 'Thanks very much.'

Tony could barely bring his hand forward. He felt the clasping hand around his own. 'I need some rope.'

'Right.'

He wanted to say something, something to equal the captain's speech of thanks. But it was impossible to admit that anything had changed in him. He said, 'I don't guarantee nuttn,' and the familiar surliness in his tone reassured him.

The captain nodded and went off into the midship section, followed by the other officer and the two sailors who had been looking on. He would be telling them ... what? That he had conned the fitter?

Hindu and Looey Baldu were coming toward him. What had he agreed to!

'What's the score?' Hindu grinned, waiting for the delicious details of how Tony had outwitted the shithead captain.

'We straighten it out.' Tony started past Hindu, who grabbed his arm.

'We straighten what out?'

'I said we straighten it out.' He saw the disbelief in Hindu's eyes, the canny air of total refusal, and he felt anger charging into his veins. 'Ax a man for a wood saw and a hammer and if they got a wreckin' bar.'

'How the fuck you gonna straighten – '

'Don't break my balls, Hindu, do what I tell you or get your ass off the ship!' He was amazed at his fury. What the hell was he getting so mad about? He heard Baldu's voice behind him, calling, 'I'll get it!' and went to the gangplank and down to the pier, no longer understanding anything except the grave feeling that had found him and was holding on to him, like the feeling of insult, the sense that he could quickly find himself fighting somebody, the looseness of violence. Hindu had better not try to make him look like a jerk.

It took minutes for him to see again within the pier where he walked about in the emptiness, shining the flashlight at random and finding only the bare, corrugated walls. Baldu came hurrying down the hollow-booming gangplank and over to him, carrying the tools. Another idiot. Son of a bitch, what did these guys do with themselves, jerk off instead of learning something, which at least he had done from job to job, not that it meant anything.

The flashlight found a stack of loading trays piled high against the pier wall. Tony climbed up the ten feet to the top tray. 'What's this for?' Baldu asked, reaching up to receive it as Tony tipped it over the edge of the stack. He came down without answering and gestured for the wrecking bar. Baldu handed him the saw, blade first, and Tony slapped it away and reached over and picked up the hammer and wrecking bar and set about prying up the boards until the two five-by-five runners underneath were free. 'Grab one,' he said and proceeded up the gangplank on to the deck.

He measured the distance between the two rails and sawed the runners to fit. It must be near eleven, maybe later, and the cold would be getting worse and worse. He cut two lengths of rope and ordered Baldu to tie the end of one around his chest, tied the other around himself, and then undid Baldu's crazy knot and made a tight one; he lashed both ropes to a frame at the root of the depth-charge rails, leaving enough slack for him and Baldu to creep out on to the rails. He took one end of a wood runner, Baldu took the other, and they laid themselves prone on the rails, then moved together, with the runner held between them, across the open water. He told Baldu to rest his end inside the L of his rail and to hold it from jarring loose and falling into the water, and he wedged his own end against his rail just behind where the bend began. He told Baldu to inch backward on to the deck, and Hindu to hand Baldu one of the sledges. But the sledges were still on the truck. He told them both to go down to the truck and bring the sledges, bring two tanks of gas, bring the burning torch and tips, and don't get wounded.

Baldu ran. Hindu walked, purposely. Tony sat on his heels, studying the rails. The sick Watch paced up and down behind him in a dream. That fuckin' Charley Mudd, up to the ceiling by his balls.

'Hey, seasick,' he said over his shoulder as the Watch approached, 'see if you can get me a tarp, huh?'

'Tarp?'

'Tarpaulin, tarpaulin. And step on it.'

Christ, one was dumber than the other, nobody knew nuttn, everybody's fulla shit with his mouth open. What was the captain saying now, what was he doing? Had he been conned, really? Except, what could the captain get out of it except the risk of his life with all those subs off Jersey? If he had been conned, fuck it, show the bastard. Show him what?

Suddenly, staring at nothing, he no longer knew why he was doing this, if he had ever known. And somebody might fall into the water in the bargain once they started hitting with the sledge.

'Coffee?'

He turned and looked up. The captain was handing him a steaming cup and had two more in his other hand.

'Thanks.'

Now Baldu and Hindu were clanking the gas cylinders onto the deck behind them. Tony drank his coffee, inhaling the good steam. The captain gave the two cups to the others.

'Whyn't you get off your feet, Captain? Go ahead, git warmed up.'

The captain nodded and went off.

Tony put down his cup. The Watch arrived carrying a folded tarpaulin whose grommets were threaded with quarter-inch rope. Tony told him to put it down on the deck. He let Baldu drink coffee for a minute more, then told him to creep out on his rail and steady the wood runner while he hit its other end with the sledge to wedge it in tight between the two rails. Sliding the sledge ahead of him on his rail, he crept out over the water. At his left, Baldu, tied again, crept out wide-eyed. Tony saw that he was afraid of the water below.

Baldu inched along until he reached the runner and held it in the angle of the L tightly with both hands. Tony stood up carefully on his rail, bent down and picked up the sledge, then edged farther out on the rail to position for a swing. The water in the light held by Hindu was black and littered with floating paper. Tony carefully swung the sledge and hit the runner, and again, and again, and it was tight between the two rails. He told Baldu to back up, and they got the second runner and inched it out with them and wedged it snugly next to the first. Now there would be something to stand on between the two cantilevered rails, although it remained to be seen whether a man could bang the bent rail hard enough with so narrow a perch under him.

He unfolded the tarpaulin and handed one corner to Baldu, took the opposite corner himself, and both inched out over the rails again and tied the tarpaulin on the two runners so that it hung to the windward of the bend and might keep the air blast from cooling the steel. It might not. He backed halfway to the deck and told Hindu to hand him the torch and to grab a sledge and stand on the little bridge he had made and get ready to hit the steel.

'Not me, baby.'

'You, you.'

'What's the matter with the admiral here?' Hindu asked, indicating Baldu.

'I wanchoo.'

'Not me, baby. I don't like heights.'

Tony backed off the rail and stood facing Hindu on the deck.

'Don't fuck around, Tony, nobody's payin' me to get out there. I can't even swim good.'

He saw the certain knowledge of regulations in Hindu's mocking eyes. His own brows were lifted, his classic narrow-eyed, showdown look was on his face, and never before would he have let a man sneer at him like that without taking up the challenge, but now, strange as it was to him, he felt only contempt for Hindu, who had it in him to hit the beam much harder than the smaller Baldu could and was refusing. It was a long, long time since he had known the feeling of being let down by anyone, as long as it was since he had expected anything of anyone. He turned away from Hindu and beckoned to Baldu, and in the moment it took for Baldu to come to him Tony felt sharply the queerness of his pushing on with his job, which, as Hindu's attitude proved, was fit for suckers and, besides, was most probably impossible to accomplish with the wind cooling the steel as fast as it was heated. He bent over and picked up the slender torch.

'You ever work a torch?'

'Well, not exactly, but . . .'

Tony turned to Hindu, his hand extended. 'Gimme the sparkler.' From his jacket pocket Hindu took a spring-driven sparker and handed it to Tony, who took it and, noting the minute grin on Hindu's mouth, said, 'Fuck you.'

'In spades,' Hindu said.

Tony squeezed the sparker as he opened the two valves on the torch. The flame appeared and popped out in the wind. He shielded it with his body and sparked again, and the flame held steady. He took Baldu's hand and put the torch into it. 'Now follow me and I show you what to do.'

Eagerly Baldu nodded, his big black eyes feverish with service. 'Right, okay.'

Unnerved by Baldu's alacrity, Tony said, 'Do everything slow. Don't move unless you look.' And he went to the bent rail and slid the sledge out carefully before him, slowly stretched prone on the rail and inched out over the water. He came to the two runners, from which the tarpaulin hung snapping in the wind, then drew up his legs and sat, and beckoned to Baldu to follow him out.

Baldu, with the torch in his left hand, the wind-bent flame pointed down, laid himself out on the rail and inched toward Tony. But with each thrust forward the torch flame swung up close to his face. 'Let the torch hang, Baldu, take slack,' Tony called.

Baldu halted, drew in a foot of tubing, and let the torch dangle below him. Now he inched ahead again, and as he neared, Tony held out a hand and pressed it against his head. 'Stop.'

Baldu stopped.

'Get the torch in your hand.'

Baldu drew up the torch and held it. Tony pointed his finger at the bend. 'Point the fire here.' Baldu turned the torch, whose flame broke apart against the steel. Tony moved Baldu's hand away from the steel an inch or two and now trained it in a circular motion, then let go, and Baldu continued moving the flame. 'That's good.'

It must be half-past eleven, maybe later. Tony watched the steel. The paint was blackening, little blisters coming up. Not bad. He raised the tarpaulin to shield the flame better. A light yellow glow was starting to show on the steel. Not bad. Gusts were nudging his shoulders. He saw the tears dropping out of Baldu's eyes, and the flame was moving off the rail. He slipped off a glove, reached over, and pressed Baldu's eyelids, clearing the tears out, and the flame returned to its right position. He saw that the Watch was pacing up and down again across the deck behind Hindu, who was standing with the flashlight, grinning.

The yellow glow was deepening. Not bad. An orange hue was beginning to show in the steel. He took Baldu's hand and moved it in wider circles to expand the heated area. He slipped his glove off again and pressed the tears out of Baldu's eyes, then the other glove, and held his hands near the flame to warm them.

The steel was reddening. Stuffing the gloves into his slit pockets, he drew up one foot and set it on the rail, leaned over to the wooden bridge he had built and brought the other foot under him and slowly stood erect. He bent slowly and took the sledge off the rail and came erect again. He spread his legs, one foot resting on the wood runners, the other on the rail, and, shifting in quarter-inch movements, positioned himself to strike. He raised the hammer and swung, not too hard, to see what it did to his stability, and the rail shuddered but his foot remained steady on it. He brought up the sledge, higher this time, and slammed it down and under against the steel, one eye on the bridge, which might jar loose and send him into the water, but it was still wedged between the rails, resting on the flange of the L. Baldu was wrapping his free arm around the rail, and now he had his ankles locked around it too.

Tony raised the sledge and slammed down. The steel rang, and he heard Baldu grunt with the shock coming into his body. He raised the sledge and put his weight into it, and the steel rang and Baldu coughed as though hit in the chest. Tony felt the wind reaching down his back under his collar and icing his sweat. Pneumonia, son of a bitch. He slammed down and across at the rail and let the sledge rest next to his foot. The bend had straightened a little, maybe half an inch or an inch. His arms were pounding with blood, his thighs ached in the awkward, frightened position. He glanced back at Hindu on the deck.

'Not me, baby.'

He felt all alone. Baldu didn't count, being some kind of a screwball, stupid anyway, he went around believing something about everything and meanwhile everybody was laughing at him, a clown who didn't even know it, you couldn't count Baldu for anything, except he was all right, lying out there and scared as he was.

He was catching his breath, coughing up the residue of tobacco in the top of his chest. He glanced down and a little behind his shoe at the steel. It was deeply red. He pounded the steel rail, all alone – and rested again. It had straightened maybe another half-inch. His breath was coming harder, and his back had tightened against the impossible perch, the tension of distributing his weight partly behind the hammer and partly down into his feet, which he dared not move. He was all alone over the water, the beam of the flashlight dying in the black air around him.

He rested a third time, spitting out his phlegm. The son of a bitch was going to straighten out. If he could keep up the hammering, it would. He dared not let Baldu hammer. Baldu would surely end in the water – him with his two left feet, couldn't do nuttn right. Except he wasn't bad with the torch, and the steel against his clothes must be passing the cold into his body. He glanced down at Baldu and saw again the fear in his face with the water looking up at him from below.

He raised the hammer again. Weakness was spreading along his upper arms. He was having to suck in consciously and hold his breath with each blow. Charley Mudd seemed a million miles away. He could barely recall what Dora looked like. If he did decide to go through with the date he would only fall asleep in her room. It didn't matter. He let the sledge rest next to his foot.

Now it was becoming a question of being able to lift it at all. Hindu, to whom he had given a dozen phone numbers, was far away.

Tony licked his lips and his tongue seemed to touch iron. His hand on the sledge handle seemed carved forever in a circular grip. The wind in his nose shot numbness into his head and throat. He lifted the sledge and felt a jerky buckling in his right knee and stiffened it quickly. This fuckin' iron, this stubborn, idiot iron lay there bent, refusing his demand. Go back on deck, he thought, and lay down flat for a minute. But with the steel hot now he would only have to heat it all up again since he could not pass Baldu, who would also have to back on to the deck; and, once having stopped, his muscles would stiffen and make it harder to start again. He swung the hammer, furiously now, throwing his full weight behind it and to hell with his feet – if he fell off the rope would hold him, and they had plenty of guys to fish him out.

The rail was straightening although it would still have a little crook in it; but as long as he could spread it far enough from the other one to let the cans pass through and into the sea, some fuckin' German was going to get it from this rail, bammo, and he could see the plates of the sub opening to the sea and the captain watching the water for a sign of oil coming up. He rested the sledge again. He felt he was about to weep, to cry like a baby against his weakness, but he was a son of a bitch if he would call it off and creep back on to the deck and have Hindu looking down at him, both of them knowing that the whole thing had been useless.

He felt all alone; what was Hindu to him? – another guy to trade girls with and buddy with in the bars, knowing all the time that when the time came he'd give you the shaft if it was good for him, like every man Tony had ever known in his life, and every woman, even Mama, the way she told on him to Grampa, which if she hadn't he would never have had to marry Margaret in the first place. He smashed the sledge down against the steel, recklessly, letting his trunk turn freely and to hell with falling in.

'That looks good enough!'

For a moment, the sledge raised halfway to his shoulder, he

could not make out where the voice was coming from, like in a dream, a voice from the air.

'I'm sure that's good enough, fella!'

Carefully turning his upper body, he looked toward the deck. The captain and two other men and the Watch were facing him.

'I think you've done it. Come back, huh?'

He tried to speak, but his throat caught. Baldu, prone, looked up at him, and Tony nodded, and Baldu closed the valves and the flame popped out. Baldu inched backward along the rail. A sailor reached out from the edge of the deck and grabbed the back of his jacket, holding on to him until he slid safely on to the deck and then helped him to stand.

Out on the rail, the sledge hanging from his hand unfelt, Tony stood motionless, trying to educate his knees to bend so that he could get down on the rail and inch back on to the deck. His head was on crooked, nothing in his body was working right. Slowly, now, he realized that he must not lie down anyway or he would have to slide his body over the part of the rail which was probably still hot enough to scorch him. Experimentally he forced one foot half an inch along the rail but swayed, the forgotten weight of the sledge unbalancing him toward his right side. He looked down at his grasping hand and ordered it to open. The sledge slipped straight down and splashed, disappearing under the black water. The Captain and the crewmen and Baldu stood helplessly in a tight group, watching the small man perched with slightly spread arms on the out-thrust spine of steel, the rope looping from around his chest to the framework on the deck where it was lashed. Tony looked down at his feet and sidled, inch after inch, toward the deck. Joyfully he felt the grip of a hand on his arm now and let his tension flow out as he stepped off the rail and on to the deck. His knee buckled as he came down on it and he was caught and stood straight. The captain was turning away. Two sailors held him under the arms and walked him for a few steps like a drunk, but the motion eased him and he freed himself. A few yards ahead the captain slowed, and glancing back made a small inviting gesture toward the midships section, and pushed by the wind went through a doorway.

He and Baldu and Hindu drank the coffee and ate the buns. Tony saw the serious smiles of respect in the sailors' faces, and he saw the easy charm with which Hindu traded the jokes with them, and he saw the captain, uncapped now, the blond hair and the way he looked at him with love in his eyes, saying hardly anything but personally filling the cup and standing by and listening to Hindu with no attention but merely politeness. Then Tony stood up, his lips warm again and the ice gone out of his sweat, and they all said good night. As Tony went through the door on to the deck the captain touched him on the shoulder with his hand.

When Hindu and Baldu had loaded the gas tanks on to the truck with the sledges, Tony indicated for Baldu to get into the cab, and the helper climbed in beside the sailor, who was racing the engine. Tony got in and pulled the door shut and through the corners of his eyes saw Hindu standing out there, unsmiling, his brows raised, insulted. 'It's only midnight, baby,' Tony said, hardly glancing at Hindu, 'we got four more hours. Git on the back.'

Hindu stood there for twenty seconds, long enough to register his narrow-eyed affront, then climbed on to the open back of the truck.

Outside the pier the sailor braked for a moment, glancing right and left for traffic, and as he turned downtown Tony at the side window saw sailors coming down the gangplank of the destroyer. They were already casting off. The truck sped through the cold and empty street toward Chambers and Brooklyn Bridge, leaving it all behind. In half an hour the destroyer would be back in its position alongside the cargo ships lined up in the river. The captain would be where he belonged. Stillwater. Captain Stillwater. He knew him. Right now it felt like the captain was the only man in the world he knew.

In the Yard, Tony made the driver take them up to the drydock where the cruiser lay on which they had been working. He went aboard with Baldu without waiting for Hindu to get off the back and found Charley Mudd and woke him up, cursing the job he had given him and refusing to listen to Charley's thanks and explanations, and without waiting for permission made his way through the ship to the engine room. Overhead somebody was still welding with the arc too far from the steel, and he raised his collar against the sparks and climbed up to the dark catwalk and found the cable passage and crawled in, spreading himself out on the steel deck. His body felt knotted, rheumatic. His smell was powerful. He went over the solutions he had found for the job and felt good about having thought of taking the runners off the loading tray. That was a damn good idea. And Baldu was all right. He visualized the kink that remained in the rail and regretted it, wishing it had been possible to make it perfectly straight, but it would work. Now the face of the captain emerged behind his closed eyes, the face uncapped as it had been when they were standing around having coffee, the blond hair lit, the collar still raised, and the look in his eyes when he had poured Tony's coffee, his closeness and his fine inability to speak. That lit face hung alone in an endless darkness.

[*1966*]

A Search for a Future

I READ where Faulkner, just before he died, was having dinner in a restaurant and said, 'It all tastes the same.' Maybe I am dying. But I feel good.

I was pasting on my beard. My mind was going back through the mirror to all the other beards, and I counted this as number nine in my life. I used to like beard parts when I was younger because they made me look mature and more sure of myself. But I don't like them so much now that I'm older. No matter how I try I can't help acting philosophical on stage with a beard, and in this part I'm a loud farmer.

That night I looked at my make-up jars, the sponge, the towel, the eye pencil, and I had a strong feeling all of a sudden: that it had always been the same jars, the same sponge, the same towel stained with pink pancake, exactly like this one is; that I had not gotten up from this dressing table for thirty-five years; and that I had spent my whole life motionless, twenty minutes before curtain. That everything tasted the same. Actually I feel I am optimistic. But for quite a lengthened-out minute there I felt that I had never done anything but make myself up for a part I never got to play. Part of it is, I suppose, that all dressing rooms are the same. The other part is that I have been waiting to hear that my father has died. I don't mean that I think of him all the time, but quite often when I hear a phone go off I think, There it is, they are going to tell me the news.

The stage-door man came in. I thought he was going to announce ten minutes (ten minutes to curtain), but instead he said that somebody was asking to see me. I was surprised. People never visit before a show. I thought it might be somebody from the nursing home. I felt frightened. But I wanted to know immediately, and the stage-door man hurried out to get the visitor.

I never married, although I have been engaged several times –

but always to a Gentile girl, and I didn't want to break my mother's heart. I have since learned that I was too attached to her but I don't feel sure about that. I love nothing more than children, family life. But at the last minute a certain idea would always come to me and stick in my brain. The idea that this marriage was not absolutely necessary. It gave me a false heart, and I never went ahead with it. There are many times when I wish I had been born in Europe, in my father's village, where they arranged marriages and you never even saw the bride's face under the veil until after the ceremony. I would have been a faithful husband and a good father, I think. It's a mystery. I miss a wife and children that I never had.

I was surprised to see a boy walk in, although he might have been twenty-two or -three. But he was short, with curly hair and a pink complexion that looked as though he never had to shave. Maybe, I thought, it is the son of the owner of the nursing home. He had a sweet expression, a twinkle in his eyes.

'I just wanted to remind you about midnight,' he said.

About midnight? What about midnight? I was completely lost. For a minute there I even thought, My father has died and I have forgotten about it, and there is some kind of procedure or a ceremony at midnight.

'The meeting,' he said.

Then I remembered. I had agreed to sit on the platform at a meeting, 'Broadway for Peace'. I had agreed in Sardi's because Donald Frost challenged me. My dresser's nephew, a musician twenty-one years old, had just had his eyes shot out in Vietnam somewhere, and I was very, very sick about it. I still haven't seen my dresser, Roy Delcampo. He doesn't even call me up since it happened. I know he'll show up one of these nights, but so far there is no sign of him. To tell the truth, I do not know who is right about this war, but I know that nobody is going to remember ten years from now what it was all for. Just as I so often sit here at my dressing table, where I am writing this, and it sometimes seems that I have never even gotten up to play, and I have had forty-three shows, forty-three openings, and who can even remember the casts, the exact kind of battles we had in production, let alone the reviews or even most of the titles? I know it all kept me alive, that's about all. But it is even hard to remember the kind of actor I had wanted to be. It wasn't this kind is all I know.

Suddenly, though, I was a little nervous about this meeting. I have always respected actors with convictions, the people in the old days who were Leftists and so on. Whatever people might say, those guys and girls had wonderful friendships between them. But I never felt it was really necessary for me to put my name on anything political. I never felt it would make a difference of any kind if I put my name or I didn't.

Besides, I felt nervous about a public appearance. But I looked at this boy and he looked at me, and I could see once again how my generation used to look way back there, that this meeting was more than a meeting, it was to stop the world from ending. Which I didn't believe, but for him it wasn't all the same, for him – and I could see he was an actor – each new show was some kind of new beginning. I could see that he still remembered every single thing that had ever happened to him, that he was on his way up, up. Actually I was quite frightened about the meeting, but I couldn't bear to say to him that it was not going to make any difference if I appeared or not. So we shook hands, and he even grasped my arm as though we were in league, or even to indicate that he felt especially good that an older man was going to be with them. Something of that kind.

When he turned around and walked out I saw that the seat of his overcoat was worn – it was a much lighter colour than the rest of the coat. An actor notices such things. It means that he sits a lot in his overcoat, and on rough places, like the concrete bases of the columns in front of the Forty-second Street Library, or even park benches, or some of the broken chairs in producers' outer offices. And here he is spending his time with meetings. I thought to myself, I cannot imagine anything I would sit and wait for, and I wished I had something like that. I ended up a little glad that I was going to be at the meeting. Exactly why, I don't know.

I think I acted better that night, not that anyone else would notice, but I found myself really looking at my fellow actors as though I had never seen them before. Suddenly it was remarkable to me, the whole idea of a play, of being able to forget everything else so that we were really angry up there, or really laughing, or really drinking the cider we were supposed to drink, which is actually tea, and coughing as though it were bitter. Toward the end of Act II some man got up from the third row and walked out, and I usually feel upset about a walkout, but this night it went through my mind that it was his role to walk out, that the whole audience was acting too; after all, the whole idea of so many people sitting together, facing in the same direction, not talking is a kind of acting. Except that some of us very soon are actually going to die.

That thought came to me also – it was just as the man was walking out – that really the only difference offstage is that you don't get up after the death scene. Even the President gets made up now for his TV talks. Everybody, every morning, gets into costume. Except that I, instead of actually marrying, stop short at the last moment every time.

As we were taking the curtain calls I thought, Maybe I never got married because it would make my life real, it would rip me off stage somehow.

The next morning I went to visit my father at the nursing home. I had been there only four or five days before, but I woke up and tried to read the scripts that had been sent to me, and I made a few phone calls, but I felt pulled. So I went.

It was a very windy day in October, a clear blue sky over New York. My father always liked strong wind and cold weather. He would put up his coat collar and say, 'Ahhh,' and even as a little boy I imitated the way he exhaled and enjoyed facing into a cold wind. He would look down at me and laugh. 'This is not a hot day, boy.'

The old man is in a cage. But the bars are so close to his face he cannot see them, so he keeps moving a step this way and a step that way. And finally he knows, for the hundredth time every day, that he is not free. But he does not know why. He feels some-one knows, and whoever it is means him harm. Something is going to happen when the time comes. Someone is keeping him here for a time, temporarily, as you might say.

The room is freshly painted and smells it – a light blue colour over many coats of paint so that the shiny surface is lumpy. A string hangs from the middle of the ceiling with a fluorescent plastic tassel on the end of it. His head strikes it whenever he moves about the room. In the dark at night he lies on his bed and goes to sleep with the bluish glow of this tassel on his retina. In the afternoons he can pull the string and make the ceiling light go on. He has never been at ease with machinery, so when he pulls the string he looks up at the ceiling fixture, a little surprised that the light goes on. Sometimes after his head has hit the tassel he scratches the spot lightly as though a fly had sat on his skin. The word 'stroke' is very right, like a touch on the brain, just enough.

The nursing home is an old converted apartment house, but an extremely narrow one. The corridors on each floor are hardly wider than a man. You come in and on the right is an office where a fat woman is always looking into a thick registry book. On the left is a slow elevator. Up one flight is my father's floor. There is always a mattress or a spring standing on edge in the corridor; someone has been moved out or died. Rooms open off the corridor, most of them occupied by old women. They sit motionlessly facing their beds, some asleep in their chairs. There is no sound in the place; they are all dozing, like thin, whitehaired birds that do not thrive in captivity. All their eyes seem blue.

A zoo smell is always in the air as soon as you walk into the building, and it gets thicker upstairs. But it is not a filthy smell. It is like earth, humid but not diseased. At my first visit I was repelled by it, as by sewage. But after a while, if you allow yourself to breathe in deeply and normally, you realize it is the odour of earth and you respect it.

The old man's room is the last one on the corridor. Opposite his door is a widened space where the nurses have a desk. They do not look up when I open his door. Nobody is going to steal anything here or do any harm. Everyone is so old that there cannot be an emergency.

He is usually asleep on his bed whatever time I come. I am already twenty years older than he was at my birth. I am an older man than the one I looked up at during the windy walks. My hair is grey at the sides. Mother has been dead a long, long time. All of his brothers and sister are dead, everyone he knew and played cards with. I have also lost many friends. It turns out that he is not really too much older than I am, than I am becoming.

I stood there looking down at him and recalled the meeting the night before. About fifteen others were sitting on a row of chairs on the stage. Donald Frost was the chairman and introduced us in turn. For some reason, when I stood up, there seemed to be heavier applause, probably because it was the first time I had ever come out for such a thing, and also because I have been quite a hit in this current play and they knew my face. But when I stood up and the applause continued, Donald waved for me to come up to the microphone. I was frightened that the newspapers would pick up what I might say and I had no idea what to say. So I came to the microphone. There was a really good silence. The theatre was packed. They said that people were jammed up outside trying to get in. I bent over to the microphone and heard my own voice saying, 'Someone went blind that I knew.' Then I realized that I did not actually know the boy who had been blinded, and I stopped. I realized that it sounded crazy. I realized that I was frightened, that someday there might be investigations and I could be blamed for being at such a meeting. I said, 'I wish the war would stop. I don't understand this war.' Then I went back to my chair. There was terrific applause. I didn't understand why. I wondered what I had really said that made them so enthusiastic. It was like an opening night when a line you never had thought about very much gets a big reaction. But I felt happy and I didn't know why. Maybe it was only the applause, which I didn't understand either, but I felt a happiness, and I thought suddenly that it had been a terrible, terrible mistake not to have gotten married.

'Pop?' I said softly, so as not to shock him. He opened his eyes and raised his head, blinking at me.

He always smiles now when he is awakened, and the lower part of his long face pulls down at his eyes to open them wider. It isn't clear whether or not he knows who you are as he smiles at you. I always slip in my identification before I say anything.

'I'm Harry,' I say, but I make it sound casual, as though I am saying it only because he hasn't got his glasses on. His fingers dance nervously along his lower lip. He is touching himself, I think, because he is no longer certain what is real and what is dream, when people he is not sure he knows suddenly appear and disappear every day. He immediately insists on getting out of bed. He is fully dressed under the blankets, sometimes even with his shoes on. But today he has only socks. 'My slippers.'

I got his slippers from the metal closet and helped him into them. He stood on the floor, tucking in his shirt, saying, 'And uh, and uh,' as though a conversation had been going on.

There are no immense emotions here but deep currents without light. He is bent a little and stiff-kneed, and he plucks at his clothes to be sure everything is on. He is very interested that someone is here but he knows that nothing, absolutely nothing, will come of it. But he wants to lengthen it out anyway, just in case something might happen to free him. He is afraid of the end of the visit suddenly being announced so he tries to be quick about everything. He says, 'Sit down, sit down,' not only to make you comfortable but to stall off the end. Then he sits in the one armchair, the fire escape behind him and a patch of city sky, and I sit on the edge of the bed facing him.

'I hear you went for a walk today with the nurse?'

'Ya. Awd the river. Doom days deen unden, but this here's a beautiful day. Some day.'

'Yes. It's a beautiful day,' I repeat so that he'll know I understand what he is talking about, although it doesn't make much difference to him. Some things he says, though, he is very anxious should be understood, and then it all gets terrible. But I am not sure he knows he is mostly incomprehensible.

He wanders his arm vaguely toward the night table. 'My glasses.' I open the drawer and hand him one of the two pairs he keeps in there.

'Are these the ones?'

He puts on the wobbly frames, which his incapable hands have bent out of shape. The lenses are coated with his fingerprints. 'Ya,' he says, blinking around. Then he says, 'No,' and roots around in the drawer. I give him the other pair, and he takes off the first pair, opens the second, and puts the first one on again and looks at me.

I realize as he is looking at me that he feels friendship between us and that he is glad to see me, but that he is not sure who I am. 'I'm Harry,' I say.

He smiles. He is still a big man even though he is very thin now; but his head is massive and his teeth are good and strong and there is some kind of force lying in pieces inside of him, the force of a man who at least has not at all settled for this kind of room and this kind of life. For him, as for me and everybody else, it is all some kind of mistake. He has a future. I suppose I still go to see him for that reason.

I never realized before that his ears stick out, that they face front. I think I was always so busy looking into his eyes that I never really saw his ears. Because there is nothing more to listen to from him or to fear, I have time to look at his body now.

His left leg is quite bowed out, more than I ever noticed. His hands are very slender and even artistic. His feet are long and narrow. He has strangely high, almost Slavic cheekbones, which I never noticed when his face was fuller. The top of his head is flatter, and the back of his neck. It was less than five years ago that I first realized he was an old man, an aged man. I happened to meet him walking on Broadway one afternoon and I had to walk very slowly beside him. A little breeze on his face made his eyes tear. But I felt then that it was not something very sad; I felt that after all he had lived a long time.

But this day I felt that it was different because he had not given up his future. In fact, he was reaching toward his future even more energetically than I was toward mine. He really wanted something.

'Linnen, I ah gedda hew orthing. Very important.'

'You want something?'

'No-no. I ah gedda hew orthing.'

He waited for me to reply. 'I don't understand what you're saying but keep talking, maybe I'll understand.'

He reached over toward the door and tested that it was shut. Now as he spoke he kept glancing with widened eyes toward the corridor outside, as though interlopers were out there who meant him no good. Then he clamped his jaw angrily and shook his head. 'I never in my life. Never.'

'What's the matter?'

'He maug lee me ounigh.'

'They won't let you out?'

He nodded, scandalized, angry. 'Hew maug lee me ounigh.'

'But you went out with the nurse, didn't you?'

'Linnen. Hew linnen?' He was impatient.

'Yes, Pop, I'm listening. What do you want?'

Something politic came over him as he prepared to speak again, something calculating. He was positioning himself for a deal. His lips, without sound, flicked in and out like a chimpanzee's as he practiced an important message. Then he crossed his legs and leaned over the arm of the chair toward me.

'Naw hen my money.'

'Your money?'

'Nay hen. Yesterday she said sure. Today, naw hen.'

'The lady downstairs?'

'Ya.'

'She asked you for money?'

'Naw hen my money.'

'She wouldn't give you your money?'

He nodded. 'Naw hen. Fifty thousand dollars.'

'You asked her for fifty thousand dollars?'

'For my money hen.'

He was leaning toward me, cross-legged, just as I had seen him do with businessmen, that same way of talking in a hotel lobby or in a Pullman, a rather handsome posture and full of grace. Of course he had no fifty thousand dollars, he had nothing any more, but I did not realize at the time what he really had in his mind even though he was telling it to me clearly.

'Well, you don't need money here, Pop.'

He gave me a suspicious look with a little wise smile. I too was not on his side.

'Linnen.'

'I'm listening.'

'I could go hime,' he said with sudden clarity. He had no home either; his wife was dead eight years now, and even his hotel room had been given up. 'I wouldn't even talk,' he said.

'It's better for you here, Pop.'

'Better!' He looked at me with open anger.

'You need nursing,' I explained.

He listened with no attention while I explained how much better off he was here than at home, his eyes glancing at the door. But his anger passed. Then he said, 'I could live.'

I nodded.

'I could live,' he repeated.

Now came the silence, which is always the worst part. I could find nothing to say any more, and he no longer had a way to enlist my help. Or maybe he was expecting me to start packing his things and getting him out. All we had in the room was his low-burning pleasure that someone was here with him, even though he did not know for sure who it was, except that it was someone familiar; and for me there was only the knowledge that he had this pleasure.

He would look at me now and then with various expressions. Once it would be with narrowed eyes, an estimating look, as though he were about to say some searching sentence. Then he would blink ahead again and test his lips. After a few moments he would look at me, this time with the promise of his warm, open smile, and once again go into a stare.

Finally he raised his finger as though to draw my attention, a stranger's attention, and, tilting back his head as though recalling, he said, 'Did you St Louis?'

'Yes, I'm back now. I was there and now I'm back.' I had been in St Louis with a show nine or ten years ago. One of his factories had been in St Louis forty years ago.

He broke into a pleased smile. He loved cities; he had enjoyed entering them and leaving them, being well served in hotels; he had loved to recall buildings that had been demolished, the marvellous ups and downs of enterprises and business careers. I knew what he was smiling at. He had once brought me a toy bus from St Louis, with a whole band on top that moved its arms when the bus moved, and inside it was a phonograph record that played 'The Stars and Stripes Forever'. He had come home just as I had gotten up from my nap. In his arms were gift boxes. This bus, and I remember a long pair of beige kid gloves for my mother. He always brought fresh air into the house with him, the wind, his pink face and his reedy laugh.

'Well, I have to go now, Pop.'

'Ya, ya.'

He hastened to stand, hiking his pants up where his belly used to be, plucking at his brown sweater to keep it properly placed on his shoulders. He even enjoyed the good-bye, thinking I had important work to do, appointments, the world's business with which no one had a right to interfere. We shook hands. I opened the door, and he insisted on escorting me to the elevator. 'This way, this way,' he said in a proprietary manner, as though he could not help being in charge. He walked ahead of me down the narrow corridor, bent, heavily favouring his bowed left leg, his face very much averted from the open rooms we passed where the old ladies sat motionless. He had never liked old women.

Outside the wind was even faster than before, but the sky was turning grey. I had some time so I walked for a while, thinking of him turning back and re-entering his room, lying down on the bed, probably exhausted, and the plastic thing on the light string swaying overhead.

It was fine to walk without a limp. I resolved again to stop smoking. I have wide hands and feet. I am not built like him at all. I crossed from Riverside Drive to the Park and caught a bus to Harlem, where I was born. But as soon as I got out I knew I had lost the feeling I had started with, and it was impossible to feel what I had felt there in my youth forty years ago.

There was only one moment that held me; I found myself facing a dry-cleaning store, which had once been one of the best restaurants in New York. On Sundays the old man would take my mother and me for dinner. There had been a balcony where a baker in a tall white hat baked fresh rolls, and whenever a customer entered he would put in a fresh batch. I could smell the rolls through the odour of benzine on Lenox Avenue. I could see the manager, who always sat down with us while we ate. He had some disease, I suppose, because the right side of his face was swollen out like a balloon, but he always wore a hard wing collar and a white tie and never seemed sick.

A Negro with a moustache was looking through the store window at me. For a moment I had the urge to go inside and tell him what I remembered, to describe this avenue when no garbage cans were on the street, when the Daimlers and Minervas and Locomobiles had cruised by and the cop on the corner threw back the ball when it got through the outfield on 114th Street. I did not go into the store, or even toward our house. Any claim to anything had slipped. I went downtown instead and sat in my dressing room trying to read.

I was just opening my pancake can when I thought of something I still don't altogether understand: that the old man is the only one who is not an actor. I am, the President is, and Donald Frost is even though his convictions are very sincere; but on the platform last night I could tell, probably because I am an actor, that he was listening to his modulations, that he was doing what he was doing because he had told himself to do it. But he is not desperate enough, not like the old man is desperate. The old man does not know enough to listen to his own voice or to ask himself what he ought to do; he just speaks from his heart, and he has even lost his hold on the language so all that is left is the sound, you might say, of his gut, which is not acting. I wondered about the young, pink-cheeked boy who had come to remind me about the meeting – whether he also was acting. Maybe in his case, with the draft grabbing for him, it was real.

I started pasting on my beard, and I thought again of my not being married. It was like all this agitation now, like everything I saw and knew about, it was a lack of some necessity. Nobody seems to have to do anything, and the ones who say they do have to, who say that something is absolutely necessary for them, may only be the best actors. Because that is what a really good actor does; he manages to make his feelings necessary, so that suddenly there is no longer the slightest choice for him. He has to scream or die, laugh or die, cry real tears or die. And at the same time he knows that he is not going to die, and this thought makes him happy while he is screaming or crying, and it may be what makes the audience happy to cry too.

I was just taking off my clothes in my bedroom that night when the phone rang. And it frightened me, as it usually does these days. It really was the fat woman in the nursing home this time; the old man had escaped. He had slipped out not long after I had left, and here it was nearly two in the morning and the police had a missing persons alarm out, but there was no sign of him yet. The worst thing was that he had gone out without his overcoat, and it was raining and blowing like hell. There was nothing more to be done now, as long as the police had an eye out for him, but I couldn't go back to sleep. I couldn't help feeling proud of him and hoping they would never find him, that he would just disappear. I have always admired his wilfulness, his blind push toward what he has to have. I have admired his not being an actor, I suppose, and he was not acting tonight, not out there in that rain and wind. I couldn't sleep, but there was nothing I could do. The clock was inching up to three by this time. I got dressed and went out.

I had walked only a block when I felt my socks getting wet so I stepped into a doorway, trying to think what to do. It was somehow strange that both of us were walking around in the same rain. But whom was he looking for? Or what? I half didn't want to find him. In fact, for moments I had visions of him crossing the river to the West, just getting the hell out of here, out of the world. But how would he talk to anybody? Would he know enough to get onto a bus? Did he have any money? Naturally I ended up being worried about him, and after a while I saw a taxi and got in.

I joke with cabdrivers but I never talk with them, but this time I had to explain myself for wanting to cruise around, and I told the driver that I was looking for my father. Cabdrivers never seem to believe anything, but he believed me – it seemed perfectly natural to him. Maybe it happens quite often like this. I don't even remember what he looked like, even whether he was white or Negro. I remember the rain pouring over the windshield and the side windows because I was trying to see through them. It was getting on toward half-past four by the time I got home again, and the rain was coming down stiff. I got into my bedroom and undressed and lay down and looked toward my window, which was running with water. I felt as though the whole city were crying.

They found him next morning at about ten o'clock, and the police phoned me. They had already returned him to the nursing home so I hurried up there. The rain was over, and once again the sky was clear, a good sharp, sunny October day. He was asleep on his bed, wrapped in his flannel robe. A bandage was plastered over his nose, and he seemed to have a black eye coming on. His knuckles were scraped and painted with Mercurochrome. He badly needed a shave.

I went downstairs and talked with the fat woman in the office. She was wary and cautious because they can probably be sued, but I finally got the story out of her. He had been found in Harlem. He had gone into a luncheonette and ordered some food, but the counterman had probably realized that he was not quite right and asked for the money in advance. The old man had a dollar but would not pay in advance, and they went looking for a cop to take care of him. When he realized they were looking for a cop he got up and tried to leave and stumbled and fell on his face.

I went up again and sat in the armchair, waiting for him to wake up. But after a while one of the nurses came in and said they had given him a sedative that would keep him under for several hours. I left and came back just before my show, and he was sitting in the armchair, eating some chicken. He looked up at me, very surprised, and felt his lips with rapid fingers.

I smiled at him. 'I'm Harry,' I said.

He looked at me without much recognition, except as before, only knowing that there was something of a past between us. I sat on the bed and watched him eat. I talked at length about the good day we were having and how hard it had rained last night. I kept wishing and wishing that even for one split second he would look at me clearly and laugh – just one shrewd laugh between us to celebrate his outing. But he sat there eating, glancing at me with a little warmth and a little suspicion, and finally I grinned and said, 'I hear you went for a walk last night.'

He stopped eating and looked at me with surprise. He shook his head. 'No. Oh, no.'

'Don't you remember the rain?'

'The rain?'

'You went to Harlem, Pa. Were you going home?'

A new attention crossed his eyes, and a sharpened interest. 'I en home raro.' He spoke the sounds with an attempt to convince me. He had one finger raised.

'You're going home tomorrow?'

'Ya.' Then he glanced toward the closed door and returned to the chicken.

Every night, sitting here putting on my beard, I keep expecting a phone call or a visitor, a stranger, and I feel I am about to be afraid.

He was trying to reach home, where ages ago he had entered so many times, carrying presents. He has a future that they will never be able to rip away from him. He will close his eyes for the last time thinking of it. He does not have to teach himself or remind himself of it. As long as he can actually walk they are going to have trouble with him, keeping him from going where he wants to go and has to go.

I'm not sure how to go about it, but I have a terrific desire to live differently. Maybe it is even possible to find something honourable about acting, some way of putting my soul back into my body. I think my father is like a man in love, or at least the organism inside him is. For moments, just for moments, it makes me feel as I used to when I started, when I thought that to be a great actor was like making some kind of a gift to the people.

[1966]